Gender and Work in Capitalist Economies

Issues in Society
Series editor: Tim May

Gender and Work in Capitalist Economies

PAMELA ODIH

Open University Press

Open University Press
McGraw-Hill Education
McGraw-Hill House
Shoppenhangers Road
Maidenhead
Berkshire
England
SL6 2QL

email: enquiries@openup.co.uk
world wide web: www.openup.co.uk

and Two Penn Plaza, New York, NY 10121–2289, USA

First published 2007

Copyright © Pamela Odih 2007

All rights reserved. Except for the quotation of short passages for the purposes of criticism and review, no part of this publication may be reproduced, stored in a retrieval system, or transmitted, in any form or by any means, electronic, mechanical, photocopying, recording or otherwise, without the prior permission of the publisher or a licence from the Copyright Licensing Agency Limited. Details of such licences (for reprographic reproduction) may be obtained from the Copyright Licensing Agency Ltd of Saffron House, 6–10 Kirby Street, London, EC1N 8TS.

A catalogue record of this book is available from the British Library

ISBN – 13: 9780 335 216727 (pb) 9780 335 216734 (hb)
ISBN – 13: 0335 216 722 (pb) 0335 216 730 (hb)

Library of Congress Cataloguing-in-Publication Data
CIP data applied for

Typeset by YHT Ltd, London
Printed in Poland by OZGraf S.A.
www.polskabook.pl

The McGraw·Hill Companies

This book is dedicated to my father William Odih, with love.

Contents

Preface	ix
Acknowledgements	xi
Series editor's preface	xiii
Illustration credits	xvii
Introduction: gender, capitalist accumulation and the political economy of time	1

Part I Industrial Times

1 Primitive accumulation and gendered histories of dispossession	27
2 Weaving time: gender and the rise of the British textile industry in the nineteenth century	42
3 Economies of time and gender in industrial capitalism	63

Part II Fordist Times

4 Gender and identity in modern times	81
5 Gender and modern work	98

Part III Post-Fordist Times

6 Post-Fordist production and the time-disciplined call centre With David Knights	115
7 Flexible work and the restructuring of gender identity	131

Part IV Global Times

8 Women, work and inequality in the global assembly-line 151

Conclusion: Towards a politics of gender, work and time 178

References 185
Index 199

Preface

Writing a book about gender and work in capitalist economies might appear to be an ambitious endeavour. The innumerable topic areas relating to gender and work would dissuade even the most fastidious scholar. While writing this Preface, my attention has been drawn to a multitude of Equal Opportunities Commission reports, detailing gender dimensions in the patterns of contemporary work. It is approximated that between 2004 and 2014 the number of paid employees in the UK will increase by 1.3 million (quoted in Walby 2007: 7). It is also generally recognized that the world of work, in the West, is dramatically changing. The 'traditional' model of the adult working life cycle is based on an archetype of full-time permanent employment, extending from the completion of full-time education into the commencement of full-time retirement, i.e., '48 hours for 48 weeks for 48 years'. But this is rapidly changing.

Innovations in the organization of work, coupled with an avalanche of new technologies, are shifting the culture of work based on 'old-fashioned jobs' to one founded on a contingent 'just-in-time' workforce. Women feature predominantly among the ranks of flexible workers. In 2005, 12 per cent of women employees worked flexitime and 42 per cent worked part-time. This compares with 9 per cent of males working flexitime and 9 per cent of males working part-time (EOC 2006: 12). Equally dramatic trends are occurring in global labour markets. In developing countries, women constitute the majority of part-time and impermanent workers (Chen *et al.* 2005: 9). With few exceptions, women in the developing world achieve a lower rate of pay than their male counterparts. And their labour market participation is, invariably, shaped by the interminable demands of care responsibilities and unpaid household work. Similarities clearly link these global patterns of female labour market participation with local trends. But how might one explore these gender dynamics?

This book argues that capitalism's political economy of time, shapes gendered patterns of work. The concept of political economy is inspired by a dedicated reading of Karl Marx's *Capital*, Volumes 1, 2 and 3. This is not to assume an adherence to some trans-historical determinant of gender inequality. Indeed, the conception of power and subjectivity that guides my analysis is more indebted to Foucauldian genealogy than Marxist dialectical materialism. Nevertheless, the concepts of political economy and time reverberate throughout the development of Western capitalism, and efficaciously highlight the irascible complexity of gender in capitalist economies. Ultimately, this book is about time. Each chapter is linked in narrative sequence in order to describe, and critically evaluate, the history and present of Western capitalism's political economy of time.

Acknowledgements

I would like to express a heartfelt thank you to Professor David Knights who supervised my doctorate and has continued to inspire my academic development. Professor Barbara Adam's prolific contribution to the study of time and society has been inspirational and I would like to pay tribute to her work.

My colleagues at Goldsmiths University, Professor Bev Skeggs, Professor Celia Lury and Professor Vic Seidler have been particularly supportive. I am immensely grateful to Professor Tim May for encouraging my initial book proposal. His editorial insights, and time invested in reading drafts of this book, have been very much appreciated. Chris Cudmore has been an extremely patient and supportive commissioning editor, and I would like to take this opportunity to thank him for his diligence. Susan Dunsmore's editorial assistance is also much appreciated. And a big thank you to my loving mother Mary and my dearest companion Simon Meats.

Additional acknowledgements are extended to Palgrave for granting me permission to reprint D. Knights and P. Odih (2002) 'Big Brother is watching you!': call centre surveillance and the time disciplined subject, in G. Crow and S. Heath (eds) *Social Conceptions of Time: Structure and Process in Work and Everyday Life*. London: Palgrave Macmillan. I would also like to thank Sage Publications for providing permission to reprint P. Odih, (2003) 'Gender, Work and Organization in the Time/Space Economy of Just-in-Time Labour'; *Time and Society* 12(2/3): 293–314 and P. Odih, (1999a) 'Gendered Time in the Age of Deconstruction', *Time and Society*, 8(1): 9–38.

Series editor's preface

The social sciences contribute to a greater understanding of the workings of societies and dynamics of social life. They are often, however, not given due credit for this role and much writing has been devoted to why this should be the case. At the same time we are living in an age in which the role of science in society is being re-evaluated. This has led to both a defence of science as the disinterested pursuit of knowledge and an attack on science as nothing more than an institutionalized assertion of faith with no greater claim to validity than mythology and folklore. These debates tend to generate more heat than light.

In the meantime the social sciences, in order to remain vibrant and relevant, will reflect the changing nature of these public debates. In so doing they provide mirrors upon which we gaze in order to understand not only what we have been and what we are now, but to inform ideas about what we might become. This is not simply about understanding the reasons people give for their actions in terms of the contexts in which they act, as well as analyzing the relations of cause and effect in the social, political and economic spheres, but about the hopes, wishes and aspirations that people, in their different cultural ways, hold.

In any society that claims to have democratic aspirations, these hopes and wishes are not for the social scientist to prescribe. For this to happen it would mean that the social sciences were able to predict human behaviour with certainty. This would require one theory and one method applicable to all times and places. The physical sciences do not live up to such stringent criteria, whilst the conditions in societies which provided for this outcome would be intolerable. Why? Because a necessary condition of human freedom is the ability to have acted otherwise and to imagine and practice different ways of organizing societies and living together.

It does not follow from the above that social scientists do not have a valued role to play, as is often assumed in ideological attacks upon their place and role within society. After all, in focusing upon what we have been and what we are now, what we might become is inevitably illuminated. Therefore, whilst it may not be the province of the social scientist to predict our futures, they are, given not only their understandings, but equal positions as citizens, entitled to engage in public debates concerning future prospects.

This international series was devised with this general ethos in mind. It seeks to offer students of the social sciences, at all levels, a forum in which ideas are interrogated in terms of their importance for understanding key social issues. This is achieved through a connection between style, structure and content that is found to be both illuminating and challenging in terms of its evaluation of topical social issues, as well as representing an original contribution to the subject under discussion.

Given this underlying philosophy, the series contains books on topics which are driven by substantive interests. This is not simply a reactive endeavour in terms of reflecting dominant social and political pre-occupations, it is also pro-active in terms of an examination of issues which relate to and inform the dynamics of social life and the structures of society that are often not part of public discourse. What is distinctive about the series is an interrogation of the assumed characteristics of our current epoch in relation to its consequences for the organization of society and social life, as well as its appropriate mode of study.

Each contribution contains, for the purposes of general orientation, as opposed to rigid structure, three parts. First, an interrogation of the topic which is conducted in a manner that renders explicit core assumptions surrounding the issues and/or an examination of the consequences of historical trends for contemporary social practices. Second, a section which aims to 'bring alive' ideas and practices by considering the ways in which they directly inform the dynamics of social relations. A third section then moves on to make an original contribution to the topic. These encompass possible future forms and content, likely directions for the study of the phenomena in question, or an original analysis of the topic itself. Of course, it might be a combination of all three.

In this spirit Pam Odih's book takes capitalism, work and gender and submits them to detailed consideration not only in terms of how they have changed in the unfolding of history, but their impacts upon everyday life. Work extends away from communal life into a disciplinary matrix in which time and effort become subject to routine calculation with effects upon all those who are its subjects. It is the clock, not the steam engine that becomes the motor of capitalist development. Time is money. Yet upon what is capitalism dependent? It is the reservoir of workers who themselves are a product of a system which is not production, but reproduction in the domestic sphere.

A special issue of the New Yorker in 1997 hailed Karl Marx as the person who has taught us most about the dynamics of capitalism and global markets and as long as capitalism persists, his books will remain relevant. Pam Odih thus devotes a section of her study to the labour theory of value. She then moves on to note its deficits in terms of understanding domestic labour and this provides her with a central basis upon which the book unfolds: that is, to see capitalism as both dependent upon the strata of domestic labour, whilst also systematically seeking to undermine that area in its drive for accumulation.

Taking the history of the British textile industry in relation to the dynamics of gender, capitalism and time bears witness to a restriction of the working hours of women by male dominated trade unions, thereby enabling the factory system to exploit domestic divisions of labour in the process of accumulation. Accompanying this was the mechanization of production with the consequence that de-skilling was manifest in the minding of machines. As craft and control were associated with facets of masculinity, this opened up possibilities for women in the factory system. However, they were paid less than men and this tended to cement, rather than challenge, domestic divisions of labour. Those who relied upon home working to supplement family incomes then found themselves subject to the economies of scale associated with manufacturing and so unable to continue in the face of the reach of capitalism into the private sphere. The issue is then raised concerning the extent to which capital is not the only determinant of gender identity, but also the interest which men have in the subordination of women in the domestic sphere.

Dispositions that inform our identities vary. A core argument of this book is that the difference between men's and women's experience of time is in terms of its relationality: time is shared rather than personal and routinely experienced through the presence and expectations constituted in interpersonal relations. Gendered time is thus investigated through a series of insightful interviews concerning the relations between work and the domestic sphere. Hence we have the phrase 'a woman's work is never done' and the experience, encapsulated in chapter five, that there is 'no time for oneself'. The attempts to constitute a domestic space in the face of pressures of time and work driven by a system that is indifferent to context are clear in the accounts of the women in this study.

As capitalism has reached out in the process of accumulation, so its effects on everyday life are ever greater. Whereas we had the textile factories, we now have call centres and global assembly lines. Two highly insightful chapters examine these issues. The first, looking at call centres, takes the issues of audit and emotional labour and finds a tension in their actual performance between the demands for output expressed in the numbers of calls taken and those of quality in terms of customer experience. Some want to evaluate their performance against others, but also clearly recognize the inherent tensions in the explicit aims of a company that seeks quality through customer satisfaction. As a result there is resistance to seeing time and performance according to quantitative indicators of throughput via the mobilization of the rhetoric of the employing organization. Time is inherently conflictual in such settings and the subject of continual negotiations, as well as practices through which employees identify themselves.

The narratives through which we convey and construct a sense of who we are vary in accordance with our experience of time. In just-in-time labour processes there is immediacy: production as instantaneity. Being subject to such processes means we experience time as different things all at once. Continuity, discontinuity and context all lead to expressions of the desire for more flexibility in order to have greater control over our lives. As this occurs, so forms of control in the process of accumulation see others, separated by thousands of miles, subjected to a 24 hour economy in which assembly lines in Asia are seen to benefit from the dexterity' associated with younger women who are paid low wages.

The indifference associated with capitalist accumulation marches on in the form of globalization. Race, class and gender inequalities are not a preoccupation for which there is an assumed responsibility, but a consequence and precondition of what is called 'success'. Free trade is not fair trade and the export-based businesses in developing world countries are forged by the disadvantage of particular groups. The clash between an increasing feminization of the workforce and domestic divisions of labour then repeats itself. Ultimately, large corporations are dependent upon both the formal and informal elements of women's labour. For this reason these dynamics need taking more seriously than they have before. The economy is dependent upon the domestic sphere and this book demonstrates, in a highly insightful manner, why this has to be taken more seriously and is a core issue in all of our futures.

Illustration Credits

Part I An industrial weaving machine. Sir Edward Baines, London 1835. Reproduced by permission of the British Library, Record Number: c7291–03 Shelfmark: 1044.g.23.

Figure 1.1 Spinning and carding wool. Illustrator: George Walker; Havell, R and D, London 1814, Reproduced by permission of the British Library, Shelfmark 143.g.1.

Figure 2.1 Power loom and cotton manufacture Swainson Birley cotton mill near Preston, Lancashire 1834. Reproduced with permission of the Science Museum/Science and Society Picture Library. Record Number: 10243006.

Part II Image Generations of scientific management in clerical work 1948. Photo by Topical Press Agency/Getty Images. Reproduced by permission of Getty Images, Record Number: HA5881.

Part III Image New Times? Post-Fordism and call centre labour process. Photo by Justin Pumfrey, Iconica. Reproduced with permission from Getty Images, Record Number Creative (RR) #200455200–001.

Part IV Twining (Her)Stories in Global Futures. Reproduced by Permission of Getty Images, Record Number Creative (RM) #200449937-001.

Table acknowledgements

Table 2.1 Average weekly wages of flax mill workers in Scotland, in 1833. Changes in the employment of women and girls in industrial centres. Part 1 – Flax and Jute Centres. Labour Department, Board of Trade. Parliamentary Papers 1898, C-8794, p. 17.

Table 2.2 Average weekly wages of flax mill workers in Leeds, in 1833. Changes in the employment of women and girls in industrial centres. Part 1 – Flax and Jute Centres. Labour Department, Board of Trade. Parliamentary Papers 1898, C-8794, p. 62.

Introduction

Gender, capitalist accumulation and the political economy of time

But in the Work we freely bear a Part,
And what we can, perform with all our Heart.
To get a Living we so willing are,
Our tender Babes into the Field we bear,
And wrap them in our Cloaths to keep them warm,
While round about we gather up the Corn;
And often unto them our Course do bend,
To keep them safe, that nothing them offend:
Our Children that are able, bear a Share
In gleaning Corn, such is our frugal Care.
When Night comes on, unto our Home we go,
Our Corn we carry, and our Infant too;
...
We must make haste, for when we Home are come,
Alas! we find our Work but just begun;
So many Things for our Attendance call,
Had we ten Hands, we could employ them all.
Our Children put to Bed, with greatest Care
We all Things for your coming home prepare:
You sup, and go to Bed without delay,
And rest yourselves till the ensuing Day;
...
In ev'ry Work to take our proper Share;
And from the Time that harvest doth begin,
Until the Corn be cut and carry'd in,
Our Toil and Labour's daily so extreme,
That we have hardly ever Time to dream.

(Mary Collier ([1739] 1985: 10–11) *The Woman's Labour*)

2 Gender and work in capitalist economies

Mary Collier presented her poem as a poignant epistle and rejoinder to a poet who seemed unaware of the arduous and prolonged hours of 'the woman's labour'. The berated poet, and object of Collier's one-sided 'flyting', was Stephen Duck who had composed the poem *The Thresher's Labour* ([1736] 1985). Duck had achieved notoriety for his heart-rending account of the desolating physical and psychological conditions endured by the rural labouring classes as a result of primitive accumulation. The development of capitalism required 'non-capitalist social strata as … a source of supply for its means of production' (Luxemburg 1971: 368). The resulting enclosure of the land caused systemic disruptions to English countryside life, and irreparably transformed the access of farmers to common land. In the wake of this upheaval, the rural community was divided into a landless labouring class, dependent for their livelihood on rapacious landlords and feckless leaseholding farmers. Duck chronicled the poverty that accompanied this 'enclosure of the commons'. Of significance is his account of the uncompromising hardship invoked by the sale of the thresher's labour as a unit of time:

> Week after week, we this dull Task pursue,
> Unless when winnowing Days produce a new:
> A new, indeed, but frequently a worse!
> The Threshal yields but to the Master's Curse.
> He counts the Bushels, counts how many a Day;
> Then swears we've idled half our Time way.
> (Duck [1736] 1985: 14)

The hard-edged reality of primitive accumulation is that capitalism, having seized possession of vital productive forces, also needs 'a reservoir of labour power for its wage system' (Luxemburg 1971: 368). This is because the greater part of surplus value is realized through the expropriation of labour time. For these purposes primitive economies, based on the shared ownership of land, directly challenge the market for surplus value. In response, capital sets out 'to liberate labour power and to coerce it into service' (1971: 369). Labour becomes integrated into a commodity economy, and time is ascribed as a measure of productivity. In this context it is 'not the task but the value of time when reduced to money [which] is dominant' (Thompson 1967: 61). 'Time is now currency: it is not passed but spent' (1967: 61). Duck is clearly cognizant of this emerging economy of time. Thus, *The Thresher's Labour* exalts the virtue of industry and condemns the tyranny of wasting time. But Duck's account of time and working-class labour, purposely, marginalizes reproductive labour and the economic materiality of women's work. Indeed, it is notable that *The Thresher's Labour* contains little appreciation, or comprehension, of the extent of women's labour. Female field workers are depicted as 'prattling Females, arm'd with Rake and Prong' (1985: 20). While the labour time of female workers is consistently derided as extraneous to material production. Duck is scornful of the talkative female hay workers. As he derisively proclaims,

'Ah! Were their Hands so active as their Tongues, How nimbly then would move the Raked and Prongs' (1985: 20). Elsewhere the marginalization of the female field worker, from the time of productive labour, is confirmed in the association of women's work with leisure:

> The Grass again is spread upon the Ground,
> Till not a vacant Place is to be found;
> And while the parching Sun-beams on it shine,
> The Hay-makers have Time allow'd to dine.
> That soon dispatch'd, they still sit on the Ground;
> And the brisk Chat, renew'd, afresh goes round.
> All talk at once; but seeming all to fear,
> That what they speak, the rest will hardly hear;
> Till by degrees so high their Notes they strain,
> A Stander by can nought distinguish plain.
>
> (Duck [1736] 1985: 20)

Again and again, Duck signifies the 'noisy prattle' of the female hay-makers, as evidence of their exclusion from the time of material production. Conversely he celebrates the 'epic heroism of the men's competitive scything' (Landry 1990: 62). As it is 'With Heat and Labour tir'd', their scythes do quit (Duck [1736]1985: 18). It is evident that the thresher's labour is bestowed a material status denied that of female labourers. This realization inspired Collier's (1739) impassioned rejoinder. Collier was a working-class rural labourer, keen to highlight women's labour as social and material. The first few lines of her rebuke to Duck make clear a case for women as especially exploited, social and material producers:

> ... My Life was always spent in Drudgery:
> And not alone; alas! with Grief I find,
> It is the Portion of poor Woman-kind
>
> (Collier [1739] 1985: 6)

Collier insistently articulates a 'discourse of "Woman" as agent of both production and reproduction' (Landry 1990: 73). Duck had ascribed the thresher's toil with a heroic determination, which raised masculine consciousness above the indignity of dispossession and the unceasing exploitation of labour time. In the concluding verse of *The Thresher's Labour*, Duck states that 'Like Sisyphus, our Work is never done; / Continually rolls back the restless Stone. / New-growing Labours still succeed the past; / And growing always new, must always last' (1985: 27). Collier's indignation at Duck's rather hackneyed proverbial tropes is particularly animated:

> For us, you see, but little Rest is found;
> Our Toil increases as the Year runs round.
> While you to Sisyphus yourselves compare,
> With Danae's Daughters we may claim a share;

4 Gender and work in capitalist economies

> For while he labours hard against the Hill,
> Bottomless Tubs of Water they must fill.
> (Collier [1739] 1985: 17)

Collier was keen to articulate gender difference in the economic hardship caused by the enclosure of land. This early form of primitive accumulation had doubly dispossessed the labouring woman; 'her body and her labor owned, but neither acknowledged nor appreciated by employer and father or husband' (Landry 1990: 60). As Collier expresses it:

> Now Night comes on, from whence you have Relief,
> But that, alas! does but increase our Grief;
> With heavey Hearts we often view the Sun,
> Fearing he'll set before our Work is done;
> For either in the Morning, or at Night,
> We piece the Summer's Day with Candle-light.
> Tho' we all Day with care our Work attend,
> Such is our Fate, we know not when 'twill end:
> When Ev'ning's come, you Homeward take your Way,
> We, till our Work is done, are forc'd to stay;
> And after all our Toil and Labour past,
> Six-pence or Eight-pence pays us off at last;
> For all our Pains, no Prospect can we see
> Attend us, but Old Age and Poverty.
> (Collier [1739] 1985: 14–5)

Not coincidently the commodification of time emerges in Collier's verse as a particularly rapacious burden. For it is in time that 'the industrious Bees do hourly strive, / To bring their Loads of Honey to the Hive; / Their sordid Owners always reap the Gains, / And poorly recompense their Toil and Pains' (1985: 17). The unbroken rhythm of Collier's prose intentionally reinforces the prolonged toil of women's labour. And this 'toil and pains', is particularly pronounced in Collier's account of the exploitation of female domestics hired, by the hour, by middle-class mistresses:

> The Washing is not all we have to do:
> We oft change Work for Work as well as you.
> Our Mistress of her Pewter doth complain,
> And 'tis our Part to make it clean again.
> This Work, tho' very hard and tiresome too,
> Is not the worst we hapless Females do:
> When Night comes on, and we quite weary are,
> We scarce can count what falls unto our Share.
> (Collier [1739] 1985: 15)

In this short extract Collier successfully conveys class, rather than sexual difference, to be the principal determinant of the uninterrupted nature of female industry. Thus, men are not the source of the woman's labouring burden. Rather, men are fellow subjects struggling to contend with a new economy of time; more structured in its rhythm and harsher in its exactitude than in previous times. To this extent 'Collier's project is one of radical defamiliarization' (Landry 1990: 65). Such intentions are evident in Collier's imaginative reflections on a passing time, in which:

> Our first Extraction from a Mass refin'd,
> Could never be for Slavery design'd;
> Till Time and Custom by Degrees destroy'd
> That happy State our Sex at first enjoy'd.
>
> (Collier [1739] 1985: 6)

Collier adopts a neoclassical mythical age for the purposes of signifying historical exigencies which precipitated the fall of women into 'slavery'. The enclosure of land had brought great capital gains for landowners and leaseholder, but this was at the expense of pre-capitalist economies. Work had once constituted an extension to communal life and workers were not subject to the time controls of capitalist production. As Engels observes, 'they were not forced to work excessive hours; they themselves fixed the length of their working day and still earned enough for their needs' (Engels [1845] 1971: 10). Collier's notion of the descent of woman, from a mythical, gilded age, signifies the asymmetrical effects of enclosure. Early forms of capitalist accumulation instantiated a 'relentless battle of capital against the social and economic ties' of pre-capitalist communities who were systematically 'robbed of their means of production and labour power' (Luxemburg 1971: 370). While vast capital gains were accrued by acquiring possession of the land, capital also needed a reservoir for the expropriation of surplus value. In due course, labour power was integrated into a commodity economy. Duck's account of his fellow countrymen eloquently describes how the local dispossessed peasantry were duly inculcated into a time-disciplined relation to work. His thresher's tale is acutely aware that 'time-keeping [has passed] into time-serving and time-accounting and time-rationing' (Mumford 1955: 5). And thus, the thresher bemoans the ability of commodified work time to galvanize every passing moment of the working day. As Duck puts it:

> The Spacious Fields we now no longer range;
> And yet, hard Fate! Still Work for Work we change.
> Back to the barns we hastily are sent,
> Where lately so much Time we pensive spent:
> Not pensive now, we bless the friendly Shade;
> And to avoid the parching Sun are glad.
> Yet little Time we in the Shade remain,
> Before our Master calls us forth again.
>
> (Duck [1736] 1985: 22)

6 Gender and work in capitalist economies

The notation of time, which emerges with primitive accumulation, embodies a clear distinction between labour and capital. Labour becomes subject to the mechanical schedules of capital and its value is now remunerated according to the linear quantitative units of clock time. Thus, the thresher's labour is integrated into a political economy of time, which demands that his labour generates more value than he needs to survive. The dialectics of capitalist accumulation depend on the commodification of time and the expropriation of surplus labour time. But capitalism is never content 'with the means of production which it can acquire by way of commodity exchange' (Luxemburg 1971: 370). And therein resides a vital limitation to capital accumulation. For in a society composed of solely workers and capitalists, the exploitation of labour time will eventually reach an economic threshold. This is because commodified labour time is a finite resource. It is an indicator of capital and revered as a scarce resource (Hassard 2001: 133). In this respect capital's key source of profitability is also its major liability. Collier's account of the unbearable burden of social reproduction is indicative of how capital is driven to expropriate social strata exterior to the dominion of capital (Luxemburg 1971). Capitalism's political economy of time needs the non-economic times of social reproduction as a reservoir for its development. It is the central contention of this book that the association of women with social reproduction has the effect of situating gender at the heart of capitalism's political economy of time. Capitalism requires that 'We Labour hard before the Morning's past / Because we fear the Time runs on too fast' (Collier [1739] 1985: 13).

Theorizing capitalist accumulation and the political economy of time

The tempo of industrial life had been steadily transforming long before the beginning of the Industrial Revolution. Nevertheless, between 1760 and 1790 a clear distinction had arisen between the old era of agrarian production and the new era of technological change and industrialization (Plumb 1968: 77). The beginning of this revolution had witnessed the fortuitous expansion of British trade and the inception of new markets, both home and abroad. Demand had instantiated the need for increased productivity and the mercantilists had the capital requirements to invest in industrial enterprise. Increased capital and technological developments rapidly transformed traditional methods of industrial organization. The isolated enclaves of domestic production dissipated as the institution of national transport networks bound commercial interest in closer unity. By 1790, it was clearly evident that a profound revolution had taken place, both technical and social.

The Industrial Revolution was driven by a discourse of growth that equated time with technological progress and economic change. To perceive time in these terms implies a construct with linear directionality, cumulative change and rational instrumentality. Such notions were resonant with the intellectual ideas of the European Enlightenment. Scientific thinking advanced a conception of economic progress intent on elevating rationality. Central to this enterprise was the vision of achieving regulated continuous production. This necessitated the development of productive technologies capable of exceeding the limitations of 'natural instruments of production', i.e., the human body (Marx, *Capital*, Vol. 1 [1887] 2003: 354). It also required the acculturation of workers into the time-discipline of industrial capitalist production. Innovations in steam engine-powered production had enabled the large-scale automation of tasks previously performed by craftsmen. Gradually the development of interconnected automation processes precipitated the systematic linkage of machine technologies, and the extensive mechanization of the productive process. With the rise of industrial capitalism, a new time consciousness emerges. Time becomes 'a commodity of the industrial process' (Hassard 2001: 133). Central to this transition is the commodification of productive labour and the economic imperative equating 'acceleration and accumulation' (2001: 133). Technological innovations in manufacturing consolidated the hegemony of linear time to the productive economy and the notion of scarcity. Human agents were now 'obliged to display good stewardship; time was scarce' and as a powerful sign of capitalist progress, therefore, it must be used rationally (2001: 135). Mumford famously observed that 'the clock, not the steam engine [was] the key machine of the industrial age' (Mumford 1934: 14). Large-scale mechanical production and new economies of scale meant that 'sophisticated temporal schedules were necessary to provide a satisfactory degree of predictability' (Hassard 2001: 134). Time became 'a commodity of the industrial process' (2001: 133). By uniting linearity and value, employers come to realize the imperative to efficiently 'use the time of his labour, and see it not wasted' (Thompson 1967: 61).

Labour theory of value

Karl Marx (1818–1833) chronicled historical transformations in the tempo of economic life. In *Capital*, Vol. 1, Marx identifies how in capitalist regimes of accumulation the labour process operates as a generalized system of commodity production, based on wage-labour and the conversion of surplus-value into profit. As he puts it: 'The rate of surplus-value is . . . an exact expression for the degree of exploitation of labour-power by capital, or of the labourer by the capitalist' (Marx, *Capital*, Vol. 1 [1887] 2003: 209).

According to Marx, the consciousness of human being achieves fulfilment through labour. This is to recognize that human beings are, first and foremost, material beings existing in relation to the natural world. Our consanguinity with nature is active, as opposed to passive, for it is based on production. And this productive activity guides human beings into relations with each other. Consequently, human beings in association with each other actively produce 'the means of the reproduction of their material life' (Harris 1983: 180).

Marx elaborates upon this materialist conception of humanity to include an account of self and subjectivity. For it is through labour that human beings control the 're-actions' between the self and nature (Marx *Capital*, Vol. 1 [1887] 2003: 173). By applying labour to the external world, and transforming it, human beings at the same time change their own nature (2003: 173). To this end, Marx contends that:

> At the end of every labour-process [the labourer] not only effects a change of form in the material on which he works, but he also realises a purpose of his own that gives the law to his modus operandi, and to which he must subordinate his will.
> (Marx, *Capital*, Vol. 1 [1887] 2003: 174)

Such dedication is 'no mere momentary act' (2003: 174). It demands 'that during the whole operation the workman will be steadily in consonance with his purpose' (2003: 174). In these circumstances the 'labour has incorporated itself with its subject: the former is materialised, the latter transformed' (2003: 176). Whenever labour is engaged in the whole process of production, this has the effect of creating an embodied, meaningful relation to the labour process. However, the propensity of human beings to achieve the fullness of their humanity, in work, is contingent on the conditions under which labour is performed. Throughout history, human action has constantly advanced its capacities in the 'appropriation of natural substances to human requirements' (2003: 179). Hence the relation of humankind to production is a dynamic process of historical materialism. Following Hegel, Marx asserts the existence of an inherent dialectic in the development and displacement of modes of production. This dialectic produces contradictions and incongruences betweens structural elements of the labour process (i.e., between owners and non-owners of the means of production). According to Marx, the labour process in capitalist production is distinct in its capacities to imbue both economic production and human reproduction with the logic of commodity production. Thus, in capitalist regimes of production, the labour process is transformed 'into the process by which the capitalist consumes labour-power' (2003: 180). Labour power becomes a commodity and 'the labour-process is a process between things that the capitalist has purchased' (2003: 180).

Buying and selling productive labour time

Marx contends that it is labour which produces value, and surplus labour is converted into monetary profit by the capitalist during the circulation of products on the market. Pivotal to Marx's concept of value is an important distinction between 'useful' and 'abstract' labour (Meek 1979). Use-value can be defined objectively as the utility of the product or subjectively as the usefulness of the labour required to produce it. When use-value is considered subjectively, the concept of 'useful' labour emerges (1979: 165). Marx defined 'useful' labour as 'productive activity of a definite kind and exercised with a definite aim' (Marx *Capital*, Vol. 1 [1887] 2003: 49). Labour in this form creates use-value, but the labour which finds expression in profit, according to Marx 'does not possess the same characteristics that belong to it as a creator of use-values' (2003: 49). Commodity production's primary aim is not the creation of use-value as such, but the manufacture of goods for sale. In this sense, use-values are of relevance to the commodity producer in so far as consumer expectations need to be taken into account.

Marx distinguishes 'useful' labour from 'abstract' labour. The latter's distinguishing characteristics are axiomatic to production within modern capitalist societies. As Marx puts it, the concept of 'abstract labour' is 'truly realised only as a category of the modern society' where 'individuals pass with ease from one kind of work to another, which makes it immaterial to them what particular kind of work may fall to their share' (Meek 1979: 165). This abstraction expresses a relation which in fact dates back to a much earlier time when products first started to be turned into commodities. Indeed, the exchange of goods for money designated the essential precondition for capitalism and marked a historical disjuncture with the mode of production which had occurred in the feudal era. The economic and social structure of pre-industrial Britain was organized around a system of feudal agriculture in which land was given as a reward for service. Goods produced in pre-capitalist social formations were typically for immediate consumption and not to be exchanged in a market place. Thus, in feudalism, it is precisely because 'personal dependence forms the ground work of society, there is no necessity for labour and its products to assume a fantastic form different from their reality' (Marx, *Capital* Vol. 1 [1887] 2003: 81). After the Industrial Revolution, and with the inception of factory-based production, the goods produced were legally defined as the property of the owners of the means of production. With growing commodity production, where tasks began to be performed for future needs or for trade, there occurred a more rigid demarcation between the workers and owners or controllers of capital. This was a time when labour first started to 'acquire its social character from the fact that the labour of the individual [took] on the abstract form of universal labour' (Marx 1971: 29, quoted in Meek 1979: 165). The point of significance here is that whereas labour begins to assume a social character from the moment men (*sic*) begin to work for each other, the special form in which this social character manifests itself differs from epoch to epoch (Meek 1979: 165). Following this, Marx identifies how in a commodity-producing society, the social character of each producer's labour manifests itself in the fact that this labour is reduced to abstract labour, and:

> the social character that his (*sic*) particular labour, has of being the equal of all other particular kinds of labour, takes the form that all the physically different articles that are the products of labour, have one common quality, viz that of value.
>
> (Marx, *Capital,* Vol. 1 [1887] 2003: 78)

The distinction between useful and abstract labour is axiomatic to Marx's account of the expropriation of profit through surplus value. If a use-value derives value 'only because human labour in the abstract has been embodied or materialised in it', the magnitude of this value is therefore measured by 'the quantity of the value-creating substance, the labour, contained in the article' (Sayer 1989: 52). The quantitative measure of labour is derived by the expenditure of time and 'labour-time in its turn finds its standard in weeks, days and hours' (1989: 52). Thus:

> Labour has been equalized by the subordination of man to the machine or by the extreme division of labour ... the pendulum of the clock has become as accurate a measure of the relative activity of two workers as it is of the speed of two locomotives ... Time is everything, man is nothing; he is at most, time's carcass. Quantity alone decides everything; hour for hour, day for day.
>
> (Marx 1967: 151)

If human labour creates value, the clock is its measurement. The mechanistic metaphors of time used by Marx are commensurate with the objectification of labour in capitalist production. The logic of the capitalist mode of production 'is and remains – the mass of direct labour time, the quality of labour employed, as the determinant factor in the production of wealth' (Marx 1973: 704). Labour power is defined by Marx as 'the aggregate of those mental and physical capabilities existing in a human being, which he [*sic*] exercises whenever he produces a use-value of any description' (Marx, *Capital,* Vol. 1 [1887] 2003: 164). In capitalist production, what Marx calls 'the dull compulsion of economics' coerces individuals to sell their labour power as there is little other means of survival other than to enter into a subordinate relationship with capital. Conversely, the owners of the means of production retain control over capital and in so doing possess – for the working day – the bodies tied to labour power. The worker for a proportion of the working day is paid back, in the form of wages, the value which is generated from their labour. The capitalist, however, only pays the worker the value of the reproduction of labour power (the sum cost of maintaining the worker at a socially determined level of subsistence). But labour has the curious ability to generate more value than it needs to survive and reproduce itself. The difference between the value of the commodity, created by labour power and the salary supplied to the labourer is surplus value. Thus, in capitalist production, the exchange of equivalences has been turned around to produce a generalized system of commodity production, based on wage-labour and the conversion of surplus value into profit.

Marx's analysis of capitalist production equates capitalist accumulation with the expropriation of surplus labour time. Marx argued that the value of a commodity is determined by 'the quantity of the value-creating substance, the labour, contained in the article' (Marx, *Capital*, Vol. 1 [1887] 2003: 46). Marx further argued that 'the quantity of labour ... is measured by its duration and labour-time in its turn finds its standard in weeks, days and hours' (2003: 46). Thus the primary determinant of a commodity's value is the amount of labour time invested in its production. For Marx, the expropriation of surplus labour time forms the basis of capitalist accumulation. But in Marx's theory the analysis of labour time is relevant only in so far as it has direct relation to capital and the making of profit. Thus, in a society based on commodity production, labour, which exists outside of trade and the market place, is conspicuously absent from Marx's economic categories. In this sense capitalist accumulation materializes 'at the point of production' between the time the worker enters and leaves the factory gate (Williams 1988: 37).

Theorizing gender, capitalist accumulation and the political economy of time

Social relations outside of the point of production are regulated, in Marx's analysis, to the realm of the 'superstructure' and thus not perceived as determinants of the capitalist's expropriation of surplus labour time. Small wonder then that Marx's analysis has been described as resonating with the eighteenth century understanding of 'private and public', in which the private sphere is associated with reproduction and familial relations (Harris 1983: 179). Conversely the public sphere is the basis of economic life. Since domestic labour is situated outside the realm of economic production (as it does not involve the direct exchange of labour power for wages), the economic dimension of domestic labour is conspicuously absent from Marx's analysis of capital (Williams 1988: 40). Marxist feminist writers suggest that forms of work conventionally considered as 'outside the commodity system' and outside of 'economic calculation' invariably relate to work carried out by women (Rowbotham 1973: 68). To this extent, Marx's tendency to exclude domestic labour as a category of capitalist accumulation 'is part of the more general economic dominance and cultural hegemony of men over women' (1973: 68). Marx's failure in this respect stems from his assumption that capitalist accumulation systematically transforms 'social structure as it transforms the relations of production' (Hartmann 1981: 10). The family and domestic labour time expended in the reproduction of the working class are merely discerned as 'by-products of the accumulation process itself' (1981: 10). Feminist writers have been keen to address the marginalization, in orthodox

Marxism, of domestic labour time. In Marxist theory, domestic labour time is, by default, functional to and determined by capitalism (Williams 1988: 40). This is because Marx's focus on the capitalist–proletariat relationship provided little space for an analysis of how the times of reproductive labour relate to capitalist accumulation. But feminist attempts to incorporate gender into Marx's political economy of time have, often, compounded the displacement of 'woman' from a discourse of material production (see Chapter 3). This is because their valorization of domestic labour time, as equating with capital's expropriation of surplus labour time, produces a technically flawed account of Marx's economic categories. To this extent, feminists have, inadvertently, constituted domestic labour time as 'Other' to the economic times of the productive economy. An alternative position is to develop the tendency that Rosa Luxemburg observed, for capitalist expansion to, on the one hand, depend on the preservation of non-economic strata and, on the other, to systematically erode these areas as part of capital accumulation. Similar dynamics are evident in the organization of gender in capitalism's political economy of time. This book argues that the dialectics of capitalist accumulation situate gender at the heart of capital's political economy of time.

Axiomatic to capitalist accumulation 'is the transformation of the commodity into money and retransformation of money into the condition of production' (Marx 1973: 537). The circuits through which capital progresses constitute divisions of circulation, 'and these sections are travelled in specific amounts of time' (1973: 538). In this respect, an important factor determining the realization of capital is not distance to market (space) but the speed travelled. This is because the speed of circulation directly determines 'the speed with which the production process is repeated' (1973: 538). Since this is the case, the fundamental operation of the capitalist economy is to multiply 'how often capital can be realized in a given period of time' (1973: 538). Indeed, businesses which fail to accelerate turnover time, risk surrendering their profits to competitors. Consequently capital must, on the one hand, strive to eradicate spatial barriers to exchange and, on the other hand, strive to 'annihilate this space with time, i.e., to reduce to a minimum the time spent in motion from one place to another' (1973: 593). This is because the velocity of circulation is both a determinant of productivity and a limitation on how often capital 'can reproduce and multiply its value' (1973: 538).

In as much as capitalist accumulation depends on the production of surplus value, the circuit which capital travels 'appears as the time of devaluation' (Marx 1973: 538). Thus any deviation from a circulation time of zero is a deviation from a maximum level of value creation and an obstacle to the realization of labour time. This is because deceleration has the affect of increasing necessary labour time and therefore decreasing the expropriation of surplus labour time. But the intention of capital is not merely surplus value extraction within a given amount of time. It is the purpose of capital accumulation to achieve 'surplus value ad infinitum'

(Luxemburg 1971: 39). And this is a particularly apposite description of the generation, by capital, of 'absolute surplus value'. In this situation, socially necessary labour time contained within the working day remains constant while surplus labour time is significantly increased. It 'is conditional upon an expansion, specifically a constant expansion, of the sphere of circulation' (Marx 1973: 407). Consequently absolute surplus value also has a direct bearing on the technologies of production, as it attempts to yield an increased magnitude of output, while retaining the rate of variable capital inputs to a level which does not threaten the rate of surplus value. To this extent, capitalist accumulation 'cannot exist without constantly revolutionizing the instruments of production' (Marx and Engels 1985: 37). This translates into continuous transformations in the modes of production as all fixed relations are swept away and 'all newly-formed ones become antiquated before they can ossify' (1985: 37). Expanding production, by individual producers, soon becomes a contagion 'which spreads automatically like a tidal wave over ever larger surfaces of reproduction' (Luxemburg 1971: 41).

The creation by capital of absolute surplus values strives towards the universal maturation of the forces of production. And this expanding 'spatial orbit of its circulation' suggests that we must enquire as to how it is that capital is able to sustain an even greater extension of the means of production. 'If labour time is regarded not as the working day of the individual worker, but as the indefinite working day of an indefinite number of workers' (Marx 1973: 539), then the universal expansion of the forces of production would be limitless. But, in so far as necessary labour time is a condition of reproduction, an increase in the forces of production 'suspends capital itself' (1973: 543). From this point of view, the appropriation of surplus labour time is a natural barrier to the repetition of production. Marx recognizes this exigency in his account of 'relative surplus value'. He argued that the 'production of relative surplus value' is based on 'the increase and development of the productive forces' (1973: 408).

The transition to monopoly capitalism in the 1900s, witnessed a systemic transformation in capitalist accumulation from a strategy of 'absolute surplus value' to relative surplus value. Relative surplus value extraction entails reducing working hours through an increased productivity of labour and the development of technology in the mechanization and rationalization of the labour process (Goldman 1995: 16). The more advanced the capital, the more predicated it is upon the continuous expansion of market relations and the more it strives for the accelerated appropriation of surplus value through 'greater annihilation of space by time' (Marx 1973: 539). But in relative surplus value production, the accelerated pace of surplus value creation requires both a quantitative and qualitative expansion of existing consumer markets. This is because the creation by capital of absolute surplus value involves making deductions from 'a given quantity of [value-creating] labour' (1973: 554). In these circumstances capital is continually maximizing the expropriation of objectified labour through extended working hours and this enables 'capital to renew this profitable bargain . . . on a more enlarged scale' (1973: 550). Conversely, in relative surplus value, an increase in the productivity of work is accompanied by a decrease in the number of hours worked. This leads to an accumulation of undifferentiated commodities and the need for the 'creation of new use values' (1973: 408). This suggests the creation of values which exceed the notion of useful values and encompass a spectrum of qualitative differences. To this extent, 'the surplus labour gained does not remain a merely quantitative surplus, but rather constantly increases the circle of qualitative differences within labour' (1973: 408). It is, therefore, apparent that the production of relative surplus value must be augmented by the expropriation of an additional non-capital reservoir of time. Marx provides some indication of this when he states that:

> This creation of new branches of production, i.e., of qualitatively new surplus value time, is not merely the division of labour, but rather the creation, separate from a given production, of labour with a new use value; the development of a constantly expanding and more comprehensive system of different kinds of labour, different kinds of production, to which a constantly expanding and constantly enriched system of needs corresponds.
>
> (Marx, 1973: 409)

It is evident that capitalist accumulation requires a reservoir of non-economic times as a basis for the production of relative surplus value. In contemporary regimes of capitalist accumulation, this translates as 'the universal appropriation of nature as well as of the social bonds itself by the members of society' (1973: 409). Just as production founded on absolute surplus value expropriates the objectified time of 'value-creating labour', so the production of relative surplus value entails 'the exploitation and exchange of natural and mental forces' (1973: 410). Consequently the qualitative times of social reproduction are an integral resource of capitalist accumulation. It is my contention that the association of feminine identity, and women's work with social reproduction, has the effect of placing gender at the heart of capitalism's political economy of time. This book develops this contribution through an analysis of gender and work in industrial times, modern times and post-Fordist times.

Part I Industrial Times

The invention of the steam engine and of machines for weaving and spinning, in the mid-eighteenth century, transformed Britain from being a primarily agricultural society to an industrial nation (Engels [1845] 1971). These early technical innovations 'gave the impetus to the genesis of an industrial revolution' (1971: 9). In 1733, John Kay invented the flying shuttle, which substantially increased the speed of weaving and by the 1750s was widely used in weaving fustians (Rose 1996: 39). Elsewhere, new technology put in motion the mechanization of spinning. Imports of raw cotton had substantially increased during the mid-eighteenth century, reflecting 'a steadily-rising demand for fustians and cotton-linens' (1996: 39). This increase marked the rapid ascent of the British textile industry. But it also brought about a significant threat of labour shortage among a mostly female workforce of hand spinners. Traditionally spinning was carried out in the homestead using a spinning wheel. Technological advances in textile production precipitated new forms of labour market organization. The revolutionary new textile machines could be operated by unskilled women or children who invariably would be paid less than a skilled male labourer. Such profit margins encouraged an unprecedented shift in the participation of women in the labour process. For example, it is estimated that of the 10,000 textile workers employed in 41 Scottish mills in 1816, two-thirds were female and a significant proportion of these were under the age of 18 (Davies 1975: 41). Life in the factories was discordant and harsh. Of concern were the abrasive forms of time discipline administered by the 'frugal-minded overseers' (Bryant 1971: 56). Women and children often fared worse, as they were more likely to be disempowered by an extended division of labour which confined them to the least skilled sectors of the labour market (Honeyman 2000).

Historical records highlight significant difference in the wages of male and female industrial workers. According to Burnette, 'the female-male wage ratio generally varied from one-third to two-thirds, depending on the type of work and location' (1997: 257). But, significant controversy exists over the role of wage discrimination as a determinant of this wage gap. It has been suggested that, for much of the industrial period, normative assumptions about the dynamics of the family meant that employers were disinclined to offer a 'living wage' to females (Valenze 1995: 89). Women were presumed to be economically dependent upon 'a household headed by a male and therefore did not depend only on her wages for subsistence' (1995: 89). Historians, adopting this position, have argued that female industrial workers received a 'customary wage' rather than 'market wages'. The concept of a 'customary wage' suggests that 'women did not receive "market wages" – wages equal to their marginal product – but rather received wages determined by custom and gender role' (Burnette 1997: 261). If this is accepted, it can justifiably be argued that women in the labour market during the Industrial Revolution experienced wage discrimination. Joyce Burnette systematically challenges this orthodoxy. Burnette has applied neoclassical economic theory to the analysis of the female-male wage gap. According to neoclassical economic theory, 'wages equal the marginal product of labour' (1997: 257). Thus, in conventional neoclassical economic theory, any disparities in wages are interpreted 'as evidence of productivity differences' (1997: 257).

Burnette's detailed secondary data analysis of key historical records, sets out to confirm this neoclassical economic model. According to Burnette, historical records consistently suggest that 'the large "wage gaps" historians have used as evidence of discrimination are often simply differences in earnings resulting from differences in hours worked' (1997: 263). She claims that 'during the period conventionally termed the industrial revolution women were less productive than men in most types of work' (1997: 272). According to Burnette, these sex differences in productivity partly stem from differences in human capital (1997: 272). Women were often excluded from apprenticeships and thus acquired less training and skills than males. Females were also less inclined to receive a formal education and had lower levels of literacy than their male counterparts. While recognizing these features to be aspects of pre-market discrimination, Burnette claims that 'they still represented differences in human capital which would have affected productivity and thus women's market wages' (1997: 272). Such conclusions collaborate with conservative discourse, which assumes that disparities in the wages of men and women during the Industrial Revolution were a consequence of market factors (Honeyman 2000: 55). What is lost in such perspectives is an engagement with the dynamics of power which systematically devalued the labour time of female textile workers.

Chapter 1 historically investigates the significance of gender to primitive accumulation. Specifically, this chapter examines the transition from domestic production to the proto-capitalist production of textiles from the 1500s–1800s. Historical changes in the mode of textile production exemplified how, with the emergence of industrial capitalism, productive activity is linked to the 'production for exchange' and associated with the market place (Alexander 1989: 40). Conversely 'production for use' was associated with female labour and the less culturally recognized private sphere of home and family. The emergence of factory-based textile production mapped onto these processes, thus ensuring the economic dependence of women upon the male members of the household. Of particular relevance were the demise of the handicraft's system and the rise of family factories. Both of these were interim stages in the transition from domestic to industrial production. And both of these stages emerged as a consequences of a new political economy of time, which in its early incantations was directed at devaluing the qualitative rhythms of domestic production. Chapter 1 develops this contribution through a combination of theoretical formulations, and the documentary analysis of parliamentary papers derived from the nineteenth century.

Chapter 2 traces the economies of time which established the British textile industry in the nineteenth century. This chapter contends that, in the nineteenth century, capitalism conceded to pressure from men to restrict the working hours of women. Male trade unions were successful in persuading the state to pass legislation restricting the employment of women and children. Male workers capitalized on the restricted working hours of female workers most especially in their claim for 'the so-called family wage' (Walby 1990: 40). Using documentary evidence, Chapter 2 describes how the factory system traded upon gender inequalities in the domestic division of labour time, and exploited this as a basis for capitalist accumulation.

Chapter 3 theoretically develops the empirical theme of Chapters 1 and 2. It critically examines feminist perspectives that have linked the rise of industrial capitalism with the exploitation of domestic labour time. This chapter examines the theoretical complexities encountered when attempting to reformulate domestic labour time as 'productive labour'. According to Margaret Benston (1989), 'the amount of unpaid labour performed by women is very large and very profitable to those who own the means of production. To pay women for their work, even at minimum wage scales, would involve a massive redistribution of wealth' (1989: 41). Maria Dalla Costa and Selma James (1975) make a similar claim in *The Power of Women and the Subversion of the Community*. They argue that the expropriation of domestic labour time is an integral component of capitalist accumulation. Domestic labour time not only produces use-values (i.e., goods and services that have tangible utility) but also surplus value, which is exploited by the capitalist as a source of profit. To this extent, Dalla Costa and James argue that:

> within the wage, domestic work produces not merely use-values, but is essential to the production of surplus value. This is true of the entire female role as a personality which is subordinated at all levels, physical, psychological and occupational, which has had and continues to have a precise and vital place in the capitalist division of labour, in the pursuit of productivity at the social level.
> (Dalla Costa and James 1975: 33)

Dalla Costa and James's account of the family, as a social factory, provoked seismic fissures in Marxist feminist analysis. Chapter 3 problematizes feminist attempts to force an affinity between domestic labour and the economic categories of productive labour time. Domestic labour is indeed 'socially necessary labour' but it does not meet either of Marx's criteria for discerning productive labour (Seccombe 1974: 11). The relation of domestic labour with capital is neither direct (i.e., it is not salaried) nor a source of surplus value (does not create more value than it possesses). To this extent, 'domestic labour is unproductive labour' (in the economic sense) and conforms to Marx's description of an unproductive labour 'exchanged not with capital but with revenue that is wages or profits' (1973: 11). A crucial mistake of trying to force domestic labour into Marx's economic categories is to prompt the mistranslation of domestic labour time as unproductive labour. This only reinforces the tendency for orthodox Marxists to constitute domestic labour time as marginal to the economic categories of capitalist accumulation. An alternative position is to emphasize that capital's political economy of time depends upon the expropriation of domestic labour time as a non-economic resource.

Part II Modern Times

The establishment of wage relations in the second half of the nineteenth century, ensued the rise of the 'employment society' and a movement towards Taylorized, synchronized work. Frederick Winslow Taylor (1856–1915) had formulated the principles of 'scientific management'. Taylor's technological interventions into the 'natural' flow of work events were geared towards achieving the wholesale rationalization of the labour process. Taylorism describes how labour productivity can be dramatically increased by 'breaking down each labour process' into narrowly specialized, unskilled tasks performed according to 'rigorous standards of time and motion study' (Harvey 1990: 123). Time was translated into economic terms and 'it became the medium in which human activities, especially economic activities, could be stepped up to a previously unimagined rate of growth' (Nowotny 1976: 330). Henry Ford applied Taylor's scientific management principles in an attempt to achieve complete and consistent interchangeability of parts and ultimate simplicity in assembly.

Fordist production epitomized the modern definition of time as predicated on the sequential organization of synchronized activities. Fordist industrialism was based on the expropriation of working time and its distinction from one's own time (leisure). The component elements of Fordist production have been described as 'a search for massive internal economies of scale based on assembly line methods, technical divisions of labour and standardization of outputs' (Scott 1988: 173). Fordism entailed the concentration of utilized labour power in minimal units of time, which maximized the extraction of surplus value in its most rational economic form (Braverman 1974).

Ford's use of time and motion studies to calculate the speed of individual task provides further indication of capital's desire to control the rate of production. Indeed, Fordism is indicative of a rapid deskilling and insidious degradation of work. Chapter 4 locates this analysis of Fordism within an overall observation of clerical and service occupations. During the early twentieth century, a vast proportion of Western capital was concentrated in the enterprises of corporate entrepreneurs (Braverman 1974). One consequence of this rapid corporate growth was the demand for expanded office structures and the dramatic increase in general office work (Morgall 1986). The vast expansion in the volume of office work encouraged the pursuit of techniques capable of making office work more efficient (1986: 117). Taylorist processes of scientific management were adopted to measure office work and eventually to control the work process (1986: 117).

Feminist writers have variously suggested that the conception of time embodied in Fordist production is in contradiction with the 'cyclical' and 'relational times' of childcare (Davies 1990, 1994; Deem 1996; Leccardi 1996). Davies (1990, 1994) and Leccardi (1996) have, for example, argued the incompatibility of 'women's time' with a linear perspective which separates work from leisure, the public from the private, and task-based from clock-based orientations to time. But many of these feminist challenges are epistemologically grounded in the very same representational tradition which has secured the hegemony of linear time. For these feminist discourses tend towards either a strategy of reversing the phallocentricity of linear time and/or synthesizing the binary elements of their discourse (i.e., its male/female opposition) into mutually inclusive dualistic pairs. The problem that unites these respective strategies is that they fail to displace the dualistic epistemology that is at the heart of Enlightenment thought. Chapters 4 and 5 present an alternative discourse of time, modern work and gendered subjectivity.

The empirical research, which forms the basis of Chapters 4 and 5, employed an eclectic fusion of in-depth unstructured interviews, observations and group discussions. Respondents were selected through 'theoretical sampling' (Strauss and Corbin 1990). This sampling approach eschews representation for a pursuit of respondent selection based on analytic deduction. In my research, the process of sampling aimed to develop theory by selecting respondents who maximized the theoretical development of key conceptual ideas. Collectively, this amounted to approximately 60 in-depth discussions. The qualitative interviews were informed by a feminist epistemology in which the search for authentic meaning and an authentic account of social reality is a profound methodological challenge. This is because the epistemological foundations of Western discourse implicitly, or explicitly, silence marginalized groups. It does this whenever the experiential differences which distinguish researcher (knowing subject) and researched (unknown object) are obscured (Stanley and Wise 1983). Feminist epistemology identifies mainstream social research as saturated by an androcentric bias. While purporting to speak for human beings, traditional social research is 'grounded in, derived from, based on and reinforcing of the experience, perceptions and beliefs of men' (Du Bois 1983: 106). Conversely, feminist research is research 'on, by and for women' (Stanley and Wise 1983: 17). The sharing of subjectivity through feminist research practice and 'dialogue' (Collins 1991) constitutes a 'conscious partiality'; a partial identification with the research object. Conscious partiality is distinct from mere subjectivism or simple empathy. It seeks to achieve a two-way discussion, between the researcher and interviewee, which widens the consciousness of both, the researcher and the researched. Despite its emancipatory intentions, conscious partiality has been the object of extensive criticism. Game (1991: 30) describes this notion as presuming a unified category 'women' and even more significantly, privileging a certain consciousness 'which knows what it is to be a woman'. In this sense, feminist consciousness constitutes a regime of 'truth' and subjugation, as it 'authorises a representation of those who do not as yet have this [consciousness], but might become one of "us"' (1991: 30).

Feminist epistemology defines the specific form and function of feminist research. Writers variously identify feminist research design as informed by an attention to 'realism'. That is a standpoint motivated towards accessing women's essential material experiences. It is assumed that the material inequalities (e.g., gender difference in pay) experienced by women, define their daily lives in ways that fundamentality differ from the experiences of men. Material inequality mirrors the subordination of women in the public and private spheres. Feminists argue that gender inequalities, in wider society, provide women with a subjective realism which is perceptible to the contradictions and limitations of material culture. But claiming access to knowledge of 'reality' from any standpoint is an inherently problematic exercise. Consequently, it is of no surprise that feminist research premised on methodological realism has experienced significant challenges. Researchers have questioned the tendency for feminist research within this tradition to overly theorize women's daily lives. My research, was therefore, cognizant of how the imposition of sociological categories can overshadow women's experience or force these experiences into existing gender stereotypical categories (Ribbens and Edwards 2000: 2). This involved the need to 'listen closely to accounts of "mundane" everyday domestic activities in detail' (2000: 2). While women's experiences constituted an important starting point for my research, the production of sociological knowledge necessitates that these first person narratives are theorized. The problem is then one of ensuring that the narrative accounts, provided by women, are not limited and that these accounts are used efficaciously.

The design of my study was ultimately motivated by a commitment to engage with a society which traditionally neglects the role of the private sphere in reproducing gender inequality. Thus my empirical research was guided by a studied commitment to making transparent power relationships in personal relationships and family life. Chapters 4 and 5 detail my empirical findings with respect to time, modern work and gendered subjectivity. Chapter 4 defines masculine and feminine times as elements that represent multiple differences, pluralities of characteristics that cross and re-cross the alleged boundary between the two. Chapter 5 uses this alternative discourse of gendered time to directly challenge the masculine fiction of unity that is rational work time, and in so doing reveals how this unity has repressed an Other.

Part III Post-Fordist Times

Harvey (1990) defines post-Fordism as involving a transition from Fordism to 'flexible accumulation', which precipitates the rise of flexible labour markets and flexible geographies of production. Disaggregated labour constituted through 'decentralised forms of labour process and work organisation' forms the principal conceptual basis of Neo-Marxist definitions (Hall 1988: 24). Conversely, 'flexible specialization' ascribes a more sanguine role to economic evolution (Piore and Sabel 1984). Transforming markets, coupled with the rise of non-specialist, highly flexible manufacturing technologies, are assumed to have enabled smaller batch production and flexible working practices (1984). Elsewhere post-Fordism is characterized by 'decentralised management and versatile technologies and workforces to satisfy increasingly volatile markets' (Amin 1995b: 2). As economies of scale are displaced by economies of scope, so flexible specialization evidences heightened competition between firms eager to capitalize on new market niches. Of course, heightened desire for competitive advantage is not new to market dynamics, but what is new is the application of flexibility to define the worker.

Flexibility at work infers empowerment and autonomy in the organization of labour time/space. But advances in information technology have enabled sophisticated methods of regulating the post-Fordist flexible working space. Often alluding to Orwellian imagery, writers variously suggest technological advances in the monitoring of the production process, performance and the management of quality, have given rise to seemingly impenetrable 'electronic panopticons' (Sewell and Wilkinson 1992; Fernie and Metcalfe 1997). They eagerly, if not too hastily, draw attention to the extensive surveillance possibilities of these 'white-collar factories'.

The organizational ethnographic research, presented in Chapter 6, significantly challenges technologically deterministic accounts of call centre labour processes. Chapter 6 details an organizational ethnography carried out in the call centre of a leading financial services provider. This study was informed by postmodern research methodologies. Consequently it challenged the notion of determinacy in the products of empirical analyses. Meanings and actions were less likely to be defined as the determinant manifestations of intentioned social actors. Rather, our analyses established new bases for empirical knowledge focusing on the 'textual strategies' social actors employ to construct versions of reality (Linstead 1999: 49). Knowledge is no longer a product of 'thick description'. Rather, knowledge is relative and fractured as it is dispersed between the realities of discursively produced 'selves'.

A central distinction in our postmodern ethnography was the intention to de-centre the subject of analysis. The subjects of our analysis were not considered as naturalistic objects of our ethnographic gaze. Rather, we recognized self, subjectivity and identity as shifting and multivocal. The subject is constituted 'through a symbolic system which differentiates and fixes them in place whilst remaining outside their control' (Linstead 1999: 59). The consequences of this position for the production of ethnographic research are profound. In our observations, the organization of the call centre was not interpreted as a material artefact inhabited by purposeful subjects. Rather, we perceived the relations between organizational members as symbolically iterative textual artefact. Organization is written, and there is no original author (1999: 59). But the textual content of the organization cannot exist outside of the processes of reading, thus, organizations depend on the reader or recipient for their existence. In this sense, the textual existence of organizations evidences their embeddedness in specific social historical contexts. By emphasizing the sociohistorical embeddedness of knowledge, our postmodern ethnography challenged mainstream efforts to provide a unifying reality of surveillance and time discipline. Our observations focused on the interpretative character of all knowledge and removed the privileging of the representational model that characterizes realist ethnography. Forms of knowledge, including realism, play a large part in determining or legislating what the world consists of through the various procedures they embody as human practices (Lemert 1994: 56). Conversely, our postmodern ethnography challenged the illusionary detached observer of modernist research. In this sense, our observations are situated within the uncomfortable space in which knowledge is no longer a source of fixed meaning.

It was from this methodological position that we empirically defined the tendency for mainstream writers to neglect gender differentiation in their analysis of call centre surveillance and the labour process. In so doing, they fail to recognize the profound implications of a gendered subjectivity and a masculine-driven interest in transforming self-disciplined individuals into time-disciplined corporate subjects.

New times?

Formidable changes are occurring in the present-day organization of work, production and the labour process. The emerging world of flexibility and 'just-in-time labour' has invoked systemic disruptions in the sequential ordering of time/space. Feminists have been less than sanguine in their resistance to the placeless, timeless logic of 'just-in-time labour'. The flexible fragmented present of post-Fordist production is variously argued to be in contradiction with the embodied social relations through which women 'weave' their own autobiographies. While sympathetic to the concept of feminine time, its application to the present labour market context requires intense inquisition and critical reflection. The modern episteme consisted of a constellation of discourses linked to narrative realism. This is to appreciate that basic to all forms of gendered subjectivity is a conscious subject living in time and capable of uniting the literal with the virtual or linking one temporal order (the present) with others (the past and future). The 'timeless times' and dislocated 'spatial flows' of our current era threaten the ability of gendered subjects to form their identities into sustained narratives. Chapter 7 theorises gender and post-Fordist flexible specialization. It challenges the fixed, unitary, relational subject of feminist critique and addresses the problematics of gender and work in the time/space economy of contemporary 'just-in-time' labour.

Part IV Global Times

In recent decades there have been unprecedented transformations in capitalist economies of time and space. Capitalism is now global capitalism and its mode of production 'shapes social relationships over the entire planet' (Castells 2000: 471). It is evident that the more advanced the capital, the 'more extensive the market over which it circulates' (Marx 1973: 539). And the more expansive 'the spatial orbit of its circulation', the greater the necessity for capital to strive for the 'annihilation of space by time' (1973: 539). The global expansion of capitalism is consistent with the necessity for advanced capital to speed 'towards the universal development of the forces of production' (1973: 540). But the universalizing proclivity of capital 'drives it towards dissolution' (1973: 540). This is because 'capital is a limited form of production' (1973: 540). Nevertheless, global capitalism continues to increase the velocity of circulation and multiply its value. This suggests the need to re-examine capital's political economy of time and its relation to the global distribution of labour.

New technologies enable transnational corporations (TNC) to set up decentralized production networks, by outsourcing to different parts of the globe (Peterson and Lewis 1999: 403). Such forms of 'vertical disintegration' (Sayer 1989) coincide with a drive towards export-oriented industrialization by Third World nations. Neo-liberal economics is convincing in its claim that developing nations can only prosper once they have harnessed their economies to the international division of labour. Indeed, the integration of Third World labour markets into the global economy has been axiomatic to a revolution in information technology and the emergence of global textile production. These flexible forms of decentralized production have precipitated spectacular advances in the velocity of circulating capital. In global capitalism, profit is generated, increasingly in decentralized production networks embedded 'in the timeless space' of the 24-hour global economy (Castells 2000: 472).

In the 24-hour global economy, decentralized production intensifies the systematic use of subcontracting as a mechanism for 'deskilling, wage depression and labour intensification' (Taplin 1996: 192). This is because subcontracting establishes patterns of decentralized production, in which firms can 'export labour-intensive and low valued-added tasks' to other firms integrated in a global hierarchical network (1996: 192). In such circumstances flexibility means the speedy delivery of goods in working conditions and where skill development is seen as a costly and time-consuming luxury. Chapter 8 argues that women are the primary workers in the global economy's 'vertically disintegrated' (Sayer 1989) methods of production. This is because the technology used in decentralized production depends on the existence of labour market differentiation among the skilled and unskilled (Balakrishnan 2002). Firms downsizing and subcontracting to smaller operators create 'labour market segmentation between firms in networks' (Taplin 1996: 192). The extent to which this segmentation translates into gender segregation depends on the distribution of skills between the sexes and the resilience of prevailing labour law. Given that the compulsive logic of 'vertical disintegration' is towards the automation of high skilled, high paid jobs, the emerging labour processes tends towards a blend of work intensification and low skilled batch production. Consequently, work in these markets 'is inevitably seen as part of secondary labor markets, with low pay, few benefits and little job security' (Taplin 1996: 197). Women are particularly over-represented in these labour markets. This is because skill distribution is often differentiated by sex, and on a global scale, most subcontracted, labour-intensive work is carried out by women, who have historically been marginalized from skill development training. Of particular concern is the experience of women in the global textile industry. Chapter 8 provides a case study of the international clothing company, Burberry, and the closure of its textile factory in Treorchy (Rhondda Valley, South Wales). In March 2007, this plant was closed and production was relocated to Asia. The case study contains a detailed document analysis of parliamentary papers and witness evidence presented by Burberry to the Welsh Affairs Committee. It argues that a majority of the 309 workers, who lost their jobs, were female and the relocation of production to plants in Export Processing Zones is directly linked to the feminization of labour in the 'new international division of labour'. Indeed, Chapter 8 argues that globalization precipitates the 'spatial degradation' of the production process. It is a disconcerting fact of contemporary textile manufacturing that accelerated turnover gains have become increasingly dependent on the exploitation of a spatially disaggregated, feminized global assembly line. It is important, therefore, to recognise that the 24 hour global economy's 'new international division of labour', is driven by a reservoir of female labour power. As advances in information technology accelerate rates of production, to previously unimaginable levels, this book advances a politics of gender and time.

PART I

Industrial Times

An industrial weaving machine.
Source: Sir Edward Baines, London 1835.
Reproduced by permission of the British Library.

Primitive accumulation and gendered histories of dispossession

Accumulation by dispossession

Writers have often romanticized about the experience of the labouring classes in domestic textile production. Gaskell's (1836) *Artisans and Machinery* contains frequent romantic reminiscences of domestic production and the family division of labour. Gaskell describes how:

> removed from many of those causes which universally operate to the deterioration of the moral character of the labouring man, when brought into large towns ... the small farmer, spinner, or handloom weaver, presented an orderly and respectable appearance. It is true that the amount of labour gone through was but small, – that the quantity of cloth or yarn produced was but limited – for he worked by the rule of his strength and convenience. They were, however, sufficient to clothe and feed himself and family decently, and according to their station; to lay by a penny for an evil day, and to enjoy those amusements and bodily recreations then in being. He was a respectable member of society; a good father, a good husband, and a good son.
>
> (Gaskell 1836: 13–4)

Similar nostalgic reminiscence is evident in Engels' ([1845] 1971) account of domestic textile production. Prior to the revolution in mechanized textile production, the spinning and weaving of raw materials were carried out within the homestead. Engels describes a domestic idyll in which 'wives and daughters spun the yarn, which the men either wove themselves or sold to a weaver' (1971: 9). Substantial numbers of these weavers' families resided in rural areas and earned enough to subsist. And these small-scale, pre-capitalist industries, although labour-intensive, offered the worker 'a stake in the country' (1971: 10). Workers owned the instruments of production and were therefore property owners. In the absence of mass-market demand, working conditions bore little resemblance to the 'dark satanic mills' (Blake [1804] 1991) of factory production. According to Engels, 'in those days the demand from the local market, which was virtually the only outlet for cloth, was steady and satisfactory' (1971: 9). Home markets operated in equilibrium with population increases, and consequently demand mirrored the supply of labourers. And work was not purely an economic activity. In pre-capitalist industry, the worker 'owned property and was a step higher in the social scale' than the labourer in capitalist production (1971: 10). Rural isolation among pre-industrial workers markedly reduced the potential for competition, thus limiting class-based antagonism. These circumstances defined a pre-industrial cultural homogeneity, in which 'workers enjoyed a comfortable and peaceful existence' (1971: 10). Work constituted an extension to communal life and workers were not subject to the time controls of industrial capitalist production. As Engels observes, 'they were not forced to work excessive hours; they themselves fixed the length of their working day and still earned enough for their needs' (1971: 10). It is clearly evident that Engels' observations preference a particular narrative of existence involving benevolent wholesome rural courtship as the basis of village life. Indeed, it is noticeable that in pre-capitalist societies 'work, religion, recreation and amusements, were confined to a small relatively undifferentiated community' (Smelser 1959: 183). It is also evident that by the eighteenth century changes were rapidly taking place and these would irreversibly change the pre-capitalist rhythms of working life. The following extract contains witness testimony presented to a Select Committee established to address the petitions of handloom weavers in the early 1830s. The extract provides an indication of how dispossession was integral to the mechanized times of industrial textile production:

> The Committee understand that you have devoted some time to statistical inquiry? – I have.
>
> In the course of that inquiry, has your attention been at all directed to the condition of the handloom weavers? – It has.
>
> What do you consider their condition to be at present time, in comparison with their condition in former periods, say 40, 30 or 20 years ago, and in comparison with the condition of those employed in other branches of manufacture and agriculture? – I have their condition to be very bad, as well by some personal acquaintance with their condition, as by examination of all the evidence that has been given before Committees of House of Commons within the last 10 or 15 years. I find that they have been getting progressively worse in condition since 1793, but more uniformly so since the year 1816, and

worse than any other class of labourers, except the agricultural labourers in some districts ...

Have you been led to any conclusion with regard to the cause of the increased privation which now prevails among the handloom weavers? – I assign the cause mainly to the uncontrolled and extended application of mechanical power ... The census of 1831 confirms the conclusions to which I had been led by that inquiry, which had no reference to and was formed in ignorance of what that Return would lead to; but it now proves that the extended application of machinery has annihilated all the domestic industry or domestic manufacture which used to prevail among at least from 800,000 to 1,000,000 of families, and which were carried on, not to a large extent, but to such an extent as supplied all the domestic comforts of the family.

(Parliamentary Papers 1835: 28)

The enclosure of land and development of capitalist mercantilism privatized hitherto public resources and precipitated 'a more exacting labour discipline' (Thompson 1967: 78). Work now embodied a new time consciousness which distinguished the employer's time from the labourer's time. Indeed, the enclosure of the commons and early capitalist production 'were both, in some sense, concerned with the efficient husbandry of the time of the labour-force' (1967: 78). The concept of 'husbandry' highlights gender distinction in the articulation of time. Close examination of primitive accumulation reveals significant gender disparities in the development of capitalist mercantilism. Pre-industrial domestic production was patriarchal in structure. The father was the head of the family and his craft defined the household's domestic trade (Alexander 1989: 40). Each member of the family participated in the household's production and thus contributed to the family income. A distinct gender division of domestic labour distinguished a woman's labour within the home from her husband's. The woman assumed responsibility for the well-being of the family and 'her time was allocated between domestic labour and work in production for sale, according to the family's economic needs' (1989: 40). Home was very much a workplace for women and their input to the family economy was considerable. Nevertheless, the woman's domestic labour took precedence over her work in social production and in a patriarchal culture this was assumed 'to follow naturally from her role in biological reproduction' (1989: 40). But the transfer of production to the market place irreparably disrupted this equilibrium. For this involved a shift in the logic of production away from the 'production for use' towards the 'production for exchange' (1989: 40). This shift in productive activity linked the 'production for exchange' with the private sphere and the market place. Conversely 'production for use' was associated with female labour and the less culturally recognized private sphere of home and family. The emergence of industrial capitalism mapped onto these processes, thus ensuring the economic dependence of women upon the male members of the household. Of particular relevance were the demise of the handicrafts system, the rise of the family factory system and the centralization of capitalist production in industrial times. These events collectively ensured that 'women moved into the subordinate and auxiliary positions' within the industrial capitalist labour process (1989: 40–1). This chapter argues that the transition from domestic production to proto-capitalism fostered gender inequality in capitalism's emerging political economy of time.

Enclosure and textile production

> In the times of Ancient Britons, Romans and Saxons and ever since the spare moments of the housewife, her maids and daughters had been devoted to spinning the supposed occupation of our mother eve.
> (Trevelyan 1973: 35)

The impetus for the formation of the English textile industry can be traced back to the arrival of the Cistercian Order in 1138 (Addy 1976). The Cistercian monks followed an especially strict form of Benedictine rule, which led them to inhabit uncolonized areas in the north of England and the Welsh valleys. This land was unsuitable for arable farming, as the soil was poor and shallow. It was, nevertheless, suitable for sheep grazing and abbeys were soon able to maintain flocks up to 12,000 in number (1976: 3). The Cistercians soon generated a reputation for the high quality of their wool, attracting the attention of European merchants. By the mid-twelfth century, the Cistercians were entering into contracts with local lords so as to expand their capacities and create new forms of enclosed farming called granges. Alongside the wool exporters emerged a new class of merchants, called 'woolmen', who travelled to the scattered farms collecting wool, which they sold to the exporting merchants.

By 1337, the export of wool had become so important that Edward III (1312–77) used it as a diplomatic weapon against France in the Hundred Years War. Edward III also mobilized the export of wool as a source of taxation revenue to fund the war. In order to achieve the efficient collection of duties he designated specific towns to be 'the centres of the staple market for wool exports' (Addy 1976: 4). The Staple was an area where English goods for export were collected, taxed and sold. By 1390, the majority of raw wool was exported through the Staple at Calais. The customs levied on export of raw wool from Calais became a substantial source of royal revenue, until this centre was captured by the French in 1558. Additional areas designated as staple towns for the collection of wool included Winchester, York, Lincoln, London, Newcastle and Bristol. King Edward, in an act of creative taxation, turned to these new Merchant Staplers to bargain for loans and levies and in return provided these companies with a monopoly on the export of wool (Trevelyan 1973). King Edward's fiscal ingenuity in the creation of mercantile provinces for the purposes of taxation is recognized to have contributed to the generative conditions for English capitalism. As Postan (1939: 165) puts it:

> The great breeding season of English Capitalism was in the early phases of the Hundred Years War, the time when the exigencies of Royal finance, new experiments in taxation, speculative ventures with wool, the collapse of Italian finance and the beginning of the new cloth industry, all combined to bring into existence a new race of war financiers and commercial speculators, army purveyors and wool monopolists.

The development of capitalist financiers and public creditors in the wool trade was later accompanied by the emergence of capitalist organizers of cloth manufacture. In Ancient Britain, the leisure activities of housewives was mainly devoted to spinning. Conversely, weaving was practised by men, who were specially trained as websters to weave cloth in their own cottage for the local peasantry. By the Middle Ages, the majority of towns and villages produced cloth of some variety. In the fourteenth century, the production of standardized cloth began to transfer to the country districts, particularly to the West regions of England. This was because of the invention of the fulling stocks, driven by waterpower for the accelerated finishing of woollen cloth (Addy 1976). Prior to this, the fuller using human labour; hand, foot and club had carried out one of the central processes of cloth making. With the invention of the fulling stocks, this practice was being conducted by waterpower. Consequently, the industry began to move from the towns towards areas with fast, flowing streams. By 1337, the Cotswold, Pennine valleys and the Lake District were developing a cloth industry, which began to compete seriously with the king's investment in East Anglia. Government legislation during the mid-sixteenth century further strengthened the growth of the cloth industry. Merchant Adventurers, supported by weavers guilds, lobbied the Edwardian government to pass the Weaver's Act of 1553 and later the Marian Act of 1558. Both of these acts were intended to overcome the rapacious effects of a decline in the wool trade. It was a condition of these Acts that weavers in the old towns could not possess more than two looms each and in rural area weavers were restricted to one loom. Conveniently these Acts did not apply to the north, thus Manchester, Huddersfield, Halifax, Leeds and Bradford were exempt from these restrictions and 'received an impetus to develop their woollen trade' (1976: 5).

The expansion of the textile industry necessitated new forms of economic organization. A division of labour began to emerge which segregated the textile manufacturing process into specialist crafts – carding, spinning, weaving, fulling, dyeing and cloth finishing. In 1563, the Statute of Artificers restricted the practice of the craft to 'those who had served an apprenticeship of seven years and empowered the Justices of the Peace to forbid all engaged in the craft who had not served such an apprenticeship, to cease manufacture' (1976: 5). The industry benefited from these quality controls, but the rapid expansion of the cloth trade for the market, at home and abroad, inevitably meant that the power of the Craft Guilds would decline. In place of the local interests of Craft Guilds, emerged the entrepreneur 'with a more than local outlook and with money at his command' (Trevelyan 1973: 37). The entrepreneur was a central component of the putting-out system. In this system, raw material and equipment were rented out to the peasant labourer and the half manufactured and finished articles, which were passed on from craftsman to craftsman from place to place, until marketed and sold. This form of economic organization needed capital investment. And thus we find the emergence of the capitalist clothier 'employing many different people in many different places' (1973: 37). By the end of the seventeenth century most home-based industries operated according to a putting-out system and artisans were paid according to piece rates. This early stage in the evolution of the textile industry is often defined as the proto industrial era, because 'textile production largely took place in rural cottages' (Rose 1996: 31). These geographically dispersed rural proto-industrialists 'were linked to adjacent areas by a web of mercantile credit' (1996: 15).

Women and domestic textile production

Merchants from the central towns would distribute materials, on credit, to the domestic textile labourers. These 'putters out' would in turn supply domestic spinners and weavers who would be paid a piece rate. The produce was returned to the merchant for finishing, marketing and selling. This system of production was by no means uniform. Indeed, the individual units of textile production operated asynchronously across the proto-industry. Patterns of work were governed by an 'essential conditioning in different notations of time provided by different work-situations and their relation to "natural rhythms"' (Thompson 1967: 59). This is evident when we consider the processual rhythms involved in domestic spinning:

> [D]omestic manufacture used to pervade every labourer's cottage, every farmhouse, and the habitations of the handicraftsmen ... the labourer's families were more generally employed in carding and spinning of wool, given out by the shopkeepers of the villages; and the yarn, after taken back by them in exchange for the articles of the shop, passed into other hands to be wove; the farmhouses and the houses of the handicraftsmen, such as the smiths, carpenters, wheelwrights, and persons of that description, were more generally employed in the spinning of flax, the yarn of which they afterwards sent to wove, some for sale and some for domestic use.
> (Parliamentary Papers 1835: 28)

In the process of spinning, the raw wool received, by domestic producers, was first of all segregated into different qualities according to such criteria as fibre length, strength and softness. The practice of sorting had an interesting gender legacy. According to Busfield (1988), in the fourteenth and fifteenth centuries women were assigned the role of 'wool sorter'. Busfield quotes a statute legislated in 1554, which declared that 'the experience of sorting "consisteth only in women as clothiers' wives and their women servants" ' (1988: 155). However, at some point between the sixteenth and seventeenth centuries, wool sorting became a task undertaken by men. This coincided with the growing organization of the wool trade and the transition from the family-based preparation of raw material for production to the sorting of raw materials by male workshop-based employees. Having monopolized the occupation, men secured this control by restricting access to apprenticeships and 'refusing to impart their skill to women' (1988: 155).

Nevertheless, women undertook virtually all the intermediate stages of the production process. Thus they were involved in scouring the raw wool, removing foreign matter and opening out the cotton fibres. The central aim, of this latter stage, was to disentangle the wool mass so as to produce a roll (or carding) of a sufficiently even density (Rose 1996). A pair of cards (an instrument for combing wool) would be used to straighten the fibres into a manageable sliver for spinning. The process of spinning the cardings involved teasing out the fibres (drafting), while simultaneously twisting them together (Figure 1.1). The spun thread was continuously wound onto a bobbin held by a spindle or directly onto the spindle so as to

Figure 1.1 Spinning and carding wool
Source: George Walker, London 1814.
Reproduced by permission of the British Library.

form 'a cop – a cylinder of yarn with conical ends', which was fitted onto the weaver's shuttle (1996: 31). Spinning was generally recognized as woman's work along with carding, doubling and hanking, and the two finishing processes of burling and mending (Busfield 1988: 155). Men were invariably employed in the initial stages of wool sorting. Men also specialized in the finishing processes, which involved willeying and fettling, scouring and milling, raising the nap and shearing, pressing and packing. And, virtually all aspects of weaving were designated to men.

In summary, the typical textile family, in the mid-eighteenth century was involved in a putting-out system. It was unusual for a cotton weaver to be self-employed; the majority of weaving families relied upon merchant agents for the acquisition of equipment, raw materials and the sale of cloth. And yet the family maintained a certain degree of isolation as a productive unit. According to Smelser, the father was the 'occupational head' of the family and specialized in the co-ordination of the weaving process (1959: 183). The apprentice system had largely disappeared by the 1700s, leaving fathers to assume responsibility for training their sons in the art of weaving. In the domestic system, women were responsible for spinning and preparatory activities. It was this stage of the textile production process, which first felt the impact of technological innovation. This is because the period between 1740 and 1770 was pronounced by a fecundity of inventions designed to improve methods of spinning.

Textile innovation and the subject of dispossession

The invention of the steam engine, and of machines for weaving and spinning, in the mid-eighteenth century, transformed Britain from being a primarily agricultural society to an industrial nation (Engels [1845] 1971). These early technical innovations 'gave the impetus to the genesis of an industrial revolution' (1971: 9). Of particular relevance was the creation of the spinning jenny, which was patented by James Hargreaves in 1770. The spinning jenny complemented the technological improvement to looms achieved in 1733 by John Kay's flying shuttle. Legend has it that Hargreaves invented the spinning jenny after having observed an occasion in which his wife's spinning wheel had become upset on the floor. He was thus inspired to produce a machine driven with multiple upright spindles (Quennell and Quennell 1933). In contrast to its more cumbersome predecessors, a single individual could operate the spinning jenny and the inclusion of multiple spindles enabled it to produce more yarn. Richard Arkwright's water-powered frame (patented in 1769) and Samuel Crompton's mule (invented 1774–9) later accompanied the introduction of the spinning jenny.

Smelser argues that these innovations in hand operated textile machinery, initially, 'merely rearranged labour within the domestic system' (1959: 184). This is particularly evident with regards to the spinning jenny, which was sufficiently small enough to be located in the cottages of labourers, or in adjacent workshops (Chapman 1987). The improved hand operated spinning machines were, indeed, initially small enough to remain in the home. But the extent to which the cottage jenny merely reshuffled the division of labour requires critical analysis. It would appear that Smelser's observations regarding continuity in the social structure of the family, was defined solely in terms of the 'occupational head' of the family. Indeed, three premises concerning the 'occupational head' guide Smelser's observations. First, he argues that the family's primary earning power, 'at least after 1780', continued to reside with the husband in either his capacity as spinner or weaver (1959: 185). Second, the new cottage machines appeared not to have disrupted 'the traditional relationship between father and son' (1959: 185). According to Smelser, 'in either spinning or weaving the father continued to instruct his son in the trade' (1959: 185). Ultimately the domestic system was able to withstand the potential structural disruptions presented by hand operated machines, because the family economy continued to be based in the homestead, albeit under the continued supervision of the patriarch.

Smelser's account of the family's structural form, during its transition from domestic production to its entrance into the factory system, has been the subject of significant critical reflection. Of particular interest is Edwards and Lloyd-Jones's (1973) critical challenge, entitled *N.J. Smelser and the Cotton Factory Family: A Reassessment*. First of all, they claim that Smelser's account of the first stage in textile industrialization (from 1770–90) is premised on inconsistent data. Smelser's observations regarding the father's continued role in the instruction of their son in 'either spinning or weaving' failed to recognize that prior to the advent of factory spinning, child spinners were instructed by females (Edwards and Lloyd-Jones 1973: 305). This challenge is supported by Pinchbeck (1969) in her examination of *Women Workers in the Industrial Revolution*. She uses historical evidence to confirm that the father administered the weaving and the mother had primary responsibility for preparatory processes, including the training and setting to work of infants. Engels also describes how, in the domestic textile industry, 'wives and daughters spun the yarn which the men either wove themselves or sold to a weaver' (1971: 9). Thus it can be discerned that in the domestic system it was women who specialized in spinning and assumed the responsibility for instructing children in their daily tasks. It was only with the advent of the factory system that there appeared marked increases in the numbers of males involved in spinning.

This inaccuracy in Smelser's (1959) account of the initial stages in the textile revolution is consistent with a level of gender myopia throughout his analysis. Female experiences, while not entirely neglected, are defined in relation to their male counterparts. The apparent partnership between the sexes, within the domestic system of family production, was actually segregated according to a hierarchy of gender roles. Women were designated as providing the 'unskilled work' while males were assumed to be engaged in the 'skilled work' (Holloway 2005: 27). It is argued that the calibration of skill derived not from technical difference in the complexity of work, but rather as part of the patriarchal control that a man possessed over his family who were his co-workers. The factory system emerged within the interstices of these traditional working structures, which made it possible to further refine the gender division of labour.

Prior to the technical innovations in hand operated machines, weavers needed to keep several female spinners busy to sustain a steady flow of yarn. Indeed, it has been said that before innovations in the mechanization of spinning 'the force of custom prevented men from engaging in any appreciable numbers in what was regarded as women's work' (Busfield 1988: 157). Men assumed the task of spinning only when innovations in spinning, at first, produced machines which demanded considerable strength and skill. Smelser recognizes these shifts in the patterns of female labour. Thus, he details how 'through 1780 the jennies increased the gains of females in a family and of the family in general' (1959: 184). Smelser accurately claims that thereafter 'women were displaced by the waterframe factories and the skilled male jenny mule operatives' (1959: 184). For some time these males were ascribed the status of an 'aristocracy of spinners'. This accolade was also partly due to the fact that these spinners had previously been weavers who had invested capital in the new spinning machines. The accumulated affect of these changes was to eclipse the female hand spinner who 'by the nineteenth century had disappeared almost entirely' (1959: 184).

Nevertheless, for Smelser, the demise of the female hand spinner is of little relevance to the 'social structure' of the family economy. Thus Smelser is able to make the unusual claim that 'the period between 1780 and 1790 was a 'golden age' for the domestic spinner; his earnings increased, but the structure of his employment remained the same' (1959: 185). Here as elsewhere, Smelser appears oblivious to the economic disadvantages experienced by female textile labourers. In 1778, a Sisterhood of Hand Spinners at Leicester petitioned Parliament in defiance of the factory system stating that:

> The business of spinning in all its branches hath ever been time out of mind the peculiar employment of women; insomuch that every single woman is called in law a spinster ... it is with great concern your petitioners see that this ancient employment is likely to be taken from them ... This we apprehend will be the consequence of so many spinning mills, now erecting after the model of cotton mills.
>
> (Davies 1975: 53)

Innovations in spinning technology had precipitated a contraction of the domestic spinning industry and the displacement of female hand spinners. And this condition of dispossession was accentuated by the emergence of the 'jenny factories' and the 'family factory' system of manufacture, which were pervasive from 1770 to 1790.

Jenny factories

Traditional histories of textile production, focus on Richard Arkwright's factory system as the first major innovation in the organization of industrial production. In fact, the economic organization of industrial production first occurred in insignificant places, such as 'jenny factories' and 'mills', which emerged in the first quarter of the eighteenth century. The spinning jenny initially augmented the system of family-based production. The early versions of the jenny could be operated without motor power, occupied little space and thus could easily be fitted into existing domestic working patterns. Outwardly the early models of the spinning jenny presented little challenge to the organization of the industry. But this is not to assume that experimentation and innovations in the organization of the jenny were limited to the operatives in their homes (Edwards and Lloyd-Jones 1973: 306). It has been proposed that prior to the full-scale establishment of the factory system there existed factories, which operated jennies and were organized in hamlets 'where the factory would form the nucleus around which villages formed' (1973: 306). Wadsworth and Mann observed the rapid growth of jenny factories during the decade 1770–80:

> Arkwright's achievement was to apply power to the whole sequence of the operations of carding and spinning, which became a continuous process carried on under one roof. The numerous mills which were springing up, especially in Lancashire, at the same time that his factories were being established, were more varied in character. The carding engine, which was coming rapidly into use after 1770, usually formed the nucleus of these undertakings. In its first crude forms it was capable of being employed as a domestic machine to be turned by hand, and it found a place in the warehouse of the manufacturer, who could give out the cardings to be roved and spun by domestic workers ... The great demand for cotton warps, created first by velvet manufacture, and then by calico manufacture which Arkwright brought into existence ... gave strong inducement for the small capitalist to add spinning jennies, twisting and warping mills. No inconsiderable part of the cotton twist for the large production of velvets that is reflected in the export returns for the later seventies, must have been furnished by these new carding and jenny mills, since at that date Arkwright's factories were hardly numerous enough to have met the demand. Weft spinning remained for the most part a domestic operation performed on the single spindle or the smaller jennies. These carding and jenny mills were of all sizes, from the small shop with nothing but a hand card engine, to the most elaborately organized factory in which all the operations from the cleaning and picking of cotton to warping were carried on and in which horse or water power was used.'
>
> (Wadsworth and Mann 1931: 492)

It is important to emphasize that these factories operated outside the home and in so doing transferred gender inequalities, evident in the family economy, to the factory system. This proposition derives, by extension, from Smelser's claim that the advent of the spinning jenny 'eclipsed the female hand spinner, who by the beginning of the nineteenth century had disappeared almost entirely' (1959: 184). Given the direct links between the arrival of machine spinning and the decline of the female hand spinner, it is plausible that the general application of the spinning jenny in factories accelerated the plight of the wife who 'became more secondary economically' (1959: 184). The gender division of labour was beginning to exert financial penalties on the female members of the family and further developments in manufacturing technology were having similar effects.

Family factories and time-disciplined production

When James Hargreaves took out the patent for the spinning jenny in 1770, the initial design had the potential capacity for 16 spindles, in 1784, Hargreaves had increased this capacity to 80 spindles (Edwards and Lloyd-Jones 1973: 307). A consequence of the increased spindle capacity was to make the jenny too expensive, large and cumbersome for domestic workers. This development in machine manufacture encouraged the further transition of textile manufacturing away from the domestic sphere. Smelser observes that the waterframe and the mill followed the invention of the domestic jenny (Smelser 1959: 185). One of the earliest mills appeared in 1704, and was established by Thomas Cotchett of London, who obtained a lease from the Mayor and Corporation of Derby to erect a silk spinning mill (Addy 1976). Further enquiry into the types of manufacturing accommodation, categorized as a 'mill', reveals some rather ambiguous arrangements. In its early inception 'the word mill sometimes meant no more than a machine which performs its work by rotary motion' (Valenze 1995: 88). But this ambiguous arrangement was soon to change as mill production attracted increased capital investment. Shrewd entrepreneurs were efficaciously adapting textile technology to the mill setting. Mills had, of necessity, to be built where there was access to a powerful stream of water. Such preconditions saw the development of mills in narrow parts of valleys where there was a strong fall of water to power the waterframe. Consequently the mills were a large distance from the industrial centres 'often in small hamlets where the supply of labour was a problem and communications frequently difficult' (Addy 1976: 25).

These remote conditions prompted the enterprising mill owner towards the need for a 'disciplined and punctual working force, which could appear at a set time to maintain continuos production of cotton yarn' (Addy 1976: 25). According to Addy, 'the habits of the native inhabitants of these river valleys had to be changed from those of ignorant, rough men and women who worked when they desired and served no master but themselves' (1976: 25). Though domestic production was labour-intensive and arduous, labourers were less subject to time-disciplined production. It has been suggested that a labourer could select their working times and that 'the relationships between employer and employee were personal and not bound by rigid rules and regulations' (Addy 1976: 30). Some indication of this relation to time and work is evident in the following extract from a parliamentary report published in 1840:

> The domestic weaver is apt to be irregular in his habits, because he does not work under the eye of a master. At any moment the domestic weaver can throw down his shuttle, and convert the rest of the day into a holiday, or busy himself with some more profitable task; but the factory weaver works under superintendence; if absent a day, without sufficient cause, he is dismissed, and his place supplied by one of greater power of application. One hundred webs, therefore, in a factory of hand-loom weavers, would be finished, even in Manchester, in the time in which 50 would not be finished by an equal number of domestic weavers.
>
> Parliamentary Papers (1840: 10)

E.P. Thompson's (1967) seminal essay 'Time, Work-Discipline and Industrial Capitalism' identifies the transition from domestic production to industrial production, in the eighteenth century, as having created a radical disruption to the qualitative rhythms of artisan craft-based work. Thompson argues that the rise of industrial capitalism precipitated a marked transformation in the dominant 'task-oriented' temporal consciousness, towards a greater synchronization of labour and more exact time routines. These changes entailed the internalization of a more rational, quantitative 'time orientation' to labour and life. Thrift and abstemiousness were enjoined on all workers as the new time ethic combined with a Protestant work ethic to produce a utilitarian economic approach to time. To this extent, 'economy became the watchword; saving time, avoiding waste and fraud, eliminating inconvenience' – these were the vital imperatives of the new manufacturing age (Valenze 1995: 88). But factory owners faced a fundamental difficulty in implementing a regime of work time discipline. Unskilled workers, in particular, disliked the protracted uninterrupted shifts in the mills and were averse to similarities between the early factories and the parish workhouse (Chapman 1987: 46). Comparisons between the two forms of institution related specifically to 'the insistence in both on close and continuous supervision of work by overseers' (1987: 46). A consequence of this abhorrence to the disciplined schedule of factory life was that, in its early stages, the vast proportion of factory workers were casual labourers.

The 'restless and migratory spirit' of mill workers troubled employers (Chapman 1987: 46). Richard Arkwright responded to the new challenge of time-disciplined production, by building houses for whole families and so creating new communities which could be acculturated into the clock time of industrial capitalism (Addy 1976: 25). Mary Rose (1996) in her account of the Lancashire Cotton Industry, describes how in the 1820s and 1830s, many rural mill owners 'really began community building in earnest ... in so doing they created a community-based labour market which they controlled' (1996: 23). Mill owners were determined to counteract the time work patterns of domestic production. In an attempt to inculcate a time-disciplined relation to work, among labourers, mill owners set about creating family-based communities, which determined the organization of work. Similar observations are provided by Smelser. As he describes:

> Two sets of wage books illustrate this invasion of family standards into the manufactory. In the spinning mill of Robert Peel and his partners near Bury, very few of the 136 persons employed as free labour in 1801–2 were adult males. Ninety-five of the 136, however, belonged to twenty-six families, showing the opportunity for members of the same family to gather on the premises. Furthermore in every case [that employees took labour only on a casual basis] no other member of their families was employed there ... their employment was very irregular and stands in striking contrast to the steady work of the majority of the families.
>
> (Smelser 1959: 185)

Such patterns of family employment not only augmented the household income but also 'allowed for the presence of a parent with the children during working hours' (Smelser 1959: 185). This, according to Smelser, was a vital condition preventing 'the family from disintegrating into a mere aggregate of individuals in a free labour market' (1959: 188). The departure of textile production from the homestead had 'threatened to disperse the family through the factories at the cost of its tradition and its solidarity' (1959: 188). This wave of change was compounded by the influx of women and children into the workplace which had 'weakened the traditional domestic basis for child-rearing' (1959: 188). According to Smelser, the presence of women and children within the textile labour force also challenged the male as the main breadwinner. Furthermore it undermined the father's ability 'to train his children for a trade' (1959: 188). The employment of families as communities stemmed the demise in the patriarchal role of the father. In this arrangement, the factory became a community. The interests of the family functioned to discipline the conduct of employees and also provided a reserve army of child labourers. Alongside these employment structures existed the activities of humanitarian masters 'who provided several correctives – welfare, education, recreation, etc.' (1959: 188). According to Smelser, the combined effect of family employment and humanitarian education was to produce 'a network of controls based upon kinship and community bonds' which 'permeated the apparently impersonal factory' (1959: 191). Certainly the employment of entire families went some way towards ameliorating the depersonalization and differentiation of the free labour market. But it needs to be recognized that it was also efficacious for the mill owner to employ parents and relatives as a corrective in the maintenance of a time-disciplined workforce. Furthermore, adult males were often hired as 'occupational head' of the family and given the skilled jobs. These adult males would then hire immediate members of their family as assistants to 'work as piecers and scavengers' and there was a tendency for the adult male to select his wife and children to carry out these menial roles (Edwards and Lloyd-Jones 1973: 311). Consequently the male could continue to occupy his 'authoritative position as head of the family' (1973: 311).

Conclusion

As industrial change continued, entrepreneurs began to establish spinning factories, which were driven by water power (Engels [1845] 1971: 14). These innovations in spinning technology expanded unabated throughout the eighteenth century. Social commentators remonstrated about the relentless march of machine technology and the abandonment of hand techniques. Engels described the application of mechanical power as having 'brought about the victory of the machine over the hand worker in the main branches of British Industry' (1971: 14). For Engels, 'the history of the hand-workers has been one of continued retreat in the face of the advance of the machine' (1971: 14).

The transition to mechanical production was well advanced by the early nineteenth century bringing with it huge increases in output and production. Cotton production had become the main pillar of Britain's industrial profile and the expansion of mechanization had strengthened the competitive presence of British industry in foreign markets. But this process also had the effect of accelerating the 'growth in the numbers of the proletariat' (Engels [1845] 1971: 15). As weaving became a more profitable industry, part-time weavers disappeared 'and were absorbed into the class of full-time industrial workers, who had no links with the soil either as owners or tenants of smallholdings' (1971: 10). To this extent, labourers within the textile industry became 'purely members of the proletariat'. 'The industrial worker no longer owned any of the means of production, and they lost all security of employment' (1971: 15). And with the introduction of power, 'the workers became machine minders rather than machine operatives' (Chapman 1987: 17). Chapter 2 argues that the transition from family factories to depersonalized mechanized systems of textile production generated gendered social consequences, which were 'of a far-reaching character' (Engels [1845] 1971: 15).

2

Weaving time

Gender and the rise of the British textile industry in the nineteenth century

Time, work-discipline and the textile revolution (1750–1870)

In the 1800s, the great cotton mills of the Midlands and North of England became the heartland of Britain's Industrial Revolution. The cotton industry was the 'most important branch of industry' (Engels [1845] 1971: 15). In the early 1800s, the percentage of British industrial output constituted by the cotton industry had grown from an annual rate of 12.76 per cent in the 1780s to 17 per cent in 1801 (Rose 1996: 26). From 1771 to 1775 the average amount of raw cotton imported into Britain, annually, was £5 million (Engels [1845] 1971: 15). In 1841, the importation of cotton amounted to £528 million, and by 1860 it had risen to £1000 million (Thomson 1971: 13). In the industrial textile mills, raw cotton was spun and woven by steam-driven machinery capable of vastly exceeding the productive capacities of domestic manufacturing. Engels notes that in 1834 '76½ million lb. of cotton yarn and cotton hosiery to the value of £1,200,000 sterling' was being produced in English factories (1971: 15). During this time the British cotton industry employed over 8 million mules spindles, 110,000 power looms and 260,000 handlooms.

The transition to mechanical production was well advanced by the early nineteenth century bringing with it huge increases in output and production. Cotton production had developed into one of the main pillars of Britain's industrial profile and the expansion of mechanical production had strengthened the competitive presence of British industry in foreign markets. But this process also accelerated the growth in the numbers of the proletariat. As weaving was transformed into a more profitable industry, part-time weavers were absorbed into the category of full-time industrial workers who had no links with the means of agricultural production. Thus labourers in the textile industry became purely members of the proletariat.

In its early stages, mechanization set in motion marked transformations in the content and profile of the textile industry's labour force. It was against this background that women's increased participation in textile manufacture was observed to be a new social phenomenon. As Gaskell notes, 'that adult male labour having been found difficult to manage, and not more productive – its place has, in great measure, been supplied by children and women' (1836: 147). For many social commentators, increases in female labour market activity were merely an extension of the home-based skills that women traditionally assumed. It was customary for spinning to be carried out in the homestead using a spindle wheel. In this context, the handicraft of spinning merely consisted of two primary motions involving the stretching and twisting of combed cotton fibres. Women assumed responsibility for spinning and for the most part the output of spinners matched the demands of domestic weavers. With the invention of John Kay's flying shuttle, in 1733, there occurred a speeding up of the weaving process, which produced a technological imbalance between the capacities of spinners and the yarn required by weavers (Rose 1996: 39). Concerns regarding the economic impact of this technological imparity prompted the Royal Society of Arts to offer financial rewards for the invention of a loom capable of doubling a weaver's output and a spinning machine which would mechanize hand spinning (1996: 39). The resulting innovations in spinning and weaving machinery required considerable physical strength and this for Engels provided the basis as to why 'men began to replace women as spinners' (1971: 13). Technological developments in textile machinery later redressed this gender ratio in favour of female employers. To this extent Gaskell observed that a change was rapidly occurring in the profile of the operative 'and a disposition is developing itself to have recourse to the labour of women and children in preference to adults' (1836: 143). Technology removed the need for strength and, for Gaskell, this coincided with the employment of women as a cheap source of labour. In the new era of machine production, labour had become 'a subsidiary to this power'. Of particular contention was the plight of the male operative 'he is condemned, hour after hour, day after day, to watch and minister to its operations – to become himself as much a part of its mechanism as its cranks and cog-wheels' (1836: 143). But Gaskell was particularly perturbed by the denigration of a sexual division of labour which had:

> the effect of rendering adult labour of no greater value than that of the infant or girl; the workmen are reduced to mere watchers, and suppliers of the wants of machinery, requiring in the great majority of its operations no physical or intellectual exertion; and the adult male has

begun to give way, and this place been supplied by those who in the usual order of things were dependent upon him for their support.
(Gaskell 1836: 144)

Some historical evidence supports Gaskell's observations linking advances in mechanical production with the displacement of male textile operatives. In 1764, James Hargreaves revolutionized spinning technology with the invention of the spinning jenny. Adoption of the spinning jenny spread rapidly and by 1770, it had displaced its predecessor, the hand wheel (Edwards and Lloyd-Jones 1973: 306). The spinning jenny was mainly suitable for the production of coarse yarn and unsuited for producing very fine fibre. The latter continued to be spun on the one tread-wheel until, in the late eighteenth century, Richard Arkwright's waterframe developed to successfully produce a fine cotton warp thread. Arkwright technologically developed his spinning machine in Lancashire and instituted the first operational system in Nottingham (Palmer and Neaverson 1994). Arkwright later transferred the operational processes of the waterframe into large-scale premises in Manchester, which by 1782 employed over five thousand people (Pike 1966: 33). The beginnings of the factory system are often traced back to this period. Indeed, historians repeatedly cite Arkwright's business model as the typical factory form of the Industrial Revolution (Edwards and Lloyd-Jones 1973). It appears, however, that the waterframe considerably deskilled spinning. Busfield describes the operator's job as 'simply to replenish the silvers, piece together the broken ends and remove the bobbins when filled with yarn' (1988: 157). The decreased necessity for skilled labour gradually yielded to the potential capital gains derived from employing women and children. Their nimble agility was deemed more suited to the delicate process of mending broken threads and removing bobbins.

The social dislocation of male operatives traced similar patterns in the development of Crompton's mule. Samuel Crompton, in circa 1779, combined the technical features of Hargreaves' spinning jenny with the variable speed rollers of Arkwright's waterframe to produce the Crompton mule. The early model of the mule was constructed out of wood and carried 20 spindles. These features enabled the first mule to be small enough to use in a cottage (Addy 1976: 21). Between 1825 and 1830, further innovations in the design of the mule transformed it into a fully automatic machine. Up until the 1790s, women and children had been employed to operate the light mule in rural factories (Honeyman 2000: 59). Thereafter the emergence of steam-driven mules required a degree of skill and considerable manual operation. Consequently, early generations of Crompton's mule offered employment to male artisanal workers in urban mills. In due course mule spinners became renowned as the 'elite among factory workers' (Busfield 1988: 158). However, advances in mule design soon challenged this accolade. In the 1830s the self-acting mule was invented and it greatly simplified the spinning process, indeed, it is observed that its inventors 'believed that it would henceforth be operated by women and children' (1988: 158).

Parliamentary reports, derived from the ninetieth century, provide further indication of the dynamics of female labour and male displacement in textile factory production. According to Gaskell, in 1816, official statistical reports, derived from 41 Scottish textile mills, returned a total of 10,000 workers (1836: 142). Some 1370 of these were males aged 18 or younger, while 3034 were females aged 18 or younger. Statistical returns for Scotland, after the Factory Act of 1833, showed no decline in the proportion of female textile workers. In 1835, Scotland had 170 flax mills, which employed 13,409 labourers of whom 3392 were males and 10,017 were females. It was noted that female labourers constituted 'about 75 per cent of the whole' (Parliamentary Papers 1898: 15). Similar patterns were evident in the West Riding of Yorkshire. In 1835, there were 65 flax mills in this area employing 9378 labours, of whom 3603 were adult males and young boys and 5775 women and girls (Parliamentary Papers 1898: 61). By 1851, 635,000 women were employed in textile factories in Great Britain (Hollis 1979: 53).

Parliamentary reports, derived from the nineteenth century, also contain some limited analysis of gender segregation survey data. In 1898, the Labour Department, Board of Trade presented to both Houses of Parliament, a report entitled *Changes in the Employment of Women and Girls in Industrial Centres*. A central conclusion of this report was that there was no evidence of employment displacement of males by females in the weaving factory. Rather, the report suggests that developments in weaving technology precipitated a natural sex division of labour. It was the advocacy, by men, of this sexual division of labour which encouraged the increased labour market participation of women. Such conclusions are evident in the following extract derived from the 1898 report:

> The hand-loom weavers were antagonistic to the factory system, but given power looms to be worked, they seem to have regarded it as a matter of course that they should be worked by women. The only grievance against women in the matter was that they were willing to go to the factory, whereas the men strenuously opposed themselves to the inevitable, and tried to preserve their independence of an overseer in working at their own homes. They sent their girls and boys to the mills, because they could not afford to refuse the higher wages that children could earn there; but the preference for girls as weavers rather than boys was probably due to the preference of boys for the domestic loom.
>
> (Parliamentary Papers 1898: 31)

It is evident from this extract that the transition from domestic production to the factory system entailed a transfer of customary cultural codes defining the sexual division of labour. It is also evident, from the 1898 parliamentary report, that the mass employment of women was axiomatic to the development of textile factory production. What is less evident is recognition of this increased female labour market participation as inextricably linked to transformations in capitalism's political economy of time.

Economies of time and space in factory production

Primitive accumulation involved the extension of capital into non-capitalist sectors and the subjugation of domestic manufacture to the rule of capital. It was the invasion of primitive economies which bolstered capitalist accumulation and offset a declining rate of profit. At first, substantial capital gains were achieved simply by the enclosure of land and possession of natural resources. Over time, labour required to transform these resources into capital was provided by the local dispossessed peasantry. But the quantitative expansion of capital, without technological change, inevitably reaches its limitations as it exhausts labour supply and material resources. In these instances capital is compelled to channel investment into technological innovation. The revolutionary era of machine-based factory production provided capital with a powerful means for intensifying the productivity of labour 'i.e., for shortening the working-time required in the production of a commodity' (Marx *Capital*, Vol. 1 [1887] 2003: 380). Given this capacity, it is puzzling why those industries first 'invaded' by machines directed their use to 'lengthening the working-day beyond all bounds set by human nature' (2003: 380). An examination into this peculiar political economy of time provides some indication as to why the initial stages of factory production excited 'capital's appetite for the labour of others' (2003: 380).

Machinery has the capacity to automate labour and transform its implements into objects operating independently of the labourer. To this extent, machinery exists as an 'industrial perpetuum mobile' that would produce indefinitely if not for the natural barriers presented by the human body (2003: 380). Capital is thus directed to pursue innovations, which reduce to a minimum the resistance presented by the visceral body. Additional resistances to the machine's perpetuum mobility arise from built-in obsolesce. The efficiency of the machine as a productive unit is 'inversely proportional to the value transferred by it to the product' (2003: 380). The longer the lifetime of the machine, 'the greater is the mass of the products over which the value transmitted by the machine is spread, and the less is the portion of that value added to each single commodity' (2003: 381). This is because the operational lifetime of the machine is conditional on the degree of material wear and tear accumulated throughout the duration of the working day. Obsolescence is appended by technological change in the industrial sector and the development of cheaper more advanced machinery. In these circumstances, 'its value is no longer determined by the labour actually materialised in it, but by the labour-time requisite to reproduce either it or the better machine' (2003: 381). Consequently, the greater the scope of time required for the machine to achieve its total value, the increased risk that newer models will materialize and render it obsolete. Industrial capitalism's rigid economies of time and space presented capital with few options other than to lengthen the working day and thus reduce the period of time in which a machine can actualize its value. Such practices distinguished absolute surplus value extraction and corresponded with the historical development of factory production. For it was 'in the early days of the life of machinery that this special incentive to the prolongation of the working-day makes itself felt most astutely' (2003: 382).

Gender time and factory production

Although automation produces a dynamic acceleration of the productive forces, 'surplus value arises from variable capital alone' (Marx *Capital*, Vol. 1 [1887] 2003: 383). Conversely, machinery represents constant capital. The evolution of the factory system precariously adumbrated an increasing rate of constant capital. Lengthening the working day countenanced a declining rate of profit by allowing production 'on an extended scale without any alteration in the amount of capital laid out on machinery and buildings' (2003: 382). But this substitution of dead labour for living labour is in turn dependent on the continual use of machinery. This provided industry with a powerful incentive to open out 'to the capitalist new strata of the working-classes' (2003: 384). Indeed, machine production was an accrescent force, 'enrolling, under the direct sway of capital, every member of the workman's family, without distinction of age or sex' (2003: 372). Hence the remarkable change in the history of textile factory employment in which women and children are 'compelled to submit to the dictation of capital' (2003: 384).

Attention to time in the analysis of factory production also highlights how 'the most powerful instrument for shortening labour-time, becomes the most unfailing means for placing every moment of the labourer's time ... at the disposal of the capitalist for the purpose of expanding the value of his capital' (2003: 384). This chapter historically examines the intensification of labour induced by the factory system. Absolute surplus value extraction was based on an immoderate expansion of the working day. It entailed the habituation of labour to a more intensified degree of labour for an excessive duration of time. Its apparatus is directed at achieving synchronization to the chronometric rhythms of capitalist production. Nevertheless, its consequences were partial as they required the expansion of labour time, to a degree attainable only through the time-disciplined exploitation of a special class of worker, i.e., women.

Weaving time in nineteenth-century textile production

Figure 2.1 Power loom and cotton manufacture, Swainson Birley cotton mill near Preston, Lancashire 1834.
Source: Reproduced with permission of the Science Museum.

Adam Smith (1937) demonstrated in *The Wealth of Nations* that the maximum economies in manufacturing flowed from the 'division of labour'. He illustrated this by describing the manufacturing system of a pin factory which employed 16 different processes and workers. It is evident that Smith regarded the early forms of textile manufacturing as 'essentially an extension of household work' (Harte and Ponting 1973: 2). Smith observed that towards the end of the fifteenth century, labour within the English cloth industry 'was probably much less subdivided ... than it is at present' (Harte and Ponting 1973: 2). Undoubtedly the various stages of domestic textile production subdivided into processes so as to provide work for members of the family economy. But it wasn't until steam power was harnessed to the new innovations in spinning that the factory system actually did supersede the proto-industry in textile production. The power requirements of the cotton industry were initially relatively modest, and up until the 1820s water wheels satisfied most of the power demands for the industry (Chapman 1987: 18). By the middle of the nineteenth century, water wheels were increasingly unable to meet the productivity demands of increased competition and new more advanced textile technology. In previous times, local shortages of water power would compel factory owners to transfer to locations where water was plentiful. Innovations in fixed industrial machinery made such business processes prohibitively more expensive. Consequently significant energy was being exerted to produce power resources, which enabled factory owners to remain on their existing sites. Innovations in steam-driven mills largely responded to these demands. Newcomen's steam engine, developed in the first decade of the eighteenth century, was already being employed in the majority of mining districts. However, it was James Watt's rotary steam engine which precipitated the real breakthrough in steam-powered textile production.

The expansion of the steam-driven mill brought with it significant transformations in the spatial organization of production. The traditional narrow mill buildings, constructed to accommodate spinning jennies, were unsuitable for large steam-driven machines which meant that new economies of space had to be built into factory design. Moreover, the installation of steam engines meant that factory owners were no longer confined to the valley regions where water supply was plentiful. The revolution of steam power made possible the development of large-scale factories, which 'moved closer to the coalfields and the centres of population, so giving rise to the black industrial Victorian "toadstools" ' (Addy 1976: 26). The factories themselves attracted 'extraordinary bursts' in population distribution (Smelser 1959: 193). Between 1821 and 1831, the population of Lancashire increased by 300,000 an increase of 27 per cent (1959: 193). During the same period Manchester increased its population from 154,807 to 227,808, an estimated increase of 47 per cent (1959: 193). Additional industrial changes, accentuating the establishment of large-scale production, included the emergence of combined spinning and weaving firms. This combination of business processes emerged with the expansion of power loom weaving between 1825 and 1833 and 'reached its zenith about mid-century' (1959: 195). It has been observed that the average size of a combined business was far larger than the existing size of either a spinning firm or weaving establishment. The increased scale of the combined business establishment is evident when we examine employment statistics derived from this time. Factory inspectorate statistics, in 1841, identified 548 spinning firms to have employed an average of 125 full-time employees (quoted in Smelser 1959: 195). According to the factory inspectorate, 89 power-weave firms engaged an average of 100 operatives. Conversely, the 313 firms which had combined both spinning and weaving employed an average of 350 employees per firm. The size of combined firms was even greater in the cities. Manchester and Aston had 65 combined spinning and weaving firms, employing an average of 500 operatives (1959: 195).

Such increases in the scale of production contrasted markedly with the family economies of the domestic system. During the proto-industry phase of textile production 'the spinning wheel and the loom required no larger apartment than that of a cottage' (Pike 1966: 33). Conversely, the series of machine innovations which had revolutionized production 'required both more space than could be found in a cottage and more power than could be applied by the human arm' (1966: 33). The scope and size of steam

50 Gender and work in capitalist economies

driven operations necessitated the design of a new form of business premises. Factories rose to meet this challenge. But as factories multiplied in the towns and cities 'they called into being a new class of human society' (1966: 43). Mechanization and steam power had consumed virtually every stage of the production process, and workers were increasingly becoming 'machine minders rather than machine operatives' (Chapman 1987: 17). To this extent, mechanization constituted the steady progression toward 'depersonalization and anonymity' (Smelser 1959: 195).

Gender and time work discipline

The conditions of life and labour, in the new factory towns of the textile industry, were often hazardous and bleak. Early investors in cotton manufacture tended to be entrepreneurs with limited capital, who were to invest the entirety of their capital reserves into machinery. Each new advance in machine technology simplified the process of manufacture and speeded up the rate of output, thus multiplying the opportunities for the accumulation of wealth (Bryant 1971: 57). Machinery gave the speculative investor a chance for quick riches. All that was needed was for the entrepreneur to hire or buy sufficient power looms to fill a room and 'a resolve to keep his expenses and consequently his prices down against all rivals and a plentiful supply of cheap labour' (1971: 58). Absorbed by the intention to maximize immediate returns on their capital, these investors too easily neglected the employment needs of the workforce, consequently, working conditions were often abominable. The size of the early factories was invariably incapacious. Production rooms had low ceilings, which were contracted in dimensions. Windows were purposely narrow so as to maximize space 'and very little precaution was used, either as to ventilation or temperature' (Gaskell 1836: 138). The lack of ventilation was even more disgraceful in the carding room, where the air was heavily laden with fluff which exposed operatives to the likelihood of eventually developing lung disease. The quality of air was further inhibited by the burning of tallow candles, made from a fatty substance, which produced a foul heavy smoke when ignited. There were many social commentators who were appalled by the dire health conditions of factory buildings.

Even more disconcerting was the harsh forms of time-discipline administered by the 'frugal-minded overseers' (Bryant 1971: 56). In 1844, James Leach, a prominent member of the Chartist Movement, published factual evidence of the sparse conditions and coercive time-discipline regime imposed in the factory system. The following extract provides a particularly relevant account of gender, time and working conditions:

> A great number of the females employed in factories are married, and not a small number of them are mothers. It frequently happens that the husband is refused work in the same mill with the wife; under

these circumstances the poor creature is obliged to leave her husband in bed at five o'clock in the morning, while she hurries off to the mill to undergo her daily repetition of drudgery, in order to procure a scanty portion of food for her husband, herself, and her helpless children. We have repeatedly seen a married female, in the last stage of pregnancy, slaving from morning till night beside these never-tiring machines, and when oppressed nature became so exhausted that they were obliged to sit down to take a moment's ease, and being seen by the manager, were fined *sixpence* for the offence. In some mills, the crime of sitting down to take a little rest is visited with a penalty of *one shilling*, but let the masters and their rules speak for themselves.

'1st. The door of the lodge will be closed ten minutes after the engine starts every morning, and no weaver will afterwards be admitted till breakfast-time. Any weaver who may be absent during that time shall forfeit threepence per loom ...'

It often happens that when the weaver goes to work in the morning, he finds the clock fifteen minutes forwarder than when he left in the evening. The hands on the factory clock do not always move from the *internal wheels*, but very frequently from a little external aid: this always takes place after the hands have left the mill in the evening ...

At this mill, a short time ago, one of the cut-lookers was discharged, and another placed in his situation. When he had been there a fortnight, the master asked him "How it was that he had so little in his *bate book*;" the man replied, "I think there's a great deal, I 'bate the weavers so much that I can't for shame look them in the face when I meet them in the street". The master answered, "You be d—d, you are five pounds a week worse to *me* than the man that had this situation before you, and I'll kick you out of the place". The man was discharged to make room for another *who knew his duty better*'.

(James Leach (1844) *Stubborn Facts from the Factories by a Manchester Operative*, published and dedicated to the working classes by William Rashleigh, M.P., London. John Ollivier. 11–5.)

Early forms of capitalist expropriation entailed a strategy of absolute surplus value extraction, which demanded extended working hours at reduced rates of pay. In this situation socially necessary labour time contained within the working day remains constant, while surplus labour time is significantly increased. Absolute surplus value also has a direct bearing on the technologies of production, as it attempts to yield an increased magnitude of output, while retaining the rate of variable capital inputs to a level which does not threaten the rate of surplus value. Broadly speaking, absolute surplus value is defined technically 'as any increase in the sum of surplus labour-time worked, regardless of the form that this takes, and without any alteration of the rate of variable capital that is required to generate that surplus labour time' (Lee 1993: 121). It is generally recognized that factory employees experienced long hours of work, in overcrowded mills with limited leisure time. Gaskell noted that protracted working hours was a defining feature of factory production in the early eighteenth century:

> The time of labour was extended to twelve hours, with very little interval; the immense profits which accrued from their produce pushing aside all ulterior considerations. Nor was this all: unsatisfied with the day labour, the night was almost uniformly spent by one portion of the hands in the mill; the owners or occupiers thus securing twenty-three hours out of the twenty-four for making their machinery valuable.
> (Gaskell 1836: 138)

Such arduous conditions were exacerbated by the objectionable behaviour of overbearing foremen. As can often be the case with the servant turned master, 'they tended to confuse discipline with terror' (Bryant 1971: 56). Foremen had little reason to adopt a more amiable approach to shop floor management, as disgruntled employees could be easily replaced with abundant supplies of cheap labourers. And the capitalist was merely concerned with paying as little for labour as possible, while also maximizing the work output of every hour of production. It is unsurprising that the factory system earned the notorious accolade 'Dark Satanic Mills' (Blake [1804] 1991).

From the early days of the factory system it was clearly apparent that the conditions of factory life were appalling and yet industrialists appeared oblivious to these concerns. Part of the problem was the untrammelled power of the capitalist 'whose responsibility was confined to the payment of wages for work done and nothing else' (Addy 1976: 33). Capitalist avarice was corroborated by utilitarian social policies which promoted 'the greatest happiness for the greatest number'. The theory that the 'State could only delay and perhaps defeat the beneficent purposes of Providence' was expounded by Jeremy Bentham (Bryant 1971: 54). This philosophical treatise provided an excuse for the suffering and inhumanity of the factory system, for it was interpreted as meaning that 'employers and employed must be left free to make whatever bargains they chose' (1971: 55). And so it was deemed commercially legitimate to rely upon women, children, the poor and unemployed, as a source of cheap labour. Indeed, in the early stages of industrialization, low cost female and child labour 'substituted for technological improvements in the factories' (Valenze 1995: 93). While this is an often stated fact, feminist analyses of salary scales in the factory system suggest that the complex dynamics of time and gender patterned insidious levels of inequality.

Wage differentials: timely constructions or a source of lower human capital and productivity levels?

Transformations in the organization of textile work helped to identify female labourers as a specific aggregation of the industrial working class (Honeyman 2000: 54). The rapid economic development of the factory system had 'eclipsed the smaller paternalistic factories of the rural villages' (Valenze 1995: 93). According to Anna Clark, these paternalistic factories relied upon a family labour system in which 'the subordinate labour of women and children was necessary and accepted; buttressing rather than undermining patriarchal authority' (Honeyman 2000: 55). The factory system traded upon this inequality in the gender division of labour, and even exploited it as a basis for unequal rates of pay. Evidence confirms that even from the early emergence of the factory system, women were not offered a 'living wage' and that this was based on the assumption that a woman would be dependent on a male as a source of financial support. But as industrial cotton manufacturing expanded, it became obvious that the factory system offered limited opportunities for adult males to earn a 'family wage' (Rose 1996: 149). Consequently, the family unit relied upon the independent earnings of individual members of the household.

Although the factory system provided women with the opportunity to become 'independent wage earners', it cemented rather than undermined the financial dependency of women. For, women were invariably paid less than their male counterparts. According to Burnette (1997: 257), it is recognized that during the Industrial Revolution 'the female-male wage ratio generally varied from one-third to two-thirds, depending on the type of work and the location'. Valenze (1995: 90) provides evidence derived from the Factory Commission report of 1833, identifying 'women earning an average of 9s. 8¼d. per week, compared with 22s. 8½ d. for men'. Table 2.1 contains official statistical evidence charting the average weekly wage of flax mill workers in Scotland, in 1833. Table 2.2 contains official statistical evidence charting the average weekly wage of flax mill workers in Leeds, in 1833.

Honeyman (2000) details how factory owners often imposed differentials in the payment structure of female textile workers. Males tended to be paid a weekly rate; conversely female workers were paid by the unit of output and received significantly less wages than their male counterparts. This marked difference in the wages received by male and female textile workers has provoked significant debate among economists and feminist historians. While it is agreed that the salaries of female textile workers were a fraction of that received by males, some disagreement exists as to the basis of this distinction. According to neoclassical economic theory, wages reflect the productive capacities of labour (Becker 1971). Consequently a neoclassical economist would interpret wage disparities as evidence of differences in levels of productivity. Similar conclusions have been presented by Joyce Burnette (1997) in her *Investigation of the Female-Male Wage*

54 Gender and work in capitalist economies

Table 2.1 Average weekly wages of flax mill workers in Scotland, in 1833. Changes in the Employment of Women and Girls in Industrial Centres. Part 1–Flax and Jute Centre. Labour Department, Board of Trade. Parliamentary Papers 1898, C–8794, pp., 17.

Age period	Average wage		Average age	Number of persons
Males	s.	d.	Years	
Under 10 years	2	11	8.9	40
10 and under 13 years	3	3	11.2	476
13 and under 18 years	4	6	14.4	518
18 and under 25 years	10	11	20.7	204
25 and under 35 years	14	10	29.5	290
35 and under 45 years	14	1	39.1	255
45 and under 65 years	13	10	51.8	249
65 years and upwards	9	7	69.0	21
Females	s.	d.	Years	
Under 10 years	2	1	8.8	40
10 and under 13 years	3	3	11.3	647
13 and under 18 years	4	10	15.1	1,655
18 and under 25 years	5	10	20.3	1,812
25 and under 35 years	5	8	28.1	677
35 and under 45 years	5	2	38.6	208
45 and under 65 years	5	5	51.4	297
65 years and upwards	4	1	69.3	9

Table 2.2 Average weekly wages of flax mill workers in Leeds, in 1833. Changes in the Employment of Women and Girls in Industrial Centres. Part 1–Flax and Jute Centre. Labour Department, Board of Trade. Parliamentary Papers 1898, C–8794, pp., 62.

Age period	Average wage		Average age	Number of persons
Males	s.	d.	Years	
Under 10 years	2	11	9.0	16
10 and under 13 years	4	1	11.4	246
13 and under 18 years	5	7	14.5	276
18 and under 25 years	14	2	20.5	127
25 and under 35 years	19	2	29.4	121
35 and under 45 years	18	7	39.3	127
45 and under 65 years	18	10	51.6	119
65 years and upwards	13	8	70.0	20
Females	s.	d.	Years	
Under 10 years	2	10	9.0	12
10 and under 13 years	3	2	11.4	272
13 and under 18 years	5	0	15.1	683
18 and under 25 years	6	0	20.1	481
25 and under 35 years	6	2	28.0	77
35 and under 45 years	6	3	38.7	20
45 and under 65 years	6	1	50.7	7
65 years and upwards	–		–	–

Gap during the Industrial Revolution. Burnette cites Becker's (1971) *The Economics of Discrimination* as a basis for an alternative application of neo-classical economic theory. According to Burnette's reading of Becker, 'wage discrimination is more compatible with monopolistic markets than with competitive markets' (1997: 261). It is assumed that in a competitive market, 'firms that do not discriminate have lower costs and tend to expand at the expense of discriminating firms' (1997: 261). Burnette alleges that this is because wage discrimination can persist in uncompetitive markets where labourers are limited in their employment choices. Burnette presents historical data to this effect and claims that: 'women workers in more competitive industries such as agriculture and most cottage industries received market wages based on their marginal productivity, not simply a customary "women's wage" ' (1997: 261).

Burnette's position here is in contrast with cultural evidence which convincingly suggests that the female–male wage gap was a product of:

> early trade union activity, the ideology of the family wage, employers' adherence to traditional norms of what was suitable work for women, increased tensions between motherhood and economic activity, and the implications of developing areas of respectability for sex segregation at work.
> (Humphries 1991, quoted in Burnette 1997: 257)

Humphries emphasizes the significance of cultural values as a determinant of the female–male wage gap during the Industrial Revolution. Similar conclusions are presented by Berg (1993) and Jordan (1989). While 'women may also have faced discrimination before entering the labour market' and 'women's wages were discriminatory in certain parts of the labour market', Burnette claims that 'the majority of women workers were paid market wages' (1997: 262). Burnette's observations are of particular interest because of the distinction she makes between 'piece rate' and 'time rate' as a basis of wages. She claims that the majority of the suppositions made about inequality in the salaries of male and female factory workers is based on an inaccurate understanding of both types of wages. Time rate is a system by which the labourer is paid according to the amount of time worked. In the modern era time rates are standardized agreements based on a stable consistent timetable. Conversely, in the eighteenth and nineteenth centuries, time rate wages were quoted on a daily or weekly basis. This system contrasted with piece rate wages which were based on the worker's unit of output. Some illustration of this distinction is provided in the following extract from Gaskell:

> It may be supposed that the masters, in thus wishing to rid themselves of a turbulent set of workmen, were influenced by other causes – that women and children could be made to work a cheap rate, and thus add to his profits. This has had considerable weight doubtless. The mode of payment now universally adopted by the trade, which is

payment for work done, piece work as it is called, – the spinner for the number of pounds of yard he produces, the weaver for the number of cuts of yards turned off from his loom, – places the active girl upon a par with the most robust adult.

(Gaskell 1836: 146)

According to Burnette, in occupations based on piece rate, salary differentials often highlighted as evidence of sex discrimination 'are really average weekly earnings on piece rates (i.e., the average, or usual, amount that a woman doing the work would earn in a week)' (1997: 263). Burnette argues that women's domestic responsibilities within the home often meant that they had less time to dedicate to market work compared with the average man. Evidence from the Handloom Weavers Commission (1840) provides some support for this claim. In 1840, it found that women handloom weavers working in weave shops earned an average of 5s. 5d a week, while females in the same profession working at home earned an average of 4s per week (quoted in Burnette 1997: 263). The commission claimed that the lower salary earned by the female home worker was because 'their time is partly occupied by their domestic duties' (quoted in Burnette 1997: 263). Similar conclusions were included in Parliamentary Papers in 1816. The following is an extract of testimony provided by a cotton manufacturer called Henry Houdsworth:

Do you employ many women in picking cotton? – I do.
Does that employment necessarily oblige them to be constant in their attendance? – No; the doors are open during the summer the same hours that the mill works in the summer time, when it is light; but in the winter they never work by candle-light; and as they are a very irregular set of hands, time is not noticed.

(Parliamentary Paper 1816: 233)

For Burnette, this statement would provide evidence to support her claim that 'in most cases of piece rate work the female–male wage gap is purely the result of differences in output rather than of differences in the piece rate' (1997: 265). Elsewhere Burnette provides statistical tables demonstrating that women earned lower time rate wages than men. This disparity is also explained in relation to 'differences in the number of hours worked ... because women generally worked fewer hours per day' (1997: 268). Thus, in summary, Burnette claims that much of the disparities in the wages between male and females, during the Industrial Revolution, were due to the fact 'women were less productive than men' (1997: 272). Burnette is keen to attribute any remaining disparities in male and female wages to 'differences in human capital' (1997: 272). Women were often denied access to the skill and experience, which would enable them to compete with their male counterparts. Burnette alleges that women were further disadvantaged in the labour market by childbearing, which 'affected women's productivity mainly through discouraging investment in human capital' (1997: 274). Such conclusions collaborate with conservative discourse, which assumes that disparities in the wages of men and women during the Industrial Revolution were a consequence of market factors (Honeyman 2000: 55). What is lost in such perspectives is an engagement with the dynamics of power and an analysis of the systematic discrimination of female workers. These conceptual limitations are less evident in feminist historical analysis, which have focused on the interplay of patriarchy and capitalism.

From private to public patriarchy

> [T]hat factory females have in general much lower wages than males, and they have been pitied on this account with perhaps an injudicious sympathy, since the low price of their labour here tends to make household duties their most profitable as well as agreeable occupation, and prevents them from being tempted by the mill to abandon the care of their offspring at home. Thus Providence effects its purposes with a wisdom and efficacy which should repress the short-sighted presumption of human devices.
> (Dr. Ure, quoted in Gaskell 1836: 174)

It is undoubtedly true that the celebrated story of the factory's beginnings has tended to obscure the role that patriarchy and male-dominated trade unions played in the creation of a gender-segregated workforce. Men organized to create trade unions which systematically excluded women from a variety of skilled occupations (Busfield 1988: 161). Their resilience was in part based on a perceived need to defend themselves from cheap female labour (Honeyman 2000). The rapid pace of technological innovation had introduced faster machines capable of simplifying complex operations and these developments favoured the employment of cheap unskilled female labour.

Typically male trade unionists resolved to exclude women 'according to practices protected by tradition' (Valenze 1995: 95). In the nineteenth century, male cotton spinners organized to prevent women from operating the spinning mules. Such intention was achieved by the action of the Grand General Union of Spinners, which was formed in 1829 (Davies 1975). The Spinners Union was an exclusively male organization and at its inauguration adopted a resolution that 'no person or persons be learned or allowed to spin except the son, brother or orphan nephew of spinners and the poor relations of the proprietors of the mills' (Busfield 1988: 161). In so doing male spinners were able to restructure the meaning of craft status to encompass training, machine maintenance and quality controls (Honeyman 2000: 60). Skilled status was thus secured through the 'construction of an artificial monopoly', which strictly controlled entry to the trade.

Females were therefore excluded from the central vehicle for gaining training and skill, the apprenticeship (Busfield 1988). While there is limited information regarding girls and craft apprenticeships, it would appear that from the mid-fifteenth century onwards 'women were gradually excluded from the male-dominated guilds' (1988: 160). Although it is possible that some women might have received limited training from their fathers, on the whole, their expertise was insufficient to provide anything more than assistance. Alexander also identifies craft guilds as having systematically excluded women except 'for the wives and widows of master craftsmen' (Alexander 1989: 39). By the eighteenth century, the policy of exclusion, linked with the handcraft base of manufacture, provided skilled workmen with some degree of control over the labour process (1989: 39). Men organized to secure craft status by ensuring that entry to trade societies was restricted and knowledge of skills was protected by apprenticeships. Barriers to entry enabled craft unions to maintain a position of strength relative to unskilled workmen. Prohibited from claiming professional accreditation, unskilled workers lacked vital bargaining power against capital. The ability of craft-based trade unions to secure prestige and power by restricting access to apprenticeships, was particularly detrimental for women. While women and men shared in the expansion of industrialization, women had historically been 'denied access to socially recognized skills' and thus were restricted in the jobs they could perform (1989: 39). Thus, although more and more women entered the industrial economy, they did so without the trade union protection enjoyed by their male counterparts.

In due course, employment protection began to emerge. But the pace of factory reform was no doubt hindered by the contradictions of utilitarian social policy and the activities of male unionists. Indeed, it has been argued that the influx of female labourers into the industrial economy had 'destabilized the balance of capital and patriarchal interests' (Holloway 2005: 28). These tensions were compounded by pressures from commercial interests to continue existing patterns of sex discrimination in the allocation of wages. Gender inequality provided a lucrative means of both limiting the amounts paid to female workers and depressing the wage scales of male workers, as is evident in the following extract derived from a parliamentary paper published in 1892:

> The employment of women tells very much against the men. Employers feel that men's work is not worth above 6d or 1s at the outside per piece more than that of women, and use the cheapness of the latter to depress the price of the former. They have often told men who apply for work that they will employ them only if they will accept women's wages. And in some cases, unfortunately, the men have agreed to these terms. If both were to be paid at the same rate, men would probably have the preference for employment, but it is to be feared that this uniformity will be attained not by raising the wages of the women, but by reducing those of men. There are scores of able-bodied, competent men who are unable to obtain employment

in consequence of the competition of women. The result is that mothers are obliged to go to the mills, neglecting their hired nurses, while the fathers are idle. Several firms, however, recognize the evil of this state of things, and have ceased to employ married women.
(Parliamentary Papers (1892: 227)

The campaign for factory reform produced a barrage of opposition from commercial interests keen to halt factory reform on the grounds that legislative regulation would hinder the nation's economic power (Bryant 1971: 55). At the same time, male unionists were vigorously campaigning against the low cost competition represented by the influx of women and children into the labour market. Many unions sought an answer in the promotion of 'protective labour laws for women and children' (Hartmann 1981: 21). The resultant Factory Acts had the dual effect of ameliorating some of the more rapacious conditions of long working hours, but they also excluded women from many 'male' jobs. The first major Factory Act, passed in 1833, made it illegal to employ children under the age of 9 and regulated hours of work. The Act of 1833 was passed through Parliament, partly to circumvent the demands of Ashley and others lobbying for a Ten-Hour Bill restricting the working hours of adults (Thompson 1967: 47). But this was a temporary reprieve. The 1844 Factory Act extended restrictions on the hours worked to women, and in 1847 reduced these hours to ten (Holloway 2005: 29). Throughout the century a flurry of factory reforms systematically limited the number of hours women could work. Cultural historians have often referred to the campaign for factory reform, as illustrating the humanitarian convictions of prominent middle-class agitators incensed by the terrible conditions of factory work (Bryant 1971).

Feminist historians have challenged the degree to which factory reforms represented benign and progressive sentimentalities. The motivation of successive reforms, restricting the hours women worked, partly stemmed from a paternalistic philanthropy intent on extending 'the ideal bourgeois family structure to the working class' (Holloway 2005: 28). The vast army of women employed in industry presented a direct challenge to the domesticated image of women evident in cultural discourse. Working women were thought to be abandoning their appropriate gender roles and this threatened to destabilize the family. Evidence of this concern is provided in the following extract of a parliamentary paper published in 1833:

> But one of the greatest evils to the working man is the ignorance of the women of his own class, who are generally incapable of becoming either good wives or good mothers ... Brought up in the factory until they are married, and sometimes working there long after that event has taken place, even when they have become mothers, they are almost entirely ignorant of household duties, and are incapable of laying out the money their husbands have earned to the best advantage. They are equally incapable of preparing his victuals, in an

economical and comfortable manner; and it not infrequently happens that as much money is spent on a Sunday's dinner as in other and better hands would have procured a dinner for two or three days. A working man is fortunate, indeed, who happens to marry a young woman that has been brought up in service, and whose habits of cleanliness and knowledge of household duties secure him a comfortable home and economical management.

The practice of the working men in general is to entrust the laying out of their money to their wives, and hence a knowledge of household duties, combined with habits of industry, cleanliness and economy, is of first-rate importance amongst the females of this class of society to working men. In thousands of instances the very contrary of these desirable virtues prevails, and the industrious working man lives in misery and debt from the conduct of an ignorant gin-drinking woman called his wife. Every apology, however, may be offered for some of these unfortunate creatures, for they have never had the opportunity of learning better; and a most happy thing it would be for thousands, if, when the hours of labour are shortened for children, a provision were made for teaching the females sewing, knitting, ... and in some measure initiating them into the duties they may one day be called upon to perform as wives and mothers. The present ignorance of the women brought up in our manufactories is productive of an incalculable amount of poverty and wretchedness, and tends to perpetuate depravity of character as much, as, if not more than, any other circumstance.

(Parliamentary Papers 1833: 1117)

Marxist feminist historians, interpret concerns raised about factory work and the demise of traditional female roles as demonstrating fundamental interconnections between patriarchy and capitalism. According to Barratt and McIntosh (1989), the introduction of women and children into the factory system was a strategic move by capitalists to deskill the labour process and maximize profits by extending the working day. By the 1830s, it became apparent that a strategy of absolute surplus value extraction was 'incompatible' with the reproduction of a fit and healthy working class. Consequently it became imperative, from the point of view of both the capitalist and labourer, 'to protect the life and health of the industrial proletariat' (1989: 73).

According to Barratt and McIntosh, pressure from the trade unions and social reformers coincided with capitalism's self-interested intention to stem the degeneration of the family. It certainly seems the case that factory employment became a power struggle between patriarchal and capitalist forces, and the resultant factory reforms were clearly designed to restrict the hours worked by female employees. It is also evident that these reforms represented a mutually beneficial compromise between patriarchal and capitalist interests. This is particularly evident with regards to the establishment of the 'family wage'. The trade union movement used the restricted working hours, legislated by the Factory Acts, as a lever to reduce their working hours. Losses incurred by working fewer hours were circumvented by the claim that a male worker should be considered a 'breadwinner', and provided with wages sufficient to support a dependent wife and children. The capitalist state responded favourably to this claim as it preserved the idealized patriarchal family structure and also enhanced the profit margins of factory owners. Needless to say, the accumulative effect of the 'breadwinner' lobby was to further reduce the pitiful wage paid to female labourers. Sex discrimination in the levels of pay received by women could now be 'justified on the grounds that they were supported, at least partially by a husband or father' (Busfield 1988: 162). Within such a deleterious context, many women had little choice but to occupy low paid employment, requiring little technical training and providing limited job security. It is clear, therefore, that from the onset of the textile revolution female labour constituted 'the industrial reserve army', which was at once both a precondition and necessary product of the time-disciplined accumulation of capital (Alexander 1989: 39).

Conclusion

During the eighteenth century the expansion of commercial trade, through the acquisition of markets abroad, constituted 'the economic conditions for the hierarchy of labour powers' in textile production (Alexander 1989: 40). It is conventionally recognized that market pressures, which exceeded the capacities of pre-industrial production, precipitated the revolution in textile production. Merchant capitalists found the wide geographical dispersal of pre-industrial production units prohibitively expensive. The costs involved in distributing raw materials to home-based producers were further compounded by the logistic difficulties involved in regulating standard levels of quality (Honeyman 2000: 35). In these circumstances, the process of outwork became devalued and 'production for exchange' was increasingly transferred away from the homestead into factories and workshops (Alexander 1989: 40). Eventually this concentration of capital facilitated the development of more advanced machines, which further undermined the domestic system of putting-out carried out in the homestead. Domestic production struggled to compete with the organizational logistics and economic rationality of large-scale production. The technological challenge presented by mechanical production was self-evidently superior. And economies of scale made it inevitable that manufacturing would transfer to the factory system of production. Moreover, the technological innovations of the factory system provided capital with the ability to centralize their operations and exert greater control over the labour process. It was supposed that women were more inclined to docile servitude and thus likely to comply with the time-disciplined regime of factory production. Indeed, Gaskell advanced the belief that mechanization was resonant with the 'disposition' of women (1836: 143). While it is evidently true that female workers lacked bargaining power, it is necessary to recognize the interplay of gender, time and political economy in determining the arduous social history of the female textile worker.

3

Economies of time and gender in industrial capitalism

Engendering Marx's economic categories

Historical analysis of textile production, in the nineteenth century, highlights the part played by time-discipline in the accumulation of capital through the expropriation of the workers' surplus production. Marx argued that the value of a commodity is determined by 'the quantity of the value-creating substance, the labour, contained in the article' (*Capital*, Vol. 1 [1887] 2003: 46). Marx further argued that 'the quantity of labour ... is measured by its duration and labour time in its turn finds its standard in weeks, days and hours' (2003: 46). Thus, the value of a commodity is determined by the magnitude of labour time required in its production. And the expropriation of surplus labour time forms the basis of capitalist accumulation. Such conclusions have resonance with the pattern of industrial advancement, which pronounced the British textile revolution. The evolution of textile machinery at first subjected the labour process to an immoderate extension in the duration of the working day. This creates, on the one hand, new circumstances by which capital can sustain the metronomic rhythms of factory production and, on the other, 'new motives with which to whet capital's appetite for the labour of others' (2003: 380). In Chapter 1 it was argued that a new economy of time, precipitated by extensive accumulation, was the fundamental driving force in capitalism's mass recruitment of women into the factory system. The excessive extension of the working day necessitated the 'opening out to the capitalist new strata of working-class' (2003: 384). And it was from the ranks of dispossessed female handspinners that capitalism recruited its reservoir of unskilled workers.

Marx's concept of relative surplus value provides a means of explaining why, throughout the nineteenth century, controls over the working conditions of women succeeded in regulating their hours of work. The first generation of textile machines demanded a habituation into mechanistic rhythms which were 'repeated day after day with unvarying uniformity' (2003: 386). The capacity of humans to apprehend the metronomic rhythms of machinery inevitably produces limitations and thus the 'lengthening of the working day becomes compatible only with a lower degree of intensity' (2003: 386). In the history of capitalism, profit acts as a spur to technical innovation; and technical change is at the heart of the historical dialectic which distinguishes extensive and intensive accumulation. The latter 'consists in raising the productive power of the workman, so as to enable him to produce more in a given time with the same expenditure of labour' (2003: 386). In this respect, technological innovation is directed towards maximizing profit through the minimization of paid labour time. This criterion informed the development of textile machinery towards the 'condensation of labour to a degree that is attainable only within the limits of the shortened working day' (2003: 486). Chapter 2 argues that it was within this intensive economy of time that female labour time became an object of regulation.

Marx's economic categories clearly have relevance to explaining the political economy of time, which transformed textile production in the nineteenth century. But in orthodox Marxist theory, the analysis of labour time is relevant only in so far as it has direct relation to capital and the making of profit. Consequently, the accumulation of profits is assumed, by orthodox Marxists, to systematically transform 'social structure as it transforms the relations of production' (Hartmann 1981: 10). The family and domestic labour expended in the reproduction of the working class are merely discerned as 'by-products of the accumulation process itself' (1981: 10). As a feature of the superstructure, domestic labour is, by default, merely functional to and determined by capitalism (Williams 1988: 40). Consequently, Marx's focus on the capitalist–proletariat relationship provides little space for an analysis of how domestic labour time relates to capital.

In the 1960s and 1970s, left-wing feminists became increasingly vocal about the gender myopia of orthodox Marxist theory. But while united in their commitment to challenge Marx's gender-blind categories, feminists differed markedly in their explanations for the nature of domestic labour. Indeed, a vociferous debate has arisen, which is geared towards determining the origin of women's oppression in terms of the 'productivity' of domestic labour. These feminist authors have assumed one of two positions. The first school of thought is categorical in its claim that domestic labour is actually productive labour. Of particular concern is the tendency for orthodox Marxists to treat 'women's production of use-values' as 'outside the exchange of labour for wages even though economically part of the creation of surplus value' (Williams 1988: 46). One of the earliest Marxist feminists to make this claim was Margaret Benston in 1969 and, she was one of the first to equate domestic labour with the production of 'use-values'. Key additional contributors to this school of thought include Mariarosa Dalla Costa and Selma James (1975). They are renowned for claiming that domestic labour produces use-values and is, therefore, a source of surplus value. Dalla Costa and James's interpretation of Marx's labour theory of value generated much feminist debate during the 1970s. This feminist perspective provides important insights when examining gender, domestic labour time and political economy. Nevertheless, feminist analysis is clearly mistaken in its endeavour to force domestic labour time into Marx's economic categories. Such conclusions are presented by a second school of thought which argues that domestic labour is unproductive labour (Seccombe 1974; Harris 1983). This chapter critically examines these feminist contributions. The chapter argues that both feminist traditions constitute domestic labour time as Other to the economic times of the productive economy. An alternative position is to develop the tendency, as Rosa Luxemburg (1971) observed, for capitalist expansion to, on the one hand, depend on the preservation of non-economic strata and, on the other, to ravenously erode these areas as part of capital accumulation. Similar dynamics are evident, in the organization of domestic labour time, as a non-capitalist reservoir of supply for capital's means of production. It is my contention that the existence and development of industrial capitalism are predicated on the expropriation of domestic labour time as a non-economic resource.

The family and domestic labour time in historical context

Although Marx's own analysis is seemingly bereft of explanations for gender inequality within the family, subsequent Marxist analysis has directly considered the economic aspects of domestic labour. Friedrich Engels ([1884] 1985) argued that gender inequality in the domestic division of labour has trajectories in economic and material conditions. Indeed, the history of the family traces 'the victory of private property over primitive, natural communal property' (1985: 95). Consequently domestic labour has a definitive relation to capital. For it operates to 'maintain and reproduce the labour force and therefore the Capitalist Mode of Production' (Williams 1988: 42). But this could only be consistent with the view that 'capital and private property' was the primary cause of women's oppression in capitalist society (Hartmann 1981: 5). Engels repeatedly defends this assumption, most especially in his claim that women's participation in the public sphere of paid labour will unbridle the control men possess over women within the family. Engels optimistically claimed that women's mass participation in the labour force would irrevocably undermine patriarchal relations, thus pre-empting the eventual destruction of gender inequality. To facilitate female employment, 'private housekeeping' needed to be 'transformed into a social industry' (1985: 107). This would disrupt capitalism's reliance on women to sustain labour power through their provision of domestic labour. Engels further argued that with the 'transfer of the means of production into common ownership' the patriarchal anxieties around 'bequeathing and inheriting' would dissipate (1985: 106–7). Thus, 'the single family ceases to be the economic unit of society' and domestic labour time is no longer a burden for the individual female, but part of the social production of domestic labour. As much as Engels has been commended for identifying domestic labour as inextricably tied to formal economic production, his analysis also 'failed to focus on the differences between men's and women's experiences under capitalism' (Hartmann 1981: 5). While clearly recognizing domestic labour as a site for the reproduction of labour power, Engels neglected to address the feminist issues of 'how and why women are oppressed as women' (1981: 5). Engels predicted that women's mass participation into the labour force will undermine patriarchy. But 'patriarchal relations, far from being atavistic leftovers' (1981: 5) are accrescent in their ability to prosper alongside capitalist modes of production.

Feminists working within the tradition of historical materialism have been assiduous in their endeavours to challenge the assumption that Marx's categories can only be determined by the capitalist–proletarian relationship. For many, the central challenge has been Marx's distinction between 'productive' and 'unproductive' labour. Productive labour involves the direct exchange of labour time for capital or revenue thus, 'the labour-process is a process between things that the capitalist has purchased' (Marx, *Capital*, Vol. 1 [1887] 2003: 180). Conversely, Marx defines unproductive labour as 'paid out of revenue' and involving labour bought from the capitalist or workers for 'personal consumption' (Williams 1988: 44). For Marxist feminists, the issue of contention here is to what extent it can be argued that domestic labour is 'unproductive labour and therefore outside market production' (1988: 46). Orthodox Marxist theory highlights the rise of commodity production as a central precursor in determining domestic labour's status as unproductive labour. Pre-industrial patterns of work had emphasized an 'essential conditioning in different notations of time provided by different work-situations and their relation to "natural" rhythms' (Thompson 1967: 59).

Pre-industrial agricultural work involved a perpetual sequence of activities of varying durations defined by the qualitative cycles of the seasons. Conversely, time measurement in industrial capitalism is defined not by the task but by the value of time when reduced to money. Time becomes an economic measure of productivity and this transformation impacts on the spatial location of work. In pre-industrial society there was limited specialist segregation of work from other aspects of everyday life. The fluidity of the boundaries between work and everyday life was supported by the forms of cottage industry which existed alongside agriculture as pre-industrial forms of production (Clarke and Critcher 1990).

As commodities began to be produced for accumulation and profit, there emerged a need to synchronize the performance of work and separate it from the homestead; 'the place in which family or household matters were practiced' (Firat 1994: 207). The attributes of work performed in each sphere were deemed to be both quantitatively and qualitatively different. To the public domain was designated the production of goods and services designed for commodity markets. This became the sphere of 'value-producing' activities (1994: 207). Conversely, the homestead was the domain of recreation and consumption. Thus, the private sphere is deemed vital for the reproduction of labour power. This segregation of the labour process into private and public spheres produced a split in the labour force along sexual contours. Those people who mostly inhabit the public sphere of industry and commerce are commonly males, while females tend to be located in the private sphere of domestic activities. According to orthodox Marxism, the public sphere is the 'unit of capitalist production' and the private sphere is the 'unit of reproduction for capital' (Seccombe 1974: 6). It is in the public sphere that labour time 'enters directly into the development of productive forces' (1974: 6). Therefore orthodox Marxists argue that it is only the productivity of labour time in the public domain that is of interest to capital. Conversely, the development of privatized domestic labour removed from the direct exchange of labour time for capital means that 'the law of value does not govern domestic labour' (1974: 6). This is clearly the economic thinking of both Marx and Engels, thus explaining why the legacy of orthodox Marxism contains 'economic categories', which appear 'only relevant to the position of the proletariat at the point of production and ... the position of women in the home ... [is] somehow outside their scope' (Foreman 1978: 112).

Domestic labour time as productive labour time?

According to Marx, the value of a commodity derives from 'the labour time necessary for its production' (Marx, *Capital*. Vol. 1 [1887] 2003: 62) and surplus labour time produces profit, which is converted into monetary value by the capitalist during the circulation of products on the market. Viewing productive labour in this way has tended to exclude domestic labour from orthodox Marxist accounts of capitalist accumulation. Orthodox Marxists claim that domestic labour is unsalaried labour and therefore 'not part of the official economy' (Seccombe 1974: 4). Thus, on examining Marx's definition of value, it becomes clear why the role of the woman 'in the cycle of production remained invisible', this is because 'only the product of her labour, the labourer was visible' (Dalla Costa and James 1975: 26).

To the extent that orthodox Marxism defines capitalist relations of power entirely in terms of the capitalist–proletarian relationship, it fails to recognize that it is 'precisely through the wage [that] the exploitation of the non-wage labourer [has] been organized' (Dalla Costa and James 1975: 26). Marxist feminists have been keen to identify domestic labour as a manifestation of capitalism. Deriving from this consensus has emerged a school of feminist thought intent on highlighting how domestic labour both produces labour power and contributes to its value. Defined as the 'Domestic Labour as Productive Labour School' (DLPLS), this tradition of materialist feminism seeks to engender Marx's economic categories (Williams 1988: 44). We have already recognized that axiomatic to Marx's concept of value is the distinction between 'useful' and 'abstract' labour (Meek 1979). Against these categories is situated domestic labour. Conversely, DLPLS identifies domestic labour as 'a supplier of a series of use-values in the home' (Dalla Costa and James 1975: 31). This contention was originally voiced by Margaret Benston in 1969. Benston observes that the structure of the nuclear family is such that 'it is an ideal consumption unit' (1989: 38). This notion of the family is consistently reproduced in classical economic theory, where the housewife's primary role is constituted as a mere consumer of the patriarch's salaried wage. Alternatively, Benston (1989) argues that domestic labour is actually a producer of use-values which are consumed within the household. This supposition arises from a corresponding analysis of commodity production in capitalist society. Drawing upon the earlier work of Ernest Mandel (1967), Benston argues that in capitalist society, commodity production overshadows all other forms of production.

The rise of commodity production and its subsequent regularization has radically transformed the labour process and the organization of society. Nevertheless, while commodity production is a 'major part of production', it is not the case that 'all production under capitalism is commodity production' (Mandel 1967: 10–1, quoted in Benston 1989: 33). According to Mandel, the household produces 'simple use-values' which remain outside of the commodity nexus (1967: 10–1, quoted in Benston 1989: 33). Examples of the simple use-values to which Mandel refers include the cleaning and ironing of laundry. While significant amounts of labour time are invested in this activity, 'it constitutes production, but it is not production for the market' (Mandel 1967: 10–1, quoted in Benston 1989: 33). Thus domestic labour time involves the transformation of commodities purchased from salaried wages into consumables and the provision of domestic services for household members (Harris 1983: 187). To this extent the domestic labour time of women is first and foremost concerned with production and only secondly concerned with consumption. Indeed, it has been observed that domestic labour is located at the interface of two markets – 'the market for labour which it supplies, and the market for consumer goods (wage goods) which it consumes' (1983: 187). These observations have encouraged Benston to argue that women constitute a class of people that 'does stand in a different relation to production than the group "men"' (1983: 33). This is because the dominant form of domestic division of labour in modern society abdicates males from the production of simple use-values within the home. Thus, and according to Benston, we can 'tentatively define women ... as that group of people who are responsible for the production of simple use-values in those activities associated with the home and family' (Benston 1989: 34). Women's responsibility for the provision of simple use-values, within the home, 'constitutes a huge amount of socially necessary production' (Harris 1983: 33). Benston's observations mapped onto a pivotal conjunction in the history of materialist feminist discourse and latter inspired Dalla Costa and James (1875: 31) to argue that 'domestic work produces not merely use-values, but it is essential to the production of surplus value'.

Domestic labour time and the production of surplus value

Dalla Costa and James (1975) proposed that women needed to be liberated from capitalism's rationalization of factory labour and from the endless demands of private domestic labour. In the latter case the forces of production, which operate to privatize domestic labour also serve to constitute it as 'feminine work' and a defining feature of womanhood (1975: 33). But this identity is a source of frustration for women, partly because the relation of housework to capital 'runs directly against the factory as regimentation organized in time and space' (1975: 22). Domestic work is family-centred and defined in relation to the needs of significant others (Davies 1990). Conversely, the regimentation of work in the public sphere commands a 'respect for timetables' and disciplined aversion to any 'disruption of the productive flow' (Dalla Costa and James 1975: 22). Nevertheless, capitalism is at the root of both the privatization of housework and its separation from the chromomeric rhythms of the workplace. According to Dalla Costa and James, the advent of capitalism precipitated a transition from a pre-capitalist society of 'co-operative unity in work', to a capitalist system in which 'the unfree patriarch was transformed into the "free" wage earner' (1975: 24). Having destroyed the community production of pre-capitalist society, capital set about exacerbating the existing 'contradictory experiences of the sexes' and establishing in the form of the nuclear family 'a more profound estrangement and therefore a more subversive relation between the sexes' (1975: 24). With the rise of industrial capitalism, the homestead ceases to be a centre of production and women lose their relative power gained from the dependence of family members on their labour, which was seen as socially necessary. The burden of financial responsibility now resides solely with the patriarch and within the family:

> [R]ule of capital through the wage compels every able-bodied person to function, under the law of division of labour, and to function in ways that are, if not immediately, then ultimately profitable to the expansion and extension of the rule of capital.
> (Dalla Costa and James 1975: 28)

To the extent that the 'rule of capital' determines the division of labour, then the qualitative rhythms of housework 'function in ways' which are 'ultimately profitable' to the capitalist mode of production. This is because domestic labour is of necessity to capital, not merely as a producer of use-values, but also because it 'is essential to the production of surplus value' (1975: 33). While previous Marxist feminists stressed the socially necessary role of housework, Dalla Costa and James argue that domestic labour is the necessary condition for the 'reproduction of labour power', from which, in turn, is extracted surplus value. This is precisely because capitalism transfers a vast amount of social services into the privatized nuclear family. Women assume responsibility for these social services 'without a wage and without going on strike' (1975: 34). Thus, according to this argument, what is economically productive about housework is that capitalism, by instituting its family structure, guarantees the exploitative bases of domestic labour and in so doing sustains the capitalist organization of work. But herein resides a primary source of contradiction in this Marxist feminist contribution. For Marx, the *raison d'être* of capitalism's organization of work is the expropriation of surplus labour time as a basis for the accumulation of capital. If indeed it is the case that 'the family is the very pillar of the capitalist organization of work' (Dalla Costa and James 1975: 35), then it would be in the interest of capital to rationalize housework by integrating it with technological innovations, designed to make it more efficient.

The argument is often advanced that Marx considered a primary intention of capitalist production was to eliminate all forms of socially necessary labour and subjugate them to 'the hegemony of capital' (Foreman 1978: 117). Evidence to support this claim is provided in *Grundrisse* in which Marx explored the circumstances essential for socially necessary labour to migrate 'into the domain of the works undertaken by capital itself' (1973: 531). Marx states that 'there are works and investments which may be necessary without being productive in the capitalist sense, i.e., without the realization of the surplus labour contained in them through circulation, through exchange, as surplus value' (1973: 531). In specific circumstances, capital may decide to undertake such works based on the presumption that it will obtain 'out of the general fund of profits − of surplus values − a sufficiently large share to make it the same as if it had created surplus value' (1973: 532). Ultimately capital strives to be able to transform the process of social production into commodities produced through exchange relations. Thus, Marx argued that:

> The highest development of capital exists when the general conditions of the process of social production are not paid out of deductions from the social revenue, the state's taxes − where revenue and not capital appears as the labour fund, and where the worker, although he is a free wage worker like any other, nevertheless stands economically in a different relation − but rather out of capital as capital.
> (Marx 1973: 532)

In other words, Marx anticipated the development of capital to eventually 'subjugate all conditions of social production to itself', thus guaranteeing that all 'social reproductive wealth has been capitalized and all needs are satisfied through the exchange form' (1973: 532). Clear parallels exist here between Marx's prophetic analysis and the expansion of commodity markets into the public and private domains. With the rise of industrial capitalism, there occurs a separation of the public sphere from the private sphere and with this a 'transfer of creative activity at home (private domain) to the socially organized workplace (public domain)' (Firat 1994: 211). In industrial capitalist society, the production of commodities, within the private sphere, has been systematically superseded by the purchase of products in the market. Initially products produced in the public domain were designed to augment the creative activities within the private sphere. Examples of these products included raw wool, spinning and knitting tools, agricultural appliances and sewing machines. Gradually these products 'have been replaced by their end products' (1994: 211). Consumer markets now contain ready-made substitutes for the creative labour that previous generations invested in the production of objects. And this transfer of creative labour from the home to the public sphere has had much to do with the growth of mass production, because it was necessary for capitalists to generate corresponding mass consumer markets (Gardiner 1976; Zaretsky 1976; Firat 1994).

Indeed it has been suggested that gender segregation in the labour market is a necessary component of mass production, as the household has 'to be populated during the day in order to have continual consumption to absorb the increasing production capabilities in the public domain' (Firat 1994: 212). So although an increasing array of products now substitutes for the creative labour women performed in the private sphere, countervailing forces, within the labour market, encourage women into 'the private domain in order to consume the products' (1994: 212). From this perspective it is clear that the relationship between capitalist enterprise and housework has largely failed 'to convert private domestic work ... into a public industry' (Engels 1968: 569). This shortcoming is even more disconcerting when we consider that the restless agitation of capital operating within the industrial process has historically provided the impetus for the transformation of the labour process through the development of new technologies (Seccombe 1974: 16). Given that labour time is a primary source of value, 'any increase in the productivity of a unit of labour time results in a proportional increase in surplus value' (1974: 16). To this extent, it has been the *modus operandi* of capitalist industry to increase the productivity of every unit of salaried labour time. It is this tendency in capitalist accumulation, which has also been a source of confrontation between capital and labour. Indeed, in the history of the working class struggle, technology has been a valuable means of 'gaining free hours' (Dalla Costa and James 1975: 29). But this has not been the case for housework. It would appear that 'a high mechanization of domestic chores doesn't free any time for the woman' (1975: 29).

Marxist feminists point out that Marx's analysis of 'social reproductive wealth' falls short of explaining why housework has not been 'capitalized' and thus transformed into a system in which 'all needs are satisfied through the exchange form' (Marx 1973: 532). For some feminist writers, the problem resides with Marx's gender-blind economic analysis of value and his failure to recognize that the woman 'is always on duty, for the machine doesn't exist that makes and minds children' (Dalla Costa and James 1975: 29). For other feminist writers, the problem is less empirical and more conceptual. Thus, Seccombe (1974) argues that any disjuncture between Marx's analysis of socially necessary labour and the apparent inability of capitalist society to draw housework into a direct relation to capital has to be explained in terms of a misinterpretation, by materialist feminists, of Marx's theory of value.

Housework: necessary but unproductive labour

Marxist feminists generally agree that 'women's oppression' in the private sphere is caused by capital. Consensus also exists around the claim that domestic labour creates use-values, which are consumed within the household. Furthermore, there is little contention that 'domestic labour has been socially necessary labour, throughout history and continues to be so under capitalism' (Seccombe 1974: 10). Significant disagreement does, however, exist as to whether the general attributes of domestic labour 'make the case for it being a productive labour in the specific context of capitalist production' (1974: 10). Using Marx's distinction between productive and unproductive labour, Seccombe argues that 'domestic labour is unproductive' (1974: 11). For Seccombe there exists abundant evidence to confirm Marx's inferred designation of domestic labour as unproductive. Thus, Seccombe quotes Marx's statement outlining the productivity of labour, which Marx states is:

> not derived from the material characteristics of labour (neither from the nature of its product, nor from the particular character of the labour as concrete labour), but from the definite social form, the social relations of production within which labour is realized.
>
> (Marx *Capital*, Vol. 1 [1887] 2003: 157, quoted in Seccombe 1974: 11)

Thus, the attribute which defines productive labour is not the material characteristic of labour, but rather, 'the definite social form, the social relations of production within which labour is realized' (Marx, *Capital*, Vol. 1 [1887] 2003: 157, quoted in Seccombe 1974: 11). Furthermore, Marx argues that 'value is determined by objectified labour time' (1973: 532) and 'the labourer alone is productive who produces surplus value for the capitalist' (Marx, *Capital*, Vol. 1 [1887] 2003: 477). Marx thus defines productive labour as distinguished by two characteristics; it is performed in direct relation with capital, and it produces surplus value. According to Seccombe (1974: 11), domestic labour, while being 'socially necessary labour' does not meet either of Marx's criteria for discerning productive labour. The relation of domestic labour with capital is neither direct (i.e., it is not salaried) nor a source of surplus value (does not create more value than it possesses). To this extent, Seccombe concludes that domestic labour is unproductive labour (in the economic sense) and conforms with Marx's description of an unproductive labour 'exchanged not with capital but with revenue, that is wages or profits' (1974: 11). Seccombe's observations, concerning the unique duality of productive labour, encouraged him to examine an alternative means of expressing the value of domestic labour. To this endeavour Seccombe re-evaluated the relationships between domestic labour and the wage form. Seccombe argued that both the husband and wife 'as members of the same consumption unit' have a shared 'common interest in the wage's magnitude, while being sharply differentiated from its form' (1974: 12). But this shared interest is obfuscated by the fact that the 'husband receives a pay cheque while his wife does not' (1974: 12). According to Seccombe, the wage has a 'mystifying quality', which obscures the fact that 'the wage in reality pays for an entirely different labour – the labour that reproduces the labour power of the entire family' (1974: 12). This forms part of the *sine qua non* of capitalism, i.e., the reproduction of the forces of production (labour power). Domestic labour fulfils this function in its capacity to reproduce labour power on 'a daily basis' and also 'on a generational basis' (1974: 14).

But the 'housewife's labour cannot assert itself' as it is 'embodied in another person' and this denies it a 'direct relation with capital' (1974: 20). Instead, the housewife's labour, in its capacity to convert wage-purchased goods into use-values, 'becomes part of the congealed mass of past labour embodied in labour power' (1974: 9). Domestic labour, according to this logic, is situated 'beyond the exercise of the law of value' (1974: 16). And it is for this reason that, despite developments in the technological complexity of domestic appliances, 'the domestic labour process has stagnated while the industrial labour process has constantly advanced' (1974: 17). Labour time embodied in productivity is a source of value, and of vital interest to capital. Nevertheless, Seccombe argues that 'domestic labour is not part of variable capital', it is not hourly paid salaried wage and thus 'capital has no interest in the productivity of a unit of domestic labour time' (1974: 17). The amount of time required to complete a domestic task is irrelevant to capital as long as this domestic labour time succeeds in its overall task of reproducing the labour force. To this extent it appears unsurprising 'that the household is the least efficient organization of a labour process existent within capitalism' (1974: 17). It is certainly the case that while the productivity of labour time (expended in housework) has increased, it continues to be labour-intensive, monotonous work. Nevertheless, Seccombe's observations struggle to explain the stagnation of the domestic labour process relative to technological developments in industrial production.

According to Seccombe, the deluge of mass-produced domestic appliances into the home should not be read as 'a progressive application of technology' (1974: 17). This is because capitalism's history of building into commodities the conditions for their rapid obsolescence, means that capital's profit motive can be served 'by the most inefficient product application in order to maximise the quantity of goods consumed per person' (1974: 17). And this, according to Seccombe, explains the short product life cycles of new domestic technologies combined with their erratic development. Because domestic labour time has no direct relation to capital, 'there exists no continual impetus to reorganize domestic labour to improve its efficiency' (1974: 17). But this conclusion is unconvincing. Even the most cursory perusal of high street stores reveals the market for domestic technologies to be a fiercely competitive sphere of commodity production. Housework would indeed be made more efficient if it were fully integrated into commodity production, but this transformation in the domestic labour process appears to be tethered by forces which exceed market dynamics. Indeed, it has been suggested that the possibilities of capital automating domestic work run up against the combined forces of patriarchy and the discursive constructions of ideal feminine identity (Dalla Costa and James 1975).

In as much as ideal feminine identity defines womanhood in terms of the maintenance of the home and family, the quest for this ideal engages feminine subjects in practices which encourage 'compulsive perfection in their work' (Dalla Costa and James 1975: 37). We are all familiar with the saying 'a woman's work is never done'. Yet we are less familiar with the conditions which serve to reproduce this construction of feminine identity. Diana Gittins (1994) provides several important observations concerning feminine identity and domestic labour time in the nineteenth-century household. She argues that the demands placed on domestic labour time were invariably linked to discourses which equated cleanliness with both feminine identity and class. To the extent that cleanliness was equated with class, women often distinguished their living standard and themselves 'through the type of accommodation they have, its degree of cleanliness and maintenance' (1994: 121). Indeed, in the nineteenth century, household cleanliness signified 'respectability' and was exclusively defined as women's work (Davidoff 1976). Thus developments in technology and house work had direct implications for the production of feminine identity. Instead of saving labour time, domestic appliances became essential apparatus in the feminine quest for the immaculately furnished and polished home. Arguably advertising promotions operated to sustain this discourse (Odih 2007). For example, in the 1890s, the Steel Roll Manufacturing Company widely advertised its newly developed washing machine. The advertising copy was emblematic of advertising's dualistic engagement with both the commodity market, and the promotion of household labour-saving technologies as a source of feminine identity. Thus, the advertising copy states 'Washing Machine for the Residence. Modern and complete with ample capacity to do all the family linen and do it just right.' Within the advertising system, the productivity of domestic labour is at one and the same time a market place and a site for the production of consumer subjectivities.

The early twentieth century witnessed a further revolution in household gadgets marketed as labour-saving devices. The electrical appliances industry, buttressed by a revolution in advertising, recognized the commercial value of the household as a market for domestic appliances. By the 1950s, the blossoming advertising industry had become rapturous in its endeavours to inculcate 'the ideal of the permanently immaculate home and the need to buy more and more gadgets to keep it that way' (Gittins 1994: 122). Thus advertisements, directed at the 1950s homemaker, depicted ideal femininity as synonymous with an impeccably dressed and coiffured mother (Kates and Shaw-Garlock 1999). Homes were not just clean, but seen to be immaculately clean. Advertising collaborated in an ideology of perfectionism, which contrived to increase, rather than decrease, the amount of time dedicated to domestic chores. Consequently, although advances in domestic appliances required that less time be dedicated to completing a task, the levels of quality now required to accomplish the task operated to extend domestic labour time. These observations suggest the inadequacy of economic reductionism when examining gender and domestic labour time. Nevertheless it is impossible to have a notion of production which does not also involve reproduction (Beechey 1979: 75). Consequently an understanding of time and domestic labour requires a comprehension of the 'interrelations between production and reproduction as part of a single process' (1979: 75).

Conclusion: capital accumulation in non-economic times

In the variety of Marxist feminisms discussed thus far, there is some agreement that domestic labour is 'engaged in the maintenance and reproduction of labour power as a source of surplus labour' (Gardiner 1976: 114). With the rise of industrial capitalism, women are defined as domestic labourers and this forms the basis of capitalism's expropriation of domestic labour time as a source of value. But there is a tendency, in this form of analysis, to view the capitalist–proletarian relationship 'as a product of the universal and all-determining force of capitalism' (Williams 1988: 50). Thus Marxist feminist analysis all too often focuses on 'capital – not on relations between men and women' (Hartmann 1981: 9). Capitalism is viewed as 'an abstract entity existing independent of gender relations (Williams 1988: 50). Heidi Hartmann argues that leading exponents of the Domestic Labour as Productive Labour debate fall short of recognizing the significance of gender relations in determining the 'strategic role of women's work in this system' (1981: 9). To this extent, Hartmann is particularly critical of Dalla Costa and James. Hartmann claims that while the 'rhetoric of feminism' is present in their work, it fails to consistently highlight 'that the importance of housework, as a social relation, lies in its crucial role in perpetuating male supremacy' (Dalla Costa and James 1975: 9). Although this is a convincing critique, it is not immediately apparent that Dalla Costa and James do obscure the role of gender difference in determining the subjugation of women as domestic labourers. Indeed, Dalla Costa and James make ample reference to the acquisition of feminine and masculine identities as an important factor in the 'relation between time-given-to-housework and time-not-given-to-housework' (1975: 36). Some evidence of this is apparent in the following extract:

> it is not necessary to spend time each day ironing sheets and curtains, cleaning the floor until it sparkles nor to dust every day. And yet many women still do that. Obviously it is not because they are stupid ... In reality, it is only in this work that they can realize an identity precisely because, as we said before, capital has cut them off from the process of socially organized production.
> (Dalla Costa and James 1975: 36)

It would appear that Dalla Costa and James did recognize gender acquisition as a determinant of a woman's ability to identify with her ascribed role as a producer of use-value. Nevertheless it is clearly evident that Dalla Costa and James are focusing on capital as a primary determinant of gender identity, thus obscuring the extent to which 'men have a material interest in women's continued oppression' (Hartmann 1981: 9).

An alternative position is to argue that the acquisition of masculine and feminine identities constitutes the ideological ground for material relations to the mode of production. Clear parallels exist between the instrumental time of the productive economy and masculine ways of being. Masculinity is recognized, here, to be a dynamic process rather than a fixed quantity or unalterable subject position which conflates physiology and gender identity. Masculinity is not entrenched in time or place, nor does it endure as some trans-historical substance. What connotates masculinity, at any given moment, is itself diverse and in transition. Acknowledging that 'what counts as masculine may shift over historical periods' and even 'over the lifetime of the individual', it is evident that contemporary masculine identities are discursively bound up with high levels of purposive-rational instrumentality in relation to a world that there is an urge to control (Kerfoot and Knights 1996: 86). It is no mere accident that the discourses of masculinity and economic linear time are both aligned and dominant in modern Western society. Not only are they conditions and consequences of one another but they also reflect and reinforce Western preoccupations with economic growth and competitive success. However, neither of these discourses are exhaustive of relations of gender and of time. In the discursive struggle for the signified feminine, the meaning of femininity is both socially produced and variable between different forms of discourse. Amid the plurality of feminine subject positions, there exist versions of femininity discursively represented as the feminine ideal. While the discursive constructs of this ideal shift and are transformed according to socio-historical context, modern representations of the feminine ideal have come to be bound up with behaviours which deny the value of self and autonomy, define meaningful existence as achieved through the care of others and through displays of social and sexual passivity (1996: 87).

For many women and some men the culmination of the feminine ideal finds expression in the subordination of self to the 'needs', demands and desires of significant others, be they family members, friends, superordinates, etc. Femininity, then, is an ideal that, in emphasizing acquiescence, leaves little space for an active and autonomous subject who can place equal demands upon those whose labour and identity are serviced by contemporary heterosexual arrangements. In this sense, the feminine ideal is expressive of a relational mode of engaging with the world. It is for this reason that the phrase 'no time to call our [her] own' has an immediate resonance for many women. For unlike the projects prevalent within masculine discursive configurations that have finite time scales in which measures of achievement can be imposed, feminine work is unending and almost infinite in its ceaseless circularity.

It is evident that capital accumulation requires a reservoir of non-economic times as a basis for the production of relative surplus value. In modern regimes of capitalist accumulation, this has translated into the universal appropriation of the social times of embodied relations. For those caught up in feminine discourses, meaning and direction derive from embeddedness in embodied social relations. Just as the feminine self is defined in terms of the 'needs' of others, so experiences of time come to be defined in relation to these very same 'needs'. Put differently, the centrality ascribed to others by those caught up in feminine discourses encourages what is described here as 'relational' perceptions of time (Davies 1990; 1994).

Just as production founded on absolute surplus value expropriates the objectified time of 'value-creating labour' (Marx 1973: 410), so the production of relative surplus value entails the exploitation of a feminine self, which is defined by the 'needs' of others. Rarely in the domestic sphere can time be conceived of as existing infinite, quantitatively discrete units that are readily demarcated between, for example, work and leisure or personal time (Adam 1993: 172). A condition and consequence of women's subordinate position in the public sphere, and their ascribed domestic role in the private sphere, are that of significantly inhibiting their power to make decisions about their own time and that of others. To this extent domestic labour time is inextricably tied to the materialism of modern existence, and the social practices which flow from capital accumulation. Chapter 4 develops this proposition with an emphasis on time, work and gendered subjectivity.

PART II

Fordist Times

Generations of scientific management in clerical work
Source: Reproduced by permission of Getty Images

4

Gender and identity in modern times

When I started the job, I felt that I was doing more than I have ever done. I just felt like I wanted to sleep all the time. And even now when people come round and I am tired, or the phone rings, I just feel like saying, Oh, just go away, leave me alone! But I don't say that, instead I open the door or answer the phone, despite the fact that I am exhausted from being at work all day ... I just feel like too many demands are being made on me. Like today, for example, I had loads of patients in at one time and it's so frustrating when that happens because I can't tend to them as I would like to. Instead I could only give each patient a specific amount of attention and move on to the next. Sometimes I find myself thinking that I'm just not being fair to my patients. But when I spend too much time on them, I just get myself into a mess and overlap into other appointments and then end up having to reschedule appointments or refer them to other colleagues. And that doesn't reflect well on me, it makes me look inefficient. But that shouldn't be what it's all about anyway ... It shouldn't be about efficiency and management, chasing upgrades and scoring points. And that's even more frustrating because everyone is so wrapped up in the management side of things, and how it can benefit them, they forget the most important aspect of our work and that is ensuring the well-being of our patients!

(full-time NHS physiotherapist, single, no children)

Why can't this individual provide her patients with the attention that she would otherwise provide? What factors constrain her? Why does providing more attention to her patients encourage disarray/a 'mess'? And why is she not attracted to pursuing the career enhancing efficiency practices of her colleagues?

Although there are potentially infinite readings and meanings that might be attributed to this transcription, her actions are understood here as reflective of a struggle to accommodate an embodied attachment to her patients, with other less embodied influences. Primarily informed by empirical research, this chapter examines gender and identity in modern times. It is my contention that the discursive constructs of 'femininity' encourage an embodied, 'relational' existence to the world. A condition and consequence of this 'relational' mode of existence are that those individuals caught up in 'feminine' discourses tend to experience their time as 'relational'. 'Relational time' is defined here as an experience of time that 'exists' in relation to an embeddedness in embodied social relations. Mediated through significant others, relational time is shared rather than personal and thus sensitive to the contextuality and particularity of interpersonal relations.

In previous years, several authors (Davies 1990, 1994; Leccardi and Rampazi 1993, Deem 1996; Leccardi 1996) have variously argued that men and women use time differently due to their distinct life-situations. The routinized circularity and repetitiveness of domestic labour (encapsulated by the phrase a 'woman's work is never done') are identified as exemplifying the incompatibility of women's work with linear conceptions of time (Davies 1990; Le Feuvre 1994). This body of literature provides a highly insightful attempt to deconstruct dominant understanding(s) of time through drawing our attention to women's time as embodied in daily life. While feminist suggestions of distinct male and female times draw our attention to the significance of gender in the discursive constitution of linear time, their insufficient theorization of power and subjectivity has the unintended effect of reproducing the very phallocentric discourse that feminism seeks to challenge.

Conversely, primarily informed by the writings of Foucault (1982), the discourse of gendered time expressed here has as its premise a conceptualization of power and subjectivity as grounded in the exercise of power/knowledge through social practices in which subjects are embedded. For power exists in its exercise and is not simply a zero-sum relationship of inequality. As Foucault expresses it, 'Power exists only when it is put into action, even if, of course, it is integrated into a disparate field of possibilities brought to bear upon permanent structures' (1982: 219). To this extent 'power relations are rooted deep in the social nexus, not constituted "above" society as a supplementary structure' (1982: 222). In so far as power is embedded in the 'social nexus', subjectivity exists in reciprocal relation to power. Individual self-consciousness is configured through the exercise of power within, which apprehensions of personal identity come to be engendered. To quote Kerfoot and Knights (1994: 70):

> Where subjectivity is constructed in and through discourse, the gender identity of men and women as masculine and feminine subjects is socially constituted in and through certain sites, behaviours and practices at any one time.

Gender identities are, in this sense, historically contingent, unstable and potentially multifarious. This notion of the discursive production of gendered subjects within and between power relations, provides a means of reconciling women's time/linear time dualism inherent in feminist discourses of gendered time. For example, feminine time is conceptualized here as a form of time experienced by those whose identities are discursively constituted as feminine and therefore not exclusive to or exhaustive of women. The dualistic opposition between essential female time and equally essential male's time/linear time, evident in feminist discourses of gendered time, is dissolved when one recognizes reciprocity in the discursive constitution of gender identities and their potential multiplicity.

This chapter is divided into two main sections. The first commences with an analysis of power, subjectivity and self that is capable of advancing a discourse of gendered time, which escapes the problems of disembodied dualisms and essentialism. The section then proceeds to reveal how the discursive constructs of femininity resonate, with difficulty, with the equally discursively constituted constructs of linear time.

The second section has as its central objective that of unravelling the often conceptually problematic interconnections between women, femininity and relational time. This section identifies how the materialism of modern existence (i.e., capitalist modes of production) and the social practices that flow from it reflect and reinforce expressions of time grounded in the hegemony of commodified, economically valued, individualistic linear time. A condition of women's subordinate position in the public sphere, and their ascribed domestic responsibilities in the private sphere, is that of significantly inhibiting their power to make decisions about their own time and also that of encouraging an existence that is discursively tied to the 'needs' of significant others. More specifically, this chapter argues that feminine perceptions of time as relational, while open to resistance, tend to prevail among women by virtue of a dominant and comparatively impermeable gendered employment segregation and sexual division of labour, both in formal employment and in the home. It is in this sense, that experiences of time as relational tend to be disproportionately exhibited by female subjects.

Power, subjectivity and gendered identities

The concept of power has, and continues to be, a contentious issue in feminist discourses of women's oppression. Feminists continue to be constrained by, or in contention with, their ancestral ties to Enlightenment thought and its assumptions about the relation between power and knowledge, reality and truth, cause and effect, freedom and the nature of human agency (Hekman 1990:83). Where feminists have been concerned to theorize women's differential social and economic position in terms of patriarchal practices, this reflects and reinforces the Enlightenment's totalizing, androcentristic, conditions of truth, knowledge and power. Patriarchal power, conceptualized as existing in a variety of institutional forms, patriarchal practices and relations collectively acting to oppress the female sex, translates as men 'having power' over women (Kerfoot and Knights 1994: 70). This comprehension of power as the capital of some to the preclusion of others, 'sets up a dichotomous relationship between the individual and the social world, between powerful men and powerless women as largely internally undifferentiated categories, and imputes a passivity to all women' (1994: 70). An insistence on the all-inclusive character of female oppression in terms of the common undifferentiated enemy, patriarchy, and inability to develop differentiated analyses of cultural and historical contexts mitigates against a comprehension of complexity and diversity in female experiences. To participate in this discourse, then, would engage feminists in a discourse which homogenizes female experiences and in so doing, obscures the possibilities for female subjects to exercise agency and creativity within conditions of social constraint.

An alternative formulation (Foucault 1980, 1982) is to envisage power as 'existing only in its exercise, operating through the production of particular knowledges – around discourses of gender and sexuality...' (Kerfoot and Knights 1994: 70). In this viewpoint, power is neither unidirectional, nor does it proceed from a unitary derivation to 'shape, direct or constrain subjects' (1994: 70). Foucault articulates the relational character of power, whose existence depends on 'the recalcitrance of the will and the intransigence of freedom' (1982: 222). The diaphaneity of discourses and their material trajectories in social institutions and practices is intrinsic to the continuance of power since 'reality' derives meaning through language. Yet language, as translated through sociohistorical discourses, derives its political affectivity only through the meaningful constructions of agents who identify with the forms of subjectivity it advances and act upon them (Weedon 1987). Power, therefore, is in reciprocal relation to 'subjectivity', where subjectivity can be delimited as individual self-consciousness inscripted into ideals of normative behaviour surrounding groupings of individuals, objects practices or institutions. 'Subjectivity is constituted through the exercise of power within which conceptions of personal identity, gender and sexuality come to be generated' (Kerfoot and Knights 1994: 70). Consequently, the individual who has a 'discursively constituted sense of identity may resist particular interpollations or produce new versions of meaning from the conflicts and contradictions between existing discourses' (Weedon 1987: 106). Gendered subjectivities are, therefore, historically shifting, fractured, inherently capricious and potentially multifarious (Kerfoot and Knights 1996). Accepting that the nature of identity and subjectivity is inherently unstable, Mouffe (1992: 372) argues that the social agent is:

constituted by an ensemble of 'subject positions' that can never be totally fixed in a closed system of differences, constructed by a diversity of discourses among which there is no necessary relation, but a constant movement of overdetermination and displacement. The 'identity' of such a multiple and contradictory subject is therefore always contingent and precarious, temporally fixed at the intersection of those subject positions and dependent upon specific forms of identification.

Acknowledging the existence of multiple masculinities/femininities draws attention to the precariousness of gender identity. This is to conceive of a secure identity as an aspiration to be achieved where the final stage is always illusive, forever out of reach and constantly in flux. Gender identity must, therefore, be worked at, acquiring the status of a 'personal project' to be accomplished through continuous practice (Kerfoot and Knights 1996). Moreover, 'becoming' a gendered subject, is never a linear process because that implies a pre-social body and also a temporally discrete origin to gender, after which it is fixed in form.

To articulate 'becoming' in this way is to espouse a view that refuses certainty, universality or constancy in what it means to be a male or female subject. One might suggest that drawing attention to the potential multiplicity of gender identities invites a collapse into relativism whereby there are, for example, as many different permutations of masculinity as there are men. While it is axiomatic that masculinity, no less than femininity, is seen as manifest in a multiplicity of forms and not as a confirmed entity, it is possible to identify their prevailing manifestations. I shall now identify the discursive constructs of prevailing forms of masculinity. This leads on to a discussion of how the discursive constructs of masculinity resonate with the equally discursively constituted constructs of linear time.

Masculin(ities)

To reiterate a previous statement, gender and gender differences are conceptualized, here, as in a dynamic process where masculinity is an outcome of social practices rather than a fixed amount that any one individual may possess. Masculinity is not consolidated in time or place, nor does it exist as some trans-historical attribute. Cultural delineations of what counts as masculinity are themselves, at specific moments, diverse and in flux (Kerfoot and Knights 1996). Acknowledging that there are multiple and disparate forms of masculinity, it is suggested here, as elsewhere (Kerfoot and Knights 1996) that modern masculine identities are discursively bound up with high levels of purposive-rational instrumentality in relation to a world that there is a drive to control. Seidler (1989) describes this form of control as one that equates with detached reason, logic and rational process. Modern masculinity generates social relations dedicated to fierce competition, hierarchical authority, careerism and the language of winning, which is in turn bound up with decisive action, a logic of productivism and risk-taking. 'Only the never ending supply of new conquests, challenges and uncertainties keep those caught up in such masculine discourses forever trapped in a permanent striving to be in control' (Kerfoot and Knights 1996: 80). In this sense, masculinity is compulsive and inevitably self-defeating. While it has as its objective control, attainment of this aim is inevitably transient, forever having to be renewed by new projects, new aims, new conquests and the (inevitably unpredictable) approval of others. As Seidler (1989: 192) puts it, masculinity's preoccupation with control translates as a 'desperate striving without ever really experiencing the joy of fulfilment'.

At a level of personal social engagement, it is invariably the apprehension of capitulating control that induces rational instrumentality in those caught up in masculine discourses. An instrumental-purposive regime of action configures social relationships, conquering or reinterpreting alternative expressions of 'being', to accord with an archetype of instrumental action. Whatever enters the terrain of rational calculation must be conceived as 'other'. This instrumental relationship to social relations and compulsive desire to be in control are ultimately expressive of an instrumental relationship to self (Seidler 1989). Self, as constructed through an abjuration or devaluation of particular domains of human experience, becomes the ultimate realm of control and cohibition. Masculinity, therefore, involves the attachment to an instrumental achievement of identity through the control of self and 'other'.

Preoccupied with cognition and externalities, masculinity is expressive of a distancing or disembodiment from the contextuality and particularity of human experience. Where rational action is privileged above emotions, feelings and desires, for those caught up in masculine discourses

> this may translate into the denial or suppression of emotionality, fear and uncertainty; the denial of human intimacy or suppression of embodied experiences of pleasure and desire; and the denial of 'contented passivity' as an alternative mode of engaging with the world.
> (Burchell 1990, quoted in Kerfoot and Knights 1993: 672)

Modern forms of masculinity are discursively bound up with an estrangement and disembodiment from the particularity of human experiences. As Kerfoot and Knights put it:

> [Masculinity] is abstract and highly instrumental with respect to controlling ... objects, thus sustaining a mode of relating to externalities that is self-estranged and wholly disembodied. Rarely does masculinity embrace the world or even itself with a sense of wonderment, pleasure or estrangement, for it labours ceaselessly in the struggle to control and possess the objects of its desire, whilst at the

same time self-deceptively presuming itself to be free of desire. That is to say, the desire is so buried beneath a series of rationalities and rationalizations as to be virtually invisible to its agent. Yet it may be suggested that the hidden agenda behind masculine struggles for control is a desire to produce a stable world in which identity can feel safe and secure.

(Kerfoot and Knights 1996: 82)

In the compulsive endeavour to control self and 'other', the contextuality of the present is transcended, swept aside in the insatiable quest for new challenges, new conquests, new realms and objects of control. In this sense, masculine ways of being appear to resonate with the equally discursively constituted constructs of linear time.

On masculinity and linear time

As with dominant forms of modern masculinity, linear time entails a perpetual transcendence from the contextuality and particularity of human experience. For 'the rationalisation of consciousness that supports the continuity of past and future, cause and project necessarily supports kinds of thinking that seek to transcend the present, concrete, arbitrarily and absolutely limited moment' (Ermarth 1992: 31). Linear time, by definition, involves a kind of transcendence that trivializes the specificity of the finite moment. It requires a kind of estrangement from the present that entails dematerialization, abstraction and disembodiment. Every present in linear time is in this way also the future. Issues of present value are deprived their contextuality and reinscribed with the clockwork precision of a depth-less, disembodied expression of time.

Linear time's transcendence from the present resonates with masculinity's compulsive hyperactivity. As with masculinity, the discursive constructs of linear time's future orientation encourage ceaseless instrumental planning and compulsive 'possessive individualism' (Macpherson 1962). Masculinity's goal-oriented instrumental planning encourages the pursuit of abstract instrumental objectives that both reflect and reinforce a disembodied and estranged relationship to the world. This involves acting in such a way as to maximize one's returns with a view to the future. But the future always becomes the present at its point of realization. Consequently, masculinity strives to maximize its returns indefinitely; that is to say, into a future that will never be realized. Masculinity's propensity for instrumental rational behaviour thus involves means–ends forms of behaviour where the end is always a means towards a future end of exactly the same kind. In so far as individuals are conceived of as having ends of this nature, they must be supposed as having desires which linear time's future orientation always precludes.

The centrality ascribed to certain forms of masculinity in the discursive constitution of linear time enables masculine ways of being to align with the discursive constructs of linear time. If this is to be accepted, then by inference less instrumental forms of masculinity and feminine ways of being will struggle to resonate with the equally discursive constructs of linear time. The foregoing discussion of gender identity is pertinent here for several reasons. In contrast to other feminist discourses of gendered time (Forman and Sowton 1989; Davies 1990; Leccardi 1996), the association made here between linear time and masculinity resists any one-to-one correlation between men, masculinity and linear time. Acknowledging the precariousness of gender identities and the possibility of multiple masculinities/femininities draws attention to the need to theorize gendered time in ways more sophisticated than a simple dualism between masculine time and feminine time. Moreover, varieties of masculinity are constructed in response to, and in reciprocity with prevailing forms and definitions of femininity (Kerfoot and Knights 1996). In this sense femininity is cultivated in reciprocal relation to masculinity. In the same vein, gendered perceptions of and relations to linear time are sustained in mutually constituting reciprocal relations. However, the materialism of modern existence, and the social practices that flow from it, reflect and reinforce a resonance between particular forms of masculinity and the discursive constructs of linear time. This has specific consequences for less instrumentally masculine and feminine ways of being. These consequences are expressive of feminine perceptions of time, and relations to linear time. The remainder of this chapter provides an account, informed by extensive empirical research, of feminine relations to linear time at the level of personal experience and social relationships.

On femininity and linear time

In the discursive struggle for the signified feminine, the meaning of femininity is both socially produced and variable between different forms of discourse. Amid the plurality of feminine subject positions, exist versions of femininity discursively represented as the feminine ideal. While the discursive constructs of this ideal shift and transform according to socio-historical context, modern representations of the feminine ideal have come to be bound up with behaviours which deny the value of self and autonomy, and define meaningful existence as achieved through the care of others and through displays of social and sexual passivity (Kerfoot and Knights 1996: 87). Modern advertising, for example, offers us models of femininity which, despite their apparent plurality, converge towards representing ideal femininity in terms of acquiescing to the demands of others. For many women, and some men, the culmination of the feminine ideal finds expression in the subordination of self to the 'needs', demands and desires of significant others, be they family members, friends, superordinates, etc. Femininity, then, is an ideal that in emphasizing acquiescence leaves little space for an active and autonomous subject who can place equal demands upon those whose labour and identity are serviced by contemporary heterosexual arrangements. In this sense, the feminine ideal is expressive of a relational mode of engaging with the world. Those whose identities are discursively constituted as feminine invariably derive meaningful existence, purpose and direction in terms of an embeddedness in embodied social relations. In contrast to masculine desires to control self and 'other', 'feminine identities are dominated by attaining an impeccability of physical environment, character and bodily virtue, reflecting the indeterminable flux of everyday interactions' (Kerfoot and Knights 1998: 16). While the hyperactivity of masculinity involves a transgression of the present, which is swept aside in the frenetic pursuit of new challenges, the relational contingency of ideal femininity embraces the contextuality and particularity of the present as evident in the following transcription excerpt:

> In personal, social relationships, for example, in not having to plan what might happen in the future, it's actually valuing each contact that I have with friends at the time and recognizing that I value it, that's one thing that I've thought about quite carefully. I suppose as well, we've been talking about money, but not sort of saving vast sums of money but just being happy that I can cope month to month with things that are happening, not thumbing ahead. I suppose work-wise it's similar, I mean, although we have to have two years strategic funds, actually being able to take each element as it comes and deal with it. I cope with that by actions so that if I know that I'm doing something today, I'm not going to worry about what I was going to have to do next week until I come to it and, equally, I've not got to worry about what happened last week. I learn to cope with this week's work. So as long as I know what is planned, then I can cope with what's happening there, it's only future uncertainties that cause me problems, personal and organizational.
> (full-time paid manager of a voluntary organization, divorced, one child)

Abstracted from context, devoid of content, linear time's future orientation is bereft of any emotional energy to allow one to question the futility of 'possessive individualism' and the transience of lived experiences that this entails. Conversely, femininity's embeddedness in embodied social relations allows for a sensitivity to the specificity of, and contextuality of, social relations. Although the interviewee, in the above transcription excerpt, is cognizant of her organization's strategic plans, by dealing with each element as distinct (i.e., rather than as systematically tied to a two-year strategic plan), it is the present rather than the future of these plans which is given priority. The discursive constructs of femininity are expressive of an engagement with the world which is at once immediate, sensual and embodied. In contrast with linear time's propensity for disembodiment, feminine ways of being derive purpose and direction through a sensitivity to the situationally contingent needs and desires of significant others. For this and other reasons, raised next, feminine discourses have a tendency to be incompatible, or in conflict, with the clockwork, disembodied precision of linear time.

Our time for others!

> People ring me up in the middle of the night sometimes. A lot of people tend to think that I can solve their problems. But the people that do, tend to be the people that are still having the same problem about five or six years later. It's just a thing you get used to in the end, and you just let them talk because you know that they are not going to ever change anything, no matter what sort of advice you give them or try to help them to see. But if anybody asks me to do something or wants to talk to me, I am normally there and sometimes I get annoyed with myself and think to myself, you've done it again, you should have said no. But it's hard to say no, especially when someone wants to talk to you and it's nice to know that someone trusts you enough to want to talk to you.
>
> (Full-time Dental Nurse, Unmarried, No Children)

The above transcription is derived from a conversation with a full-time dental nurse located in a practice which I, reluctantly, frequent. It is pertinent here as it illustrates a mode of being which is not instrumentally attached to securing itself through purposive-instrumental action and causal directionality. As inferred in the transcript, she is clearly aware that the conversations described may not result in any immediate or deferred resolution. Rather, her understanding of self revolves around being available to provide solace to her confidants, even if this may run up against other aspects of her identity. This engagement with her self and others 'is at once immediate, sensual and embodied, not driven by cognitive and goal-centred designs and preoccupations' (Kerfoot and Knights 1996:87). In her desire to meet the 'needs' of others, self becomes subordinated to the particularity and situational contingency of others' 'needs'. The latter part of the transcript refers to an understanding of self which appears to be a condition, and consequence, of a subordination of self to others, in that she begins to infer the significance of interpersonal recognition to her personal identity. Although it was stated previously that masculinity involves a compulsive drive to achieve the approbation and approval of others, the distinctiveness of feminine desires for public recognition resides in its grounding in emotional validation (Kerfoot and Knights 1996). While both modes of being might well be expressive of compulsive actions, masculinity has as its intention the control of self and 'other'. In contrast, feminine desires for approval and recognition emanate from an attachment and connectedness with others and have as their intention emotional validation. This distinction is apparent in the following transcription derived from a conversation with a primary school teacher:

Two children immediately come to mind, I know that with some additional help, I could conquer their special needs. But I have twenty-four other children that also need my attention. I've tried to get additional support but my school can't afford it. So I make up for it, I stay behind during my lunch hours and hear them read to try and bring up their reading levels. I wouldn't have to give up my lunch times if I felt the children were getting a fairer deal and I don't think they are. But it is also a bit of a self-agenda really. You see, we have reading tests and it feels good to know that I have been able to bring a child up from six and a half to eight on the scale. And then I can show *** [name of the headmistress] what I have achieved. So, in fact, there are two separate reasons really. I hear the children read during my lunch time because I want them to do well. And secondly I want *** [name of headmistress] to recognize me as a good teacher. But she never seems to appreciate what I have achieved ... Apparently she told the OfSTED assessment officer, we had OfSTED several months ago, that I was very conscientious. But it would mean a lot more if she had said it to me.

(Full-time primary school teacher, unmarried, no children)

When I initially read through this transcript my thoughts were drawn to masculinity, as a source of explanation, as to why this primary school teacher was working through her lunch break to provide extra tuition for her pupils. After all, as stated above, masculinity is associated with incessant activity. At a further level of analysis, it became apparent that while the primary school teacher's action reflected the frenetic activity of masculinity, her intention was not to achieve control through the approbation and approval of others. If that had been her intention, having achieved the recognition of her senior colleague (*vis-à-vis* her headteacher's comments to the OfSTED commissioner), the teacher's actions might then have been redirected to pursuing other challenges and conquests. Rather, the primary school teacher's continued pursuit of affirmation, from her senior colleague, suggests that her actions are motivated by an embodied attachment to this colleague and her pupils. In this sense, her desire for approval is indicative of an embodied, interpersonal quest for emotional validation. It might suffice here to say that just as the masculine self can never secure the response of the other, so the feminine self's attempts at developing an embodied relation to an Other can never be guaranteed. The feminine self, in its pursuit of embodied social relations, might also find itself caught up in compulsive, frenetic activities. But while the masculine self's compulsive hyperactivity is motivated by the desire to control self and other, the feminine self's actions are motivated by a desire for emotional validation.

The transcripts converge to represent a mode of being that is fundamentally embodied in social relations. Where, as is evident in these transcripts, self is defined in terms of the needs of others, so experiences of time come to be defined in relation to these very same needs. The inextricable links between feminine embodiment and personal experiences of time are clearly evident in the primary school teacher's decision to provide reading tuition during her free time. Her subordination of self to the needs of her pupils impacts on her availability to service these needs and thus her personal experiences of time. Put differently, the centrality ascribed to others by those caught up in feminine discourses encourages what is described here as relational perceptions of time. Davies (1990: 15) defines relational time as perceptions of time that exist in relation to significant others, and identifies relational time as women's time. While I have a profound respect for, and appreciation of, Davies's (1990, 1994) theoretical and empirical contributions, the dualistic oppositions upon which her alternative discourse of gendered time is grounded are significantly problematic. For example, when referring to gendered times, Davies states:

> [L]inear time and clock time make up the dominant structure in our present-day society, and this may be used ... as an instrument of power and control over women. (This, of course, would equally apply to men who lack power.) As the dominant structure, women must of course assimilate themselves into this temporal order and indeed it is part and parcel of their way of relating to time: taken for granted and often unquestioningly accepted. Alongside this though, is another temporal pattern and consciousness which are more diffuse in nature, being process and cyclically oriented. Due to the nature of women's reproductive work and women's socialisation, women to a larger extent than men are affected by this temporal consciousness.
> (Davies 1990: 231)

Davies's discourse is clearly guided by a zero-sum conception of power as evidenced by the statement 'This, of course, would equally apply to men who lack power'. Similar conceptions of power are evident in Leccardi (1993, 1996) and Forman and Sowton's (1989) respective discourses on gendered time. The reliance of these respective discourses on a conception of power as the capital of a few, and located in a position of exteriority to the individual, constructs a dichotomous relationship between forcible men and ineffectual women as internally indistinguishable categories. Consequently, when Davies proceeds to identify the operations through which women come to identify with relational time, the zero-sum conception of power that informs her discourse is unable to articulate the significance of identity, subjectivity and agency to the maintenance of these processes. Hence, Davies is forced to resort to statements such as: 'women must of course assimilate themselves into this temporal order and indeed it is part and parcel of their way of relating to time: taken for granted and often unquestioningly accepted' (Davies 1990: 231).

Specifically, Davies's (1990, 1994) approach has difficulty recognizing how female subjects become the sites and apparatus of power by identifying with, and contesting, forms of subjectivity that are the products of specific configurations of discourse. The absence of a coherent theorization of the social processes which maintain relational experiences of time invites suggestions of essentialism (Ermarth 1989). Conversely, gendered subjectivities are conceptualized here as grounded in power/knowledge relations; they are an outcome of social processes as opposed to a quantity that any one person may acquire. Feminine and masculine modes of being are not peculiar to or exhaustive of women and men respectively. Acknowledging these caveats, relational time is defined, here, as an expression of time reflective of the embeddedness, of those caught up in feminine discourses, in embodied social relations. Mediated through significant others, relational time is shared rather than personal and thus sensitive to the contextuality and particularity of interpersonal relations. While disproportionately exhibited between the sexes, feminine conceptions of time, as relational, are neither synonymous with nor exclusive to women. Rather, it is my view that gendered perceptions of time vary between individuals and contexts but that masculine linear time is the more dominant because of its centrality in the productive economy. The materialism of modern existence and the social practices that flow from it reflects and reinforces expressions of time grounded in the hegemony of commodified, economically valued, individualistic linear time. A condition of women's subordinate position in the public sphere and their ascribed domestic role in the private sphere, is that of significantly inhibiting their power to make decisions about their own time and that of others. It is in this sense, and for reasons discussed below, that experiences of time as relational tend to be disproportionately exhibited by female subjects. The following section focuses on the discursive constructs of motherhood as an illustration of the significance of power/knowledge relations to the disproportionate experience of relational time by female subjects. In so doing, I intend through illustration to further unravel the complex interconnections between femininity, women and relational time.

Domestic division of labour: timely reminders

Motherhood is neither a unitary experience, nor is it a simple one. To be a mother demands that a woman takes on a complex identity (Richardson 1993). She is still herself but she is also a mother, with the incumbent roles, responsibilities and relationships which this entails. While women define their own expectations about mothering, they are also guided in this by cultural ideas about motherhood, about what a 'good' mother is supposed to do and be. The significance of cultural prescriptions, centred around contemporary motherhood, to women's everyday understandings of motherhood is illustrated in the following transcription:

> I think there is a physical tie. When you have a child, you are attached. I remember reading this wonderful description of the life of a woman brought up in a religious community . . . and she says that at

some point when she was not looking her mother tied a piece of string around her heart and every now and then she tugs it and draws her back. And it is about this bond that you have with your children, and it is true no matter how hard you try to fight it. It is the other way round as well when you have a baby, I have felt this with ★★★ [my daughter]. You have this physical bond to your child and you find it very difficult to believe that anyone could look after the child as well as you could, even its father.

(city council full-time (returner) Information Development Officer, married, two children)

With reference to the above transcript, while there are potentially infinite meanings available to explain and determine mothering practice, only a small proportion of what constitutes motherhood has been identified and described here. Her description of motherhood is reflective of how the role of 'mother' has been socially constructed through power/knowledge relations, which encourage women to become mothers and practise motherhood in historically specific, narrowly defined ways.

In the potential myriad of social prescriptions for motherhood certain claims to knowledge are given priority over others, pass into popular discourse and come to represent our everyday understandings of motherhood. For example, significant shifts and transformations in motherhood practices during the 1950s, 1970s, 1980s and 1990s (Richardson 1993) suggest the existence of discursive struggles to attach meaning to the signifier 'motherhood' and establish responsibility for child-rearing. These discursive struggles in turn serve to reinforce and/or challenge, the – sociohistorically contingent – relational demands made on a mother's time. An indication of the significance of power/knowledge to contemporary mothering practices can be revealed by focusing upon discursive struggles to define motherhood in the 1970s and 1980s. While the childcare literature of the 1970s and 1980s continued to emphasize the infant's immense need for maternal attention, the content of this attention contrasted with the maternal deprivation theses of the 1940s and 1950s (Richardson 1993). By the 1970s, the focus of expert attention had shifted from the child's emotional 'needs' to its intellectual development and this had significant consequences for social prescriptions centred around the relational demands made on a mother's time (Nicholson 1993).

For example, primarily informed by scientific studies (Kaye 1977), experts frequently conceptualized mother–child bonding in terms of a dialectical process of reciprocal exchange. In association with the redefinition of the child as active recipient to interpersonal stimuli, ideal motherhood came to be defined in terms of an interplay between instinctive maternal bonding and the acquired skill of responding to a particular infant in a reciprocal and synchronized manner (Richardson 1993). Scientific discourses suggesting the child's potential for reciprocal exchange and need for intellectual development served to undermine the predominance of maternal bonding discourses about child-rearing, thus sustaining the possibility that mutual parental influence might benefit childhood learning (Stoppard 1984). However, the continued significance (albeit less predominant) of maternal instinct to discourses of childhood intellectual development, also attended to discourses suggesting the existence of different and distinct roles for women and men within the family. It is the mother to whom is ascribed the capacity to recognize the child's intellectual processes and facilitate the highly synchronized patterns of interaction (Kaye 1977). Sensitive or good child-rearing is, in this sense, a skill, essentially associated with the mother and peripherally ascribed to the father. The mother's 'essential' skills enable her to respond to an infant in a reciprocal and synchronized manner and thus ascribe to her the fundamental responsibility for the child's learning experiences.

While it is axiomatic that understandings of motherhood may shift over time, over the lifetime of individuals and in differing spatial and cultural contexts, it is possible to recognize instantly some of its contemporary discursive constructs. Within academic circles, popular culture and everyday discourse, motherhood often implies some reference to self-sacrifice and the subordination of self to the needs of the infant. One should, however, recognize that these discourses of motherhood rely upon the identification of free subjects for their meaning and actualization. It is, therefore, necessary to understand motherhood in terms of the existence of complex discursive forces within which female subjects situate themselves, and are situated, and come to identify with a mode of existence which has at its centre the subordination of self to the needs of an infant. For example, as Richardson (1993: 1) states, 'though not all women perceive femininity as a reward, for some its association with motherhood is an important aspect of what they get out of being a mother'.

Where, as is evident in popular discourse, ideal womanhood is associated with becoming a 'good' mother, for many women who strive to achieve ideal womanhood, this involves them in identifying with modes of subjectivity which are the product of discourses of motherhood. Where these discourses of motherhood propose an existence which entails the subordination of self to the needs of the child, women who identify with this mode of subjectivity experience a relational existence to the needs of their infant. A consequence of the female's need-centred relational existence to her child is that of perceiving her time as relational. The mother's experience of relational time manifests itself in an infinitesimal number of ways. A familiar manifestation of the significance of relational time to motherhood is expressed in the following transcription:

> I think I had more, I did have more time then than now. You could say two, three, maybe four hours during the day. But I think I never really felt free of her because I was breast feeding her. I was therefore indispensable, she wouldn't take her bottle, and there were times that I would feel very trapped. I couldn't go anywhere, I couldn't go

shopping, at the beginning, there were times that I couldn't even go to the shops without her. I felt that I couldn't go anywhere and that was very frustrating at times. The first time I went out to get my hair cut and I came back and she had been bawling with somebody else and I thought I can't even get my hair cut !!! ... When she is awake, she requires an enormous amount of attention. It is very rarely that you can sit and read a book or the newspaper or something when she is around, she likes to be actively involved.

(full-time Admin. Officer (recent returner), married with one child)

Looking after children, especially during infancy, is a tiring, demanding, highly repetitive experience which can seem unending. Both the assumption that women have a duty to take care of their children and the expectation that they will find motherhood naturally rewarding make it difficult for women, as mothers, to openly express feelings of dissatisfaction and disappointment, anger or frustration (Richardson 1993). Moreover, the hegemony of ideal motherhood discourses is such that the stresses of motherhood may be experienced by women as their own 'inadequacies' (Boulton 1983; Brown et al. 1986). In this sense, becoming a better mother and aspiring to the motherhood ideal are often subjectively perceived as a solution to the frustrations and stresses of motherhood, as illustrated in the following transcription:

It was just the same as the feeling that I had when I was working at the tax office. A feeling of being, of my mind clogging up. I found myself acting like a radio advert on television. Sort of like ... the important things in my life was whether my husband's shirt was smelling all right! Some of my friends who have come from a similar educational background, have had children and this has completely fulfilled everything that they wanted to do. I never felt like that I got bored. I mean, physically I was actually shattered but mentally I was bored. I couldn't understand why they found it so satisfying. I couldn't tell them that it just made me feel tired all the time.

(part-time librarian (returner) married, one child)

Timely reflections

As inferred in the above transcripts, the power of mothering discourses are such that the stresses and strains of mothering are often resolved through a more resilient appeal to achieving the mothering ideal. In this sense, women often find themselves caught in a constricting cycle of relational time, motivated by the prospect of eventually achieving the subjective fulfilment associated with the mothering ideal and, in so doing, eventually alleviating their feelings of present despair. These, and factors discussed previously, converge to experientially constitute motherhood as bereft of temporal demarcation. For many women, motherhood and mothering practices often involve a fusion of personal time with the seemingly endless needs and demands of their children.

5

Gender and modern work

A woman's work is never done

> I think the general running of the household does fall more to me. *** [husband's name] does do things but usually I have to ask. He very seldom does things without being asked ... When I'm not there he switches on, but I have always found that with things like household things, he tends to switch off. He just assumes that when I'm here that I'm going to do it. It is like with the baby at night. When she cries, I'm the one who wakes first. He wakes up if I give him a nudge but then he says that she is crying for me. And then I have to get up because she is still crying and then when she stops, he says, 'See, she was crying for you' and goes back to sleep!!!
> (full-time mother, married, two children)

In 2005, two-thirds of mothers and 55 per cent of mothers with children under 5 were in employment (EOC 2006: 15). The significance of this increase is evident when compared with the figure of 28 per cent of mothers of under 5s in employment in 1975. Increasing numbers of mothers are entering the labour market for greater proportions of their lives than was the case in previous decades. At the same time women retain the well-enshrined, female responsibility for domestic work and childcare. Statistical analysis of labour market data consistently confirms the extent to which female labour market participation is configured by domestic circumstances (Walby 2007). Nevertheless, it is equally significant to understand why women freely accede to part-time working and flexible employment. There are obviously formidable discursive forces at work, sustaining the devaluation of women's financial role and reaffirming traditional models of the domestic division of labour. Indeed, the statistical concurrence of childcare obligations with part-time working suggests that the configurations of circumstances that motivate female employment are overlaid by subjective perceptions of appropriate femininity. This chapter examines the role played by feminine subjectivity in determining the hegemony of clock time to capitalism's political economy of time.

No time to call our own!

It is clear that female employment patterns are configured by domestic circumstances and the workings of the household. Within academic circles this conception of women's employment is advanced by two distinct schools of feminist thought. The first is human capital theory, which has its roots in neoclassical economics. Human capital perspectives explain female labour market participation in terms of the functionality of family obligations (Becker 1981). Women voluntarily enter into, and out of, the labour market in accordance with their functional position within the family. Women's time outside of work directly impacts on the acquisition of human capital. These disparities in human capital translate into income disparities and labour market segregation. Consequently, human capital theory argues that it is women's engagement in domestic labour which reduces their capacity to accumulate the experience and qualifications necessary to succeed in the labour market. To this extent, women's time outside of paid work is a primary determinant of inequalities in the levels of human capital possessed by males and females. Gender inequality at work is an outcome of women's lack of human capital. Clear problems exists in human capital analysis, the most significant of which is that it assumes the existence of a perfect, gender-neutral, labour market (Walby 1990).

An alternative perspective is articulated in the reserve army of labour approach. The idea here is that women constitute a long-term reserve of labour that is intermittently beneficial to capital. This perspective has its roots in Marx's general law of capitalist accumulation. According to Marx, as capital accumulates, it causes periodical changes which affect 'social capital in its totality' (Marx, *Capital*, Vol. 1 [1887] 2003: 590). In certain spheres these changes manifest in the composition of capital necessitating a 'diminution of its variable constituent'. Elsewhere increases in the magnitude of capital require a proportionate increase in labour power. Consequently, capital accumulation 'is always connected with violent fluctuations and transitory production of surplus population, whether this takes the more striking form of the repulsion of labourers already employed, or the less evident ... absorption of the additional labouring population' (2003: 591). Moreover, each historic mode of production relies on the formation of a 'special law of population'. In capitalist accumulation, the existence of a reserve army functions to suppress wage rises, which, if left unchecked, would squeeze levels of surplus value. As capital accumulation advances, increased numbers are drawn into the 'disposable industrial reserve army', thus creating 'a mass of human material always ready for exploitation' (2003: 592). Marx was little concerned to differentiate the members of the industrial reserve army. Nevertheless, Marx's analysis has inspired feminist writers to argue that women's participation in paid labour corresponds with the characteristics of a flexible reserve army, which can be brought into the labour market and expelled, in accordance with periodic alternations in capitalist cycles of accumulation (Braverman 1974; Beechey 1977). Beechey has argued that married women represent a clear example of a reserve army, because they can periodically retreat from the labour market and, during these times, rely upon their partner's salary. Bruegel (1986: 49) has extended this proposition to examine the functionality of part-time work for capitalist economies. Part-time work provides capital accumulation with a surplus population which has the capacity to correspond with capitalism's shorter and shorter periodic changes in its industrial cycle. As capitalist accumulation accelerates, it is subject to yearly fluctuations, monthly shifts and even daily changes. This magnitude of indeterminacy necessitates a correspondingly flexible labour force and 'the costs of dealing with such fluctuations for the capitalist is less when women, particularly part-time women have been employed' (1986: 49). It is clearly evident that this form of feminist analysis provides a means of contextualizing women's work as part of the exploitative relations of capital and labour. The reserve army approach, however, insufficiently addresses the issue of power, control and autonomy. Indeed, what is missing from both the human capital approach and the reserve army perspective is an appreciation of the relationality of power and subjectivity. The following discussion engages with the crucial question of gender and subjectivity at work.

Employment for women

Mothering, and for that matter housework, are practices bereft of boundaries or limits, with no clear beginning and end points, with no guaranteed space for leisure. In housework the spaces of work and non-work are indistinguishable, and so are the classifiable observances of time-and-motion study. Mothers do not clock in and clock off within a delineable context of time. Tasks are the orientating boundaries of care-centred activity, hence their capacity to occupy the entire space and time of a woman's life. 'A woman does not go to work, she wakes up to work. Home is work and work is home' (Rowbotham 1973: 71).

Mothering and housework are also, of course, unpaid. Conversely, in the sphere of employment, time is money. It is conceived of as a quantity, an economic variable like labour, capital and machinery, an abstract unit infinitely divisible and free from all reference to content and context (Adam 1993). I am obviously making reference here to the hegemony of linear time to the productive economy. The general pervasiveness of linear time reflects upon our understandings of 'free time', in that 'free time' and its correlate 'leisure time' are derived from commodified work time (Adam 1993). In this sense, free time accumulated through work time exists only in relation to the time of markets and employment. Relational time exemplifies the incompatibility of care-centred times with the prevailing economic notion of value. The commodified time of the productive economy is divisible into finite units, quantitatively evaluated, substituted for money, gathered for 'time out' and delineated against leisure (Adam 1995: 95).

The fact that domestic labour time is exterior to the commodity system and outside the realm of economic calculation makes it barely recognized as work. When, for example, mothers engage in embodied relational time, their temporal experiences are perceived, through the hegemony of linear time, as subordinate to the commodified time of the productive economy and denied equal value. This is despite the fact that domestic labour constitutes a vast volume of socially necessary production essential to the perpetuation of the capitalist economy. Nevertheless domestic labour is constituted by capital as non-productive because it resides outside trade relations and the marketplace. Furthermore, when mothers enter the productive economy, their relational experiences of embodied time remain subordinate to the hegemony of work time, thus often mitigating against social recognition for their dual domestic and working responsibilities. And therefore, limiting the possibility of 'time-out' from this double burden. My empirical findings suggest that this situation is accentuated by the intersubjective meanings attributed to pervasive forms of female employment as illustrated in the following transcription:

> Basically he gets offended if I ask him to do something, he doesn't like anyone asking him to do anything. He is working on writing a paper at the moment. A research paper. This takes up all his time and energy, so he feels he has to have his space to do that. He also says things like, Oh, you are better at cooking than I am ... but I have work that is very important to me as well. He has this very male attitude that his work is more important than my work.

> *How do you feel about this?*

> Well, according to him, his work is more important. If other men come round to the house, he will talk to them about his work, and how difficult this must be and how much work he is putting into it. I feel differently! ... But, then, I feel the need to give him space to do his work, because I know to him his work is important. I do resent the extra work load I have to do, the fact that I am doing two jobs, all the housework and I am working as well ... his work is research at the university, he feels that that is far more important than my work. So I feel I have to fit round him really. I really should be more assertive about my work but then if he gets bad-tempered, he shouts

at the kids and smacks the baby and I feel unhappy and I cannot concentrate on my work, so it is far easier for me to sort the children out and do my work ... I don't make a big thing about it but I do feel that his work is valued far more than mine.

Have you any views as to why this is so?

I think that we operate at different levels. Part of the problem is that I start to feel that my work is not as important. I don't earn as much as he does. So I get the feeling, I have to value my own work and give it priority, even though he doesn't. And I have to do it in a way that the children don't suffer, which is hard. I mean, I do tend to put the children first at home, whereas he doesn't.

(full-time paid voluntary worker, married, two children)

Mothers at work: a 'dual temporal burden'

Female participation in the labour market generally involves low paid, part-time,[1] insecure employment (Dex 1984; Rubery 1994). The converse is generally more reflective of male employment, although admittedly this is changing (see Chapter 7). Moreover, a number of studies have found that even where women make a substantial contribution to household income, the importance of their earnings may be played down so that the male is still defined as the 'breadwinner'. Women's wages, however essential, are often seen as covering 'extras' and less often seen as challenging the earning capacity of the 'male breadwinner' and the concomitant value ascribed to his financial contribution to the household (Pahl 1989; Morris 1990; Brannen and Moss 1991).

With reference to working mothers, the incongruences between their experiences of relational time and working time, coupled with their dual domestic responsibilities and subordinate position in the productive economy, often culminate in accentuating the demands made on their time and further negating the possibility for 'time-out' and/or 'own time'. This is evident in the above transcript, in which the speaker's husband's devaluation of her paid work attends to his identification with traditionalist discourses of domestic labour, a consequence of which is that of increasing the female's ascribed responsibility for child-rearing and accentuating the relational ties between her time and the 'needs' of her children. For many women, their subordinate position in the productive economy often serves to accentuate the relational demands made on their time. It is equally significant to recognize their employment patterns as a condition, and consequence, of their relational experiences of time. The significance of this latter issue to working mothers' experiences of relational time and their 'dual temporal burdens' warrants its further exploration.

Working women are usually disadvantaged in the career stakes because of their engagement in a multiplicity of simultaneous 'need'-centred responsibilities and therefore they cannot always show the same amount of commitment to paid employment as their male counterparts. It is quite often the case for males that they manage excessive time demands at work as a result of this labour being serviced domestically by a woman (i.e., partner, maid or mother). Increasing rates of formal employment by women have meant that they are faced with the task of managing the most demanding temporal constraints of economic labour during precisely the same periods of their life cycle when domestic pressure is at its greatest (Le Feuvre 1994; Deem 1996). For many women, the accumulative temporal constraints of paid and domestic work negatively impact on their promotion opportunities and frequently result in broken or part-time employment:

> Yes, I did because once you've made a move into hard science, or out of a hard science environment, it's hard to go back. I mean, I could never get into it now. Because if you're out of research, for about six months to have a baby, even if things haven't moved on that much really, people's perceptions will be such that there has been some significant advancement and thus they will be reluctant to take somebody on who has been out of the working environment for some time. You don't see many women coming back into a project or, even if they do, it is usually at a lower level ... The friends that I have that want to further themselves in their research, the price they pay is that they usually don't have kids. They may have relationships with people who are doing research or relationships that don't affect their research. But they don't have the children, although a few people do they have nannies. And then they hardly ever see their children and they end up feeling very guilty about this, as they don't spend any time with their kids. There is also the other side of the coin, a woman at work where I am, who is basically a frustrated researcher, is working where she is because she wanted to have kids and ends up resenting it, because she wants to be a researcher. I think that you have to be pragmatic about it in the end. So, yes, I did make a conscious decision not to go into research. If the conditions were different, I might have achieved more. But saying that, I wouldn't have been able to have had a family as well.
>
> (full-time lecturer, married, two children)

Working mothers consistently experience pressure from almost every sphere of their lives. Many have to reconcile subjective feelings of guilt with the financial necessity of paid employment and also the satisfactions that working might bring. Significantly, my attention has been drawn to yet another media-exaggerated academic study, widely circulated in the popular press (possibly because it coincides with concerns over school discipline), suggesting direct correlations between a mother's participation in paid employment and maladjusted children (BBC News 2003). For many women, social pressures deriving from this, and similar discourses of 'maternal deprivation', exist in conjunction with temporal conflicts, grounded in linear time, between work and home. More often than not, mothers find that they cannot afford to spend extra hours doing overtime, attending union meetings or other work-related activities. One should also consider the pressures employers place on female employers to convince them that their loyalties and priorities reside at work and not at home (Wearing 1984). For many women, the culmination of these social pressures is expressed in terms of their opting for part-time work or less temporally demanding full-time employment. It is for these, and other reasons (e.g., the reproduction of gender segregation in paid employment, see, for example, Kerfoot and Knights 1993) that women are generally disproportionately represented in the subordinate ranks of organizations. While many women tailor their working patterns around their domestic commitments in an attempt to reduce their dual burden, my empirical findings suggest that this often has the unintended consequences of increasing the demands made on their time. In that their disproportionate representation in the lower ranks of organizations often encourages experiences of 'temporal disempowerment' in relation to their superiors, as evident in the following transcription:

> The job that I'm doing at the moment in NEAB, I don't think I'm getting paid enough, for what I'm doing. But that's just how it goes ... You find that most of the low paid people at the NEAB do the most work, mind you, that's the way it is in most walks of life, isn't it?

> *Could you expand a bit more on how it is at work?*

> Well, it is just that because you work on a switchboard people might say to me, what day will the exam results be sent out? I know what day the exam results are to be sent out but I haven't the time to tell them, so I put it on to the general office. And they will tell them, they will have the time. I mean, I would just say, oh, it is going to be the 26th of August. And they might say, well are you sure about that? I have to be 100 per cent sure about it because you're talking about exams. Working in that sort of environment, it is not how I think it has got to be accurate. Because I don't have the time ... I have gone through this with ***[name of husband], he says, why don't you have the time? And I say because we don't have the time. I have a supervisor she is quite nice although very extreme. She is the kind of woman who is constantly saying, 'Come on answer the phone.' And I feel like saying to her 'Why don't you answer the phone?' She seems to spend all day telling people to answer the phone, she doesn't seem to do anything else but that ... I'm always arguing with her. You can't treat people like that, you can't just get rid of a call that quickly. Oh, yes, you can, you have got the time [referring to a conversation with her supervisor]. We are not allowed to take messages either. So

really it's funny in a way, because at the end of the day, I just laugh sometimes, because I think, oh, well, you're getting paid for it.
(full-time receptionist, married, one child)

The transcript eloquently illustrates the 'temporal disempowerment' often experienced by those occupying the subordinate ranks of organizations. The respondent makes several references to superordinates (i.e., those occupying the general office and her supervisor) whom she perceives as having more time than she. In so doing, she appears to be aware of a form of 'temporal hierarchy' of personal times within her working environment. It would appear, in this instance, and for working environments in general, that the organization of the workplace reflects and reinforces a hierarchy of time control; that is, the time of subordinates is largely controlled by superiors (the latter often have 'gatekeepers' to protect them from the pressures of others' time demands). Since women are disproportionately represented in the subordinate ranks of organizations, their time is more likely to be regulated by others than by themselves. Following on from the theme of this subsection, the disproportionate representation of working mothers in the subordinate ranks of organizations, has as its condition the effect of increasing the demands made on their time, i.e., their relational experiences of time grounded in their 'need'-centred relation to their infants coexist with experiences of temporal disempowerment consequent of their (often) subordinate position in the ranks of organizations. It is in this sense that working mothers often experience a dual temporal burden. My approach to analysing the dual temporal burden of working mothers attempts to render problematic the recourse to dualistic divisions of public and private. Rather experiences of relational time 'weave' complex patterns through every aspect of the individual's life, intertwining the public and private into an embodied existence with the world (Davies 1990).

Gendered time power/knowledge and resistance

A central aim of the discussion so far has been to identify how women's ascribed domestic role in the private sphere, and subordinate position in the public sphere, encourage a disproportionate experience of relational time by female subjects. But this is not to assume that these temporal demands are beyond negotiation and resistance. A consistent theme throughout this chapter has been that of identifying the inextricable associations between relational time and power/knowledge. Relational perceptions of time are constructed through sociohistorical discourses. These discourses are informed by culturally specific knowledges which emerge through discursive struggles and compete among each other for pre-eminence, as illustrated in the discussion of the discursive constructs of motherhood. An unintended consequence of the pre-eminence of these knowledge claims is that of marginalizing and/or subjugating alternative knowledges emanating from, for example, feminist writings or discourses on sexuality (Butler 1990; Clough 1994). It is these marginalized or subjugated knowledges that offer a point of resistance to dominant masculine, linear conceptions of time. Of course, resistance cannot assure the dissipation of dominant knowledges, and indeed resistance has the curious affect of accentuating focus around a particular power configuration whose 'existence depends on a multiplicity of points of resistance' (Foucault 1979b:95). In this sense, resistance can 'play the role of adversary, target, support, or handle in power relations' (1979b:95). Thus the relationality of power is constituted by a complex matrix 'that passes through apparatuses and institutions, without being exactly localised in them, so too the swarm of points of resistance traverses social stratifications and individual unities' (1979b:96). Consequently, 'the relationship between power and freedom's refusal to submit cannot be separated' (1982: 221). Located at the heart of 'the power relationship, and constantly provoking it, are the recalcitrance of the will and the intransigence of freedom' (1982: 221–2). While power relationships have the propensity to induce periods of stability, they are also inherently unstable: 'Every power relationship implies at least *in potentia*, a strategy of struggle' and the possibility of reversal (1982: 225). With specific reference to gender relations, feminist discourses provide a concrete challenge to androcentristic knowledges. So, for example, women's movements, the feminist press, feminist academic and even women's magazines, can circulate the foundations for alternative discourses that inspire resistance to dominant gender relations of power/knowledge. Alternative ways of negotiating the domestic division of labour, for example, bring into question the gendered status of these responsibilities in ways that could facilitate a substantial challenge to gendered divisions in the salaried labour market (e.g., job segregation, unequal pay, etc.). Consequently, the relational demands made on women's time are, at least in principal, open to negotiation, resistance and contestation.

Moreover, my empirical research findings suggest that women do not consistently and uniformly acquiesce to the relational demands made on their time. Rather, it is evident that women often adopt complex strategies and modes of negotiation in an attempt to gain some autonomy within the constraining nexus of relational demands made on them and their time. For example, the full-time voluntary worker, quoted earlier, described how she copes with the demands made of her at work and at home:

> I home in, and I say, right, I'm doing this now, and I try and block out the other things. I think, well, I can't do it all and I just have to miniaturize. It becomes like one thing after another and instead of having a wider perspective, I have to have a very narrow perspective in that I must deal with these phone calls one after another. I must get the books done. I must, you know, one thing after another and I have to simplify everything and I feel like it's narrowing.
>
> (full-time paid voluntary worker, married, two children)

The coping strategy is interesting for several reasons. At one level of analysis, it is illustrative of the potential for resistance to the demands made on her time. She tries to accumulate space and time by narrowing the boundaries of her work routines. Each operation is fragmented into distinct and separate tasks. Assuming that she is successful in this endeavour, then the entirety of obligations will be represented within a manageable context. But complex forces curtail such strategies, as women's work can 'never be a normal job routine because emotion erupts in its midst' (Rowbotham 1973: 73). Further discussion of women's work and emotional labour is provided in Chapter 7. What is of significance, here, is the respondent's method of compartmentalizing her actions. Such coping strategies appear resonant with the discursive constructs of linear time. It is as though the respondent's strategy for coping with the multiple and simultaneous demands made on her time involve adopting actions which reflect and reproduce the purposive instrumentalism discursively associated with masculinity. This might be explained by the observation that 'masculinity is neither exclusive to men nor exhaustive of their discursive being' (Kerfoot and Knights 1996: 80). But it would appear that the respondent's action is indicative of the necessity for organizational members to adopt masculine enterprise as a coping strategy. Even though this may require the denial of a more conventional feminine identity, life experience and social relations.

For individuals caught up in feminine discourses, their relational experiences of time and cries for 'time out' often find little expression unless reinscribed into the rational instrumentalism and disembodied existence of linear time. With specific reference to the working environment, although the respondents, in my empirical research, described numerous strategies of 'temporal negotiation' (e.g., extended coffee and lunch breaks, and 'appropriately timed' flexi-leave), freedom to negotiate time schedules generally varied significantly according to the individuals' position within an organizational hierarchy. So, for example, less senior staff were more constrained in terms of time discretion when compared to their senior colleagues. This is not to presume a less intense time commitment for more senior female members of staff. Many of the female managers and senior personnel, that I interviewed, spoke of having to put in longer hours, as it were, to continuously justify and maintain their status *vis-à-vis* their male counterparts and colleagues. These longer hours and extra work duties were often combined with the equally, if not more intense, domestic demands made on these women within the home. I therefore suggest that feminine conceptions of time as relational, while open to resistance, tend to prevail among women by virtue of a dominant and comparatively impermeable gendered employment segregation and sexual division labour, both in formal employment and in the home.

Timely reflections

Capitalist accumulation is premised on the rational ordering and control of space and time, and the denial of *différance*, 'a refusal to accept limits and the insistence on continually reaching out ... [to] a destiny that is always beyond; beyond morality, beyond tragedy, beyond culture' (Bell 1976: 50). Consequently, the rationalization of time in capitalist accumulation presupposes a 'metaphysics of presence' in which a substance is assumed to have a meaning in and of itself and can be present to a knowing disembodied subject. This metaphysics of presence is resonant with the structural organization of modern Western language. Derrida (1997) argues that Western metaphysics is perpetually animated by the presumption that true meaning is inherent in the spoken address. This assumes that both the word (signifier) and the meaning (signified) are directly present at the instance of a speech act. So, for example, the concept of clock time presupposes a metaphysics of presence, which invokes a universal meaning that is consistent irrespective of the immediate context. Thus, we are led to believe that a unit of work time has the same value irrespective of the biography and gender of the worker. Such is the hegemony of clock time to the productive economy that we fail to recognize that 'Without a retention in the minimal unit of temporal experience, without a trace retaining the other as other in the same, no difference would do its work and no meaning would appear' (1997: 62). Consequently, the metaphysics of presence, that is, clock time, 'carries in itself the destiny of its nonsatisfaction' (1997: 143). From the instance that representation 'claims to be presence and the sign of the thing itself' it denies the binary operation of the sign and the 'vicariousness of its own function' (1997: 144). This is because the self-evident presence of meaning is accomplished through a binary opposition between what is present and what is absent or denied. This conception of 'being as presence' (Heidegger 2006) reduces the innumerability of appearances by making them apprehensible to a sovereign phallocentric consciousness (Hekman 1990). 'Being as presence' is therefore a project of mastery, i.e., an attempt to obliterate the origin of absence. This kind of circumspection has inspired me to link the clock time of modern work with masculine legislative reason. Following Derrida, it is claimed here that the desire for a metaphysics of presence in rationalist discourses of time consists in a repression of the feminine to an absent Other. But the feminine is a 'dangerous supplement' to the presence of linear clock time. This is because 'difference produces what it forbids, makes possible the very thing that it makes impossible' (Derrida 1997: 143).

Despite its hegemony, representational clock time is struggling to contain radical challenges to the sovereignty of its Cartesian subject, its rational ordering of time and space and its subversion of *différance* (Ermarth 1992). Emerging through and contributing to fractures and fissures in the hegemony of representational time is a vibrant feminist tradition which radically challenges linear time's claim to neutrality. Linear time as a masculine project, seeking to control the future, is oblivious of any other (e.g., feminine) conception of time. Its claim to neutrality therefore arises by default. It knows no Other. In contrast to the representational assumption which claims linear time to have meaning in and of itself, these feminist discourses draw attention to linear time as grounded in gendered power relations. For example, Davies (1990, 1994), and Leccardi (1996) have variously argued that men and women use time differently due to their distinct life situation. The routinized circularity and repetitiveness of domestic labour encapsulated by the phrase 'a woman's work is never done' are identified as exemplifying the incompatibility of women's work with linear conceptions of time (Davies 1990; Le Feuvre 1994). Rarely in the domestic sphere can time be conceived of as quantitatively delineated units that are readily differentiated between, for example, work and leisure or personal time (Adam 1993: 172). These literatures variously identify 'women's time' as continuous. Here the temporal density and complexity of 'women's roles' displace any sense of 'time out' (Davies 1990). Moreover, as Chambers (1986) argues, 'women's perception of time are historically constructed within a domestic ideology in which time not spent in paid employment is used for unpaid domestic duties'. Consequently 'time out', or 'free time' is impossible or translated into other 'self-sacrificing activities'. In sum, this broad feminist critique attempts to illuminate the incompatibility of 'women's time' with a linear perspective which separates work from leisure, the public from private, and task- from clock-based orientations to time.

While feminist suggestions of distinct male and female times draw our attention to the significance of gender to the discursive construction of linear time, their dualistic suppositions need to be treated with immense caution. By transforming what are merely heuristic categories into reified ontological realities, these feminist discourses attend to representational epistemologies and in so doing, often unintentionally, reinforce the hegemony of linear time. For their male/female temporal oppositions (or even feminine time/masculine time dualisms, which assume each element to have a calcified existence in the world) partake of a tradition which constitutes the feminine as Other to the masculine order. Moreover, feminist discourses which valorize female time as that which counters male time compound the phallocentricity of dualistic representation. The theme here is directly relevant to an idea expressed by Derrida (1979) in which he equates the quest for truth with the pursuit of mastery and assigns this with the signifier masculine. Conversely, feminine identity 'takes so little interest in truth, because in fact she barely even believes in it, the truth ... For it is the man who believes in the truth of woman, in woman truth' (1979: 63). Consequently, the woman who pursues absolute truth merely succeeds in mimicking the fallacies and contradictions of logocentricism. In so doing, 'in truth, they too are men' (1979: 65). Thus 'and in order to resemble the masculine dogmatic philosopher this woman lays claim – just as much claim as he – to truth, science and objectivity in all their castrated delusions of virility' (1979:65). In this sense, feminist discourses which invert the dualistic oppositions through which linear time is constructed, are unintentionally reproducing the hegemony of linear time and in doing so marginalizing their alternative discourse. Leccardi (1996: 171), for example, identifies women's time as expressive of a 'female rationality'. Starting from the premise that rationality has been conceived as transcendence of the feminine and that women cannot easily be accommodated into a cultural ideal which has defined itself in opposition to all that is feminine, several feminist writers (Lloyd 1984) have argued that the ideal of a sexually neutral reason is radically misconceived. Moreover, these feminist writers have variously drawn our attention to the feminine as itself partly constituted by its occurrence within rationalist thought. Acknowledging this, one might argue that Leccardi's conceptualization of women's time, and her identification of this time as motivated by a distinctive kind of rational order, have been partly formed within the philosophical tradition to which it may appear to be a reaction. More specifically, the effort to valorize women's time as an essentially different kind of rationality and agency unrecognized by masculine rationalism 'will occur in a space already prepared for it by the intellectual tradition it seeks to reject' (Lloyd 1984: 104). One can only assume, therefore, that no dualistic theory – not even one which measures its adequacy in terms of justice to the complexities of 'female temporal experience' – can place itself beyond the danger of reproducing the very Same conditions to which it is Other.

Conversely, it is suggested here that to avoid this reproduction of the very discourse that feminism seeks to destroy, it is necessary not to invert, but to deconstruct the masculine/feminine opposition. Deconstruction as defined by Derrida (1984: 329) is a strategy which attacks the classical oppositions of the metaphysics of presence and in so doing undermines the phallocentric binary system that is its condition and consequence. As Derrida puts it, 'Deconstruction cannot limit itself or proceed immediately to a neutralization: it must, by means of a double gesture, a double science, a double writing, practice an overturning of the classical opposition and a general displacement of the system' (1984: 329). Deconstruction achieves this by intervening in and or violating the exclusions of 'logocentric closure', refusing to accept an elevation of the present over the absent. My alternative discourse of gendered time is premised on the discursive constitution of gender identities. There is no metaphysical conception of gender and time which has meaning in and of itself. There is no reified, unitary, rational subject. There is no essential self, which transcends culture and language. 'Deconstruction does not consist in passing from one concept to another, but in overturning and displacing a conceptual order, as well as the nonconceptual order with which the conceptual order it articulated' (1984: 329). Our own experience as women cannot be taken as an unproblematic starting point for feminist theory, because that experience has neither an essential nor a consistent meaning. For subjectivity, constituted in and through a multiplicity of (often contradictory) discursive positions, is unsystematic and always in process. To this extent 'subjectivity is at once both contingent and precarious' (Kerfoot and Knights 1996: 86). Gender identities are, therefore, inherently unstable and continually self-deconstructing. 'For if the subject is constituted by power, that power does not cease at the moment the subject is constituted, for that subject is never fully constituted, but is subjected and produced time and again' (Butler 1992: 13). The subject is neither a foundation nor a fixed immutable product, but rather the 'permanent possibility' of certain 'resignifying' processes (1992: 13). In this sense, the meaning of gender is interminably deferred and endlessly multiple.

While it is axiomatic that what counts as masculine or feminine identity is multilayered, and may shift over the lifetime of individuals, it is possible to recognize their current manifestations. Primarily informed by my empirical research, this chapter has argued that those whose identities are discursively constituted as feminine invariably derive meaningful existence, purpose and direction through an embeddedness in embodied social relationships. The centrality ascribed to others by those caught up in feminine discourses encourages a perception of time that exists in relation to significant others. Feminine time and masculine time are constituted through complementary processes of inclusion and exclusion. For example, Chapter 4 described masculine linear time as embodying high levels of instrumental rationality. This form of rationality was in turn identified as constructed through a denial, displacement and/or denigration of what is generally accepted to be feminine characteristics.

In conclusion, Chapters 4 and 5 have sought to challenge discourses of gendered time that conceptualize this phenomenon as 'existing' through the opposition of an absolute polarity between male and female. The alternative discourse proposed here is an interval that endeavours to originate not a theory of knowledge, in the sense of a replacement of Enlightenment reason, but rather to apprehend the inter-subjective relations by, which gendered subjects ascribe meaning to their life worlds. In keeping with this proposition, my alternative discourse of gendered time depicts masculine and feminine times as elements that represent multiple differences, pluralities of characteristics that cross and recross the alleged boundary between the two. It is a discourse that recognizes gender identity as inherently unstable and continually self-deconstructing. In this discourse the meaning of gender identity is constantly deferred, eternally multifarious a narrative archetype of perpetual textual reverie and yet one that does not eradicate either the masculine or feminine self. It is in this sense that discourses, of gendered time can fracture the masculine fiction of unity that is the rationalization of clock time in modern work and reveal how this metaphysics of presence depends on the repression of an Other.

Note

1 Some 42 per cent of women employees work part-time (Equal Opportunities Commission 2006: 11).

PART III

Post-Fordist Times

New Times? Post-Fordism and Call Centre Labour Process.
Source: Justin Pumfrey,
Reproduced by permission of Getty Images

6

Post-Fordist production and the time-disciplined call centre

With David Knights

Timely reflections on self, subjectivity and technological determinism

Within academic circles and in the media, call centres have often been described in distinctly Orwellian terms. In these 'white-collar factories' hundreds of employees are arranged in serried ranks to handle a seemingly endless flow of customer telephone inquiries. The new generation of monitoring technology is extremely powerful. It can analyse 'keystrokes' on terminals to determine whether employees are making efficient use of their time between telephone conversations. Employers can tap phones, read emails and monitor computer screens. The possibility, and in some cases the coercive use, of surveillance techniques for call centre personnel are dramatic, intense and secretive. This surveillance can involve not only a constant measurement of performance but also other pressures associated with the intensification of work.

As a result of this mechanistic division of labour, there has been a tendency to see call centres as a contemporary version of the nineteenth-century sweatshop or those Dickensian 'dark, satanic mills' (Apostol 1996; Garrod 1996). Theoretical support for the 'sweatshop' view of call centres and similar IT-intensive workplaces has, in part, come from an increasing use of a deterministic Foucauldian perspective on discipline at work (Sewell and Wilkinson 1992; Arkin 1997; Fernie and Metcalf 1997). Incessant dedication to electronic performance monitoring and ubiquitous accumulation of coded information are described as typifying disciplinary modes of regulating activities in time–space (Sewell and Wilkinson 1992). But there is a tendency in these accounts to read Foucault's conception of subjectivity 'as a product of controlling and dominating social bonds ... of the person as simply responding to disciplinary power' (Ezzy 1997: 428). In short, this use of Foucault fails to recognize the distinction between subjects being constituted *through* rather than *by* a variety of disciplinary technologies that reinforce and reproduce existing inequalities at work and within wider society more broadly (Knights and McCabe 1998a, 2001). Conversely, our research has been more sanguine concerning the realistic, as opposed to the theoretical, potential of using technology to control employees in this fashion. Employers' dependence on emotional labour (Hochschild 1983) and the social skills of their call centre staff to ensure high levels of customer service, means that the employee relationship has to be managed extremely carefully (Frenkel *et al.* 1998; Taylor and Bain 1998).

The ethnographic research presented in this chapter was conducted in a UK financial services call centre that historically had seemed to switch back and forth between 'hard' performance-driven and 'soft' service quality-based, management strategies. When the research began in February 1997, management stressed the quality of service encounters, and thereby within that framework, allowed staff considerable time and space to perform their jobs as they thought fit. This 'process' style of management had been in existence for five or six years, having partially replaced earlier quantitative 'task'-oriented concerns with productivity. By the end of the research in October 1998, a rekindling of the anxiety about productivity levels resulted in a demand for a stricter timing of calls and performance measurement. As we shall see, this created tensions, not least because it conflicted with quality management initiatives, that had recently been introduced but, more importantly, it violated the levels of service quality with which staff had begun to identify. Consequently, the performance programmes, which seek to increase productivity through decreasing call handling and abandonment rates, were met with a mixed reception, ranging from resistance through to reluctant accommodation. The close attachment to service quality had arisen, partly despite management, largely because of an identification with customers that could be seen as a response of staff to a situation that otherwise might have little to offer except a monotonous routine and increasing levels of work intensification. But staff had another tool in their armoury of resistance to a coercive or heavy-handed system of management control, and this was the company brand. If calls had constantly to be terminated abruptly because of standard times, what might this do for the brand reputation that had taken years to establish? There was not militant resistance to the intensification of time discipline because, like all call centre staff, they were used to the pressure to keep call waiting times down and the electronic call boards were a constant reminder of this obligation both to customers and colleagues. Also given the importance of meaningful projects to the securing of a solid sense of identity, it is not surprising to find self-disciplined individuals transforming themselves into time-disciplined corporate subjects. What is surprising is the failure of some academic literatures to recognize this aspect of

Foucault's (1979a) analysis of disciplinary technology and, perhaps more importantly, the subtle forms of resistance that often ensue.

The chapter is structured as follows. The first section provides a brief overview of the literature on call centres in so far as this has implications for work intensification and time/space discipline in the labour process. Second, the ethnography of the call centre and several key analytic themes emergent from the ethnography are defined and discussed in relation to concepts, issues and topics in the literature. Finally, some concluding reflections are offered on how the chapter contributes to the development of workplace analyses of call centres.

Time discipline at work

In recent years, several literatures have sought to challenge the prevalence of linear discourses of time to organizational analysis. Hassard (1989) and Clark (1985), for example, have drawn attention to the limitations of treating time as exclusively homogeneous and quantitative and the plural-temporality of organizational life. As Clark (1985: 6) puts it, ' "the central time problem" for organizational sociology is to penetrate behind the metaphor of clock-time, because existing approaches to the "time dimension" rely totally on "clock-time" '. Whipp in his review of Clark's contribution to organizational analysis, describes the way in which Clark shows 'how contrasting industries lead organizations to develop "repertoires" of rules, structures and forms of action to meet the varying rhythms of demand, competition and regulation' (1994: 103). Such rules rely upon everyday commonsense knowledge (Schutz 1967) but, nonetheless, are a vital means of accounting for and coping with the negotiated timetables of organizational life. Whipp (1994: 103) draws upon the notion of temporal repertoires in his work on time and management, stating that 'the notion of structural and temporal repertoires is based on the recursiveness of the irregular, sometimes cyclical, event-based trajectories of the firm'. This reading of temporality recognizes the extent to which subjectivity is a reflexive, fluid and often precarious process instantiated through the time/space events, which it also serves to constitute (Mouffe 1992: 372). In this sense, 'governable spaces are not fabricated counter to experience; they make new kinds of experience possible, produce new modes of perception, invest percepts with affects, with dangers and opportunities, with saliences and attractions' (Rose 1999: 32). Our work extends this Foucauldian–inspired proposition by identifying how call centre staff secure a sense of their own subjectivity and identity through the incessant codification and material organization of conduct in time and space.

The ethnography of the BNFS call centre

The ethnographic case study took place in the call centre of a major retail financial services company, whose brand name and reputation were well-established. For purposes of confidentiality, the company is given the pseudonym – Brand Name Financial Services (BNFS). The research was focused on the telephone service encounter although various departments were investigated on a systematic basis. The main departments were customer service, including resource and support, credit services, new business and life and pensions/savings and investment. The research took place and involved intensive fieldwork and feedback meetings with the company's management and staff (Knights, Calvey and Odih 1998, Knights, Calvey and Odih 1999). The methodology adopted combines 'critical ethnography' (Wainwright 1997) with 'organization ethnography' (Bate 1997) thus synthesizing a focus on the meanings and definitions of organizational members with a critical examination of the historical and organizational context of their production and reproduction. Our research methods were comprised of conversational analysis of tape-recorded service encounter interactions, observational techniques, discourse analysis on organizational documents and unstructured interviews. Telephone customer advisers, in BNFS, work in teams of eight with a senior adviser and a team manager. Typically an adviser will simultaneously be doing screen work and scripted call work with the customer while at the desk on a set of headphones. The average numbers of calls per hour is 26 and time spent on the phone is 80 per cent of the working day. The abandonment rate (i.e., calls not taken to a successful conclusion), the reduction of which is highly prioritized, is 7 per cent. The centre is open 8a.m. until 8p.m. with a mix of full- and part-time staff doing various 8-hour shifts. To coin a phrase, it is 'all day, everyday' (Westwood 1976).

Analytic themes, data and discussion

The shift away from a 'task'-oriented focus on productivity towards a more 'process' concern with the quality of service encounters, had occurred just prior to our arrival to conduct empirical research in BNFS. Characteristic of the 'hard' aspects of quality management (Hill 1991), the previous 'task'-oriented culture was predominantly concerned with statistical monitoring and performance measurement standards. Recognizing that statistical measurements take place within a social context, where their human interpretation remains paramount, the process approach seeks to complement quantitative calculations of performance with qualitative support for staff to improve customer service.

A series of structural changes (e.g., emergence of team managers), initiatives and strategies (e.g., tape reviews, team talks, Quality Assurance, etc.) dedicated to quality resulted from the development of a more 'process'-oriented culture. The following transcript excerpt provides for a partial insight into the impact of this approach on the service encounter:

> Those techniques are actually trained to actually help the adviser deal with the calls. Not, that is, not necessarily trained in terms of high call volume, it is overall in terms of telephone techniques in order to help the adviser. When the calls are queuing, we don't say, you better hurry up, because that is not what we are about, we are about customer service and however much that customer requires our attention, we hope that we can give it. The call control training just helps them ... but by no means is it associated with when 23 calls are queuing then you use the speed-up process, that's not what it is about at all.
>
> (trainer)

Partly as a result of this training, but perhaps also because of the relational conceptions of time held by the staff, customer service was a deeply embedded value that strongly defined the meanings, reality and sense of self-identity of customer advisers. Characteristic of the 'soft' aspects of quality management (Hill 1991), this 'process' orientation has, as its main concern, that of gearing every activity and member of the organization towards serving the final customer. Activities performed within the organization are reconstituted into interlinking segments of a 'quality chain'. Through quality initiatives, every level of the organization right down to the appraisal of individual members of staff, reflects and reinforces the corporate desire for excellent, quality service. The necessary levels of commitment and quality performance, needed to sustain the desire for excellence, are achieved through a process-centred training programme.

Process time and 'emotional labour'

It is significant that the call centre is staffed predominantly by young women although BNFS has begun to see the benefit of recruiting more mature women, especially because of their potential to assume informal leadership roles in teamworking (Kerfoot and Knights 1996). This gender division of labour conforms to a well-established tradition of service industry employment. However, it could be argued that women's experience of surviving in a male-dominated and often macho culture has meant that they have acquired social skills that prove highly effective in service and sales encounters (Hochschild 1983). One particular skill that was heavily emphasized by training and personnel managers was 'empathy'. The concept of 'empathy' is eloquently expressed in the following excerpt:

> [Empathy] which is all about looking at you and the customer's relationship, [and asking] what else can we do for the customer? So it is going beyond APTUS (consultant techniques of how to handle the customer, how to control, how to keep the customer informed). It

was looking at, OK, you have got the customer on the line. You have got your techniques, your telephone procedures but what else can we do to exceed their expectation with BNFS so that they will always remember us, with, yes, BNFS have always provided me with an excellent customer service.

(trainer)

'Emotional labour' is an integral feature of achieving empathy. Following Hochschild (1983: 7) we define emotional labour to mean 'the management of feeling to create a publicly observable facial and bodily display'. It is our contention that empathy's emotional labour encourages a 'process-orientation' where:

> time is enmeshed in social relations. Several processes may intertwine simultaneously and the fabric of life is patterned by the multiple criss-crossing chains of processes. In some cases, schedules and clock time may have structured the activity originally but unexpected exigencies frequently call for the abandonment of a clock-time relationship and bring process time to the fore instead.
>
> (Davies 1994: 280)

This involves a more flexible relation to time where 'the task itself defines the amount of time to be consumed, rather than a time limit or temporal demarcation being placed on the task' (Davies 1990: 37). These literatures provide for highly insightful attempts to deconstruct dominant understanding(s) of time (see especially Davies 1990 and Leccardi 1996) through, for example, drawing our attention to 'women's time' as embodied in daily life (Davies 1990). While feminist suggestions of distinct 'male/linear' and 'female/process' times draw our attention to the significance of gender in the discursive constitution of time, their insufficient theorization of power and subjectivity has the unintended consequence of reproducing the very phallogocentric discourse (Irigaray 1980) that feminism seeks to challenge. Conversely, primarily informed by the writings of Foucault, the discourse of gendered time, expressed here, has as its premise a conceptualization of power and subjectivity as grounded in the exercise of power through social practices in which subjects are embedded. Subjectivity is constituted through the exercise of power within which conceptions of personal identity come to be generated. To quote Kerfoot and Knights (1994: 70):

> Where subjectivity is constituted in and through discourse, the gender identity of men and women as masculine and feminine subjects is socially constituted in and through certain sites, behaviours and practices at any one time.

Gender identities are, in this sense, historically contingent, unstable and potentially multiple. This notion of the discursive production of gendered subjects within and between power relations provides a means of reconciling the 'women's time'/linear dualism inherent in feminist discourses of gendered time (see chapter five). Instead of polarizing the masculine and feminine conceptions of time along the lines of biological/social gender, we conceptualize 'feminine' time as discursively constituted as 'feminine' through particular identities but not in such a way as to be exclusive to, or exhaustive of, the lives of women. The dualistic opposition between an essential 'female time' and equally essential 'male/linear time', evident in feminist discourses of gendered time, is dissolved by a recognition of the discursive constitution of gender identities and their potential multiplicity. However, the materialism of modern existence and the social practices that flow from it reflect and reinforce expressions of time grounded in the hegemony of commodified, economically valued, individualistic, linear time (Odih 1998). Game (1991: 26) describes how 'a conception of time as homogenous and empty, or abstract is associated with a desire for identity and a whole, a desire to know what the social is in its totality'. For it is only when time is conceived of as homogenous can it be held still in order that the 'whole' can be revealed to the 'objective' observer (1991: 26).

Linear discourses of time, therefore, reflect and reproduce conceptualizations of the social world which seek to represent the world as an intelligible whole, rendering it readily manipulable for instrumental purposes. Clear parallels exist between this instrumental manner of relating to the world and 'masculine' ways of being. Writers have variously identified contemporary discourses of masculinity as discursively bound up with an estrangement and disembodiment from the particularity of human existence (Seidler 1989). Kerfoot and Knights (1996: 86) describe this form of masculinity as 'abstract and highly instrumental with respect to controlling its objects, thus sustaining a mode of relating to externalities that is self-estranged and wholly disembodied'. Linear time by definition involves a kind of transcendence that trivializes the specificity of the finite moment. It requires a kind of estrangement from the present that entails dematerialization, abstraction and disembodiment (Ermarth 1992). In the writings of Foucault (1979a, 1982) we come to recognize the inextricable links between subjectification and linear conceptions of time. *Discipline and Punish* (Foucault 1979a) is replete with references to subjectification as necessitating the 'control' of time/space in strategies such as the separation of individuals, the homogenization of physical being, activity and the installation of permanent and intensive forms of surveillance.

Returning to our case study, masculine preoccupations with control and conquest are routinely reproduced by task-oriented demands for quantitative results in improved performance, productivity and profitability. An incessant dedication to electronic performance monitoring and ubiquitous accumulation of coded information typifies masculine preoccupations with transforming everything and everyone into an object of control and conquest (Kerfoot and Knights 1996).

The introduction of processual working practices implied a challenge, discontinuity and/or disruption of the hegemonic linear rationalities associated with task-oriented production. Process time is both a condition and consequence of specific management practices, geared towards the achievement of 'empathy' with consumers. Accountability and self-discipline are central to the production of 'empathy'. But the demand for empathy means that adviser–customer relations and interactions, rather than productivity performance measures, are more likely to condition the time that is spent in service or sales encounters. This generates some tensions, if not contradictions, in the management of call centre staff.

Task and process tensions

The organization's task orientation and its process orientation, are productive of two specific modes of relating to the duration of the call. The task orientation assumes the call to occur within a predefined amount of time (i.e., a 200 seconds average handling time). The duration of the call in this sense is a specified quantity, an abstract singular unit, homogenous though divisible into discrete elements (i.e., 200 seconds). According to this task orientation, the duration of the call translates directly into money; it is a commodity – a resource that can be used to co-ordinate activities. But this task-oriented perception of the duration of the call is deployed without reference to content or context. It is unable to recognize that empathy is a relational quality and not a numeric quantity.

By contrast, the process orientation has no predefined perception of the duration of the call. The service encounter/call itself defines the amount of time to be consumed rather than a time limit or temporal demarcation being placed on it. For the customer advisers, a process orientation to the service encounter facilitates a holistic comprehension of their role and its significance to the organization as a whole. Furthermore, a process orientation can ameliorate some of the repetitive monotony of telephone work, the separation of employees from one another, and the routinized processing of abstract or depersonalized pieces of data or information. The benefits and advantages of a process orientation to the service encounter are expressed in the following transcript:

> I think that the only way that I can get overall satisfaction is to really know that I have done the job properly. In a way you become a robot. You do generally, I'm not saying that I achieve it every time. You do have to feel that you have done that right and that you have done everything that you possibly can. It is the only way that you get satisfaction. Otherwise it does get very, very repetitive. And even sorting out queries, you know, if there is an ongoing thing. To sort of trace it up. I quite like doing that. Usually it is quite nice to have to see where it leads. To come in on Monday morning it is quite nice to start that off.
>
> (customer adviser)

While customer advisers are trained to be processual in relation to the service encounter and prioritize the needs of the customer, this often runs up against the task-related pressures of call volume. As the following excerpt makes clear, the conflict between call volume and quality of service present a continuous dilemma:

> [T]here is in the fact that if they do follow something through and it is something which is a little bit unusual, then we say keep a note of it so when you go for your review to the team manager, they are aware that you are taking customer service a step further ... But timewise call volumewise doesn't allow them to. But again if you have somebody that really takes and you have a customer that is really upset and you take it upon yourself to sort it out it is going to make your job more interesting, isn't it?
>
> (trainer)

Towards the end of our research it was noted that the readoption of a task-oriented approach (evidenced by productivity measures) was encouraging a rigid time perception of the duration of the call and this contradicts the processual time perceptions promoted during training. There is a sophisticated management control system, including monitoring technology, which forms part of the disciplinary apparatus for staff. The call centre is clearly an environment where staff are under pressure to perform, in terms of both quality and quantity of output. In terms of quantitative measurement, the staff operate under a timed pressure system where everything is routinely measured and monitored. The number of calls queuing (NCQ), average delay in queuing (ADQ), average speed of answer (ASA), number of agents signed in (NAGNT) are calculated instantly and visually displayed on electronic call boards in the centre for all the teams to see. From such measurements, a range of productivity statistics are produced relating to individual and team performance on a daily, weekly and monthly basis. Although there are no formal statements, an informal understanding of around 20 calls handled per hour has emerged as the norm. This ultimately serves to discipline the staff in a competitive way since they attempt to reach the norm and, indeed, feel guilty if falling below it with any regularity. Equally, to miss a queuing call is frowned upon by the staff themselves as not only under-performing but, more importantly, 'letting the customer down'. Here we can see how there is a collective commitment to customers that operates to discipline performance in a way that requires no explicit sanctions from management. In this sense, telephone performance becomes individualized and competitive even though there is no formal system of reward, such as commission-based salaries, to support it. In terms of the quality of performance, service encounters are taped regularly for purposes of appraisal monitoring and quality audits. Within such tape reviews ordinarily between the adviser and her supervisor (see also Frenkel *et al.* 1998: 965), staff are marked according to scripted responses and techniques, such as politeness, conversational control, clarity of information, addressing service opportunities and standard opening and closings. Throughout the exchange, staff are expected to adhere consistently to the missionary messages of 'quality, value and service'.

Temporal clashes, resistances and attrition

Motivation and staff training have become a big issue within the call centre industry although, according to Frenkel *et al.* (1998: 965), companies typically only spend 5 per cent of their business unit budgets on training. The recruitment consultant, Austin Knight, conducted a study into call centre management and staff motivation in 1997. The survey of 1000 call centre employees revealed that more than half felt morale was low. While some companies have labour turnover rates as low as 4 per cent a year, in others it is above 30 per cent. Burnout varies depending on the company and the product but, on average, call centre operators last 18 months before moving on to another job, albeit in exactly the same line of business. While presently experiencing attrition levels at lower than average levels, BNFS's customer service employees spoke of low morale and significant levels of stress and frustration. Our findings suggest these emotions to be in part the consequence of temporal clashes between task and process orientations to the service encounter. This conclusion is further confirmed by the following reports of dissatisfaction as regards the role of senior advisers.

Senior advisers, role status and temporal ambiguity

The role of senior advisers is critical in the call centre culture. They act as a buffer zone between advisers and the management layers. Half of their time is spent on calls and half on escalated problem calls and project management. They are being encouraged to become multiskilled across various functions to increase their flexibility and ensure service quality. A central objective of quality management is that of involving every member of the organization in the corporate pursuit of excellent service quality. But when the metaphorical 'quality chain' is directly competing with call volume, then task becomes paramount. Senior customer advisers are currently being encouraged to subordinate their quality exercises to more task-oriented activities during periods of high call volume.

> Well, at the moment, I think that it is almost to do with the TCS and the monitoring of the seniors' roles. I can understand that I ought to get on the phones, on the other hand, I think that they ought to take us out of the phone equation and any time we can get on to the phone, it is a bonus. Rather than try and sort of say that you have got to be on the phones for 25–60 per cent of the time. Because I think

my prime part of the job is helping the other people not just in my team but throughout the whole company.
(senior customer adviser)

This process versus task clash is even more evident when one enquires into the Senior Customer Adviser's (SCA) role in Quality Assurance (QA). Quality Assurance (QA) refers to the period immediately after training in which the newly qualified Customer Advisers (CA) are quality checked to ensure that their work is up to the necessary standards. According to their original role description, the SCAs are responsible for Quality Assurance. But we have found that SCAs are not being allocated sufficient time to provide the QA coaching prescribed by their role. Moreover, it is quite often the case that, in the absence of SCAs, other less experienced members of the team are providing the quality assurance for new starters. This situation, and the resulting tensions, would appear to be a consequence of a growing conflict between output/performance and quality/service cultures within the organization. But what is particularly interesting here is how employees negotiate the conflicting temporal and other demands of a re-emerging task-oriented organizational culture. This is evidenced in the following transcription excerpt where the respondent discusses her forthcoming performance tape review:

> You do have choice on whether they tell you or not. Sometimes you prefer not to be told about it. It is good to get appraised because it confirms that you are doing the right things once its pointed out to you.
> (customer adviser)

Significantly, by opting not to be told when her performance manager would be listening to her transactions to assess their quality, this individual had inadvertently extended the realms of her regulation to any time during the performance review. Our point is that, through identifying with an idea of quality inscribed in organization culture, ideology and practice, employees contribute to the intense forms of surveillance that serve to regulate their conduct. Integral to these conditions of subjectification is the articulation of what staff commonly refer to as 'the company way', which is a combination of commitment to exemplary standards of customer service quality and ongoing customer focus. Although partly organizational mythology, the 'company way' is simultaneously a descriptive category used by many of the staff to reconcile the tempo-spatially conflicting shifts, transformations and contradictions in organizational dictates and procedures.

Discussion

For a generation of sociologists, advances in information technology provide a near-perfect analogy of the principle of discipline. The incessant dedication to electronic performance monitoring and ubiquitous accumulation of coded information, evident in call centre operations, are often cited as typifying disciplinary modes of regulating activities in time/space (Sewell and Wilkinson 1992). But there is a tendency here to interpret Foucault's account of disciplinary technologies as hyper-rational tempo-spatial systems capable of 'electronically tagging', tracing and regulating passive bodies within insidiously coercive 'information panopticons'. Axiomatic to this techno-determinist reading of Foucault (1979) is an absolutist conception of linear time/space as well as a heavily circumscribed, if not deterministic conception of subjectivity. But this limited reading fundamentally fails to recognize Foucault's *Discipline and Punish* as detailing technologies and techniques constituted through the co-operation of linear and social times. As he puts it:

> The disciplinary methods reveal a linear time whose moments are integrated, one upon another, and which is orientated towards a terminal, stable point; in short, an 'evolutive time'. But it must be recalled that, at the same moment, the administrative and economic techniques of control reveal a social time of a serial, orientated cumulative type; the discovery of an evolution in terms of 'progress'.
> (Foucault 1979a: 160)

Foucault's account of discipline is clearly not limited to the quantitative dimensions of linear time. Rather social times involve a 'discovery of an evolution in terms of genesis . . . of individual' (1979a). While linear time makes possible the 'serration of activities . . . in each moment of time', the 'possibility of accumulating time and activity, of rediscovering them, totalised and usable in a final result . . .' (1979a). Social times enable the subjectification of subjects, whereby 'the small temporal continuum of individuality-genesis certainly seems to be, like the individuality-cell or the individuality organism, an effect and an object of discipline' (1979a: 161). The copresence of objectifying linear and subjectifying social times induces 'a macro- and a micro-physics of power', a 'temporal unitary, continuous, cumulative dimension in the exercise of controls and practices of domination' (1979a: 160). It is at this interface that 'power is articulated directly into time' (1979a: 160), assuring its control and guaranteeing its use.

Our case study to varying degrees illustrates subjectification as concerning the establishment of forms of relations of self with self through disciplinary practices and the incessant codification and material organization of conduct in time and space. It illustrates how subjectivity is constituted in and through the embedded temporalities of management practices in general and quality processes in particular. Consistent concerns with achieving 'empathy', through person-centred service delivery encouraged a 'processual'-orientation to both the content and duration of the service encounter. Reconstituted as a care-centred activity, the service encounter is neither linear, continuous nor entirely measurable, rather, it is part of several different ongoing, non-abstract processes, whereby, 'the task itself defines the amount of time to be consumed, rather than a time limit or temporal demarcation being placed on the task' (Davies 1990: 37). The language and timing of empathy enabled employees to secure a sense of meaning and identity by acting in accordance with the norms and values that the quality programme conveyed.

But this process of identification also served to reproduce the employee's conditions of regulation and subjugation. For empathy, as a form of emotional labour, demands an engagement with self whereby 'she [sic] offers personalised service, but she herself becomes identified with the –ized part of it' (Hochschild 1983: 187). Constructed and reconstructed through the qualitative embodied times of process, the subject becomes self-disciplined to securing work conditions which, on the one hand, offer a means of ameliorating the stultifying monotony of call centre work, while, on the other, subjecting the employee to increased performance regulation. For empathy to be productive, it has to be standardized. Or as one team manager expressed it, 'Efficiency linked with quality ... at the end of the day, with the nicest will in the world it is still a business. It still has to make money.' Consequently, there is no question of quality programmes resulting in the abandonment of performance as a control in our case study. Indeed, our work further confirms that the distinctively social character of call centre work demands a greater reliance on managing through identity and this is often a process dependent on comparative performance. The team manager quoted earlier, described at length how customer advisers had increasingly sought quantitative measures with which to compare their progress. As he expresses it:

> Conversations I have had, it becomes apparent to me that people want to measure themselves against something. They feel starved of some kind of, I don't whether it is efficiency measure but they feel starved of some kind of target. They want something to work towards.
>
> (team manager)

Munro (1998: 53) describes how in the post-bureaucratic organization 'what counts is both singing from the same hymn sheet as your superiors and delivery of the auditable numbers for which you have agreed to be responsible'. Dividing practices (Foucault 1982) then separate the good performers from the bad, extra training from the former often being given to the latter in case the identity of performance delivery has not quite 'caught on'. It is necessary to recognize that, despite considerable tension and some conflict surrounding working intensification demands, resistance to the new productivity and performance measures is comparatively constrained. Rather, employees willingly engage with training programmes geared at producing normative standards of delivery. But here resides a perplexing paradox. If the social times of quality management have effectively transformed individuals into self-disciplined subjects who are involved in their work body and soul, why is the call centre industry currently beset by high rates of attrition?

Knights and McCabe (1998b: 192) identify quality innovations as frequently failing to reconcile 'an internal drive for control over processes and people' with 'the trust, teamworking and creative processes that are also asserted to be a condition of quality management'. Consequently, the conditions of quality innovation are simultaneously contradicted by management's preoccupation with control translated as the standardization of quality service delivery. While alleviating the repetitive and routinized conditions of call centre work, the embodied qualitative times of process provide little protection against the quantitative disembodied times of 'speed up'. No doubt variations exist with regard to employees' means of reconciling the conflicting temporal demands of quality and increasing levels of performance measurement. But for those employees seduced by the promise of a secure sense of self, the choices are limited. If they persevere with trying to meet the performance targets until the self is depleted and no longer able to achieve empathy, the quality of their work will suffer irretrievable deterioration. But if they try to preserve the quality of service encounters, it is likely they will miss their volume or performance targets and be subject to management discipline or dismissal. Either they reject the meaningful embodied social relations of quality or risk losing their jobs.

The management of the call centre labour process is therefore caught on the horns of a dilemma. On the one hand, managers are attracted to an intensification of work through information technology supported, performance measures and techniques of surveillance. On the other hand, however, call centre employment is characterized by a uniquely social mode of work where staff performance is dependent on socially sensitive communication and involves the whole person and not just the employee's physical participation. Meeting call volume performance targets, for example, may totally contradict the demands for quality and customer service.

Conclusion

This chapter has been concerned to examine the conduct of call centre staff in one case study and, in doing so, has come to question the labelling of these new, admittedly work-intensive, developments in the workplace organization as a modern equivalent to the nineteenth-century sweatshop. Part of the analysis is focused on developing our understanding of the self-disciplined subject and call centre workplace subjectivity. In some recent research on call centres there is a recognition of subjectivity as both the medium and outcome of time–space events (Collinson and Collinson 1997; Baldry 1998; Taylor and Bain 1998). Of particular interest to our work, Collinson and Collinson (1997: 35) examine the processes of negotiation and resistance through which global processes of time/space come to be translated within particular workplaces, into surveillance practices that have significant gender effects. Cognizant of a tendency for gendered discourses of time to 'romanticize' and 'essentialize' women's differences, Collinson and Collinson avoid conceptualizing 'gendered time/space'. Consequently, gendered time struggles to avoid an association with essentialized gender difference. Conversely, gendered time has been conceptualized in this chapter as discursively constituted through socially contingent gendered power/knowledge relations. Process time is both a condition and consequence of specific management practices, geared towards the achievement of 'empathy' with consumers.

Gendered time enables an understanding of the social process, whereby BNFS staff willingly turn themselves into self-disciplined subjects who put in performances without management having to use up resources in distributing rewards and sanctions. It was argued that the principle and practice of achieving empathy encouraged a processual relation to the service encounter. Integral to this orientation is an engagement with self and the exercise of emotional labour. These features enables the employee to attribute a sense of meaning and value to their work, and in so doing, to limit the negative effects of their participation in routinized and repetitive tasks. But the capture of self in a culture of identifying with the customer and the emotional labour that this involves were also highly vulnerable to burn-out, frustration and even resistance. So, for example, there was muted if not open resistance to the 'speeding up' or accelerated work processes that were consequent on the re-emergence of a task-oriented culture. Part of this 'muted resistance' and/or resigned accommodation appears to be the consequence of subjective identification with BNFS's organizational commitment to quality, customer service and the brand. One might argue that inherent conflicts between the company's process and task-orientation were reconciled by a renewed identification with and commitment to achieving the company's desire for quality customer service. This was evidenced by the desire among some employees for the reintroduction of quantitative measures to enable comparative assessments of their progress.

Our case study, at BNFS, may be seen as unique because of the distinctive role of the brand, the discretion, and the ease with which the company achieves its competitive success but the arguments arising from the case could have analytical purchase elsewhere. By understanding call centre workplace subjectivities in terms of their embeddedness in organizational imagery, branding, service ideology and work, we can begin to unravel the conditions and consequences of staff's self-subjugation. If nothing else, it encourages the analysis of call centres to move beyond the abject pessimism of research that sees call centres only in terms of the technologies of surveillance, on the one hand, and the uncalled for optimism of the quality and virtual reality gurus, on the other. While not necessarily endorsing Frenkel *et al.*'s (1998) thesis regarding call centres being a hybrid form of organization that they call 'mass customized bureaucracy', we certainly share their view that current representations of their practices are far from satisfactory.

7

Flexible work and the restructuring of gender identity

Gender identity and just-in-time production

The postmodern condition suggests that we are experiencing an intense phase of time/space compression and their fragmentation both globally and locally (Harvey 1990). Unparalleled advances in communication technology have intensified, fragmented and dramatically delineated complex value chains inducing systemic disorder in the chronology of time and space, whereby, 'split-second capital transactions, flex-time enterprises, variable life working time ... systematically mix tenses in their occurrence' (Castells 2000: 464). Advances in information technology enable the 'software universe' of modern capitalist production to traverse space, literally and in 'no time' (Bauman 2001: 117). Networks pervade the new social morphology disaggregating capital, labour and global institutions into diverse tempo-spatial contexts. Flows of capital, information and technology, produce 'timeless time' as 'things are happening instantaneously and linearity is broken in the discontinuity of hyperlinks, menus, etc.' (Van Dijk 1999: 373).

Postmodernity marks the demise of representational time and this invokes a loss in the narrative chronology of everyday modern experience. We no longer live our lives through identities imbued with coherent narrative meaning. Rather, the flexibilization of postmodern existence enables a disengagement of free agents from co-operative projects and endeavours. Time in modernity is not only a narrative temporality but also axiomatic to the reflexive construction of modern subjectivity (Giddens 1991). Thus, 'self-identity is not a distinctive trait possessed by the individual. It is a self as reflexively understood by the person in terms of her/his biography' (1991: 53). A crucial effect then of modern narrativity is the 'handing down of possibilities from the self to the self' which has the effect of 'stretching' our 'Being across time' (Thomas 1996: 45). This is to say that the reconnection of the self through time is a crucial source of self-identity. But the excessive ephemerality, fragmentation and time/space compression of postmodernity, radically disrupt the signifying continuities that characterize narrative time. One indication of this disjuncture is evident in the writings of Bauman (1997), when he identifies the postmodern self as characterized by the avoidance of fixed identity. As he puts it, 'The hub of postmodern life strategy is not making identity stand – but the avoidance of being fixed' (1997: 89).

There is clearly intensity and tension (Cooper and Law 1995) around postmodern temporal/spatial relations that were perhaps not so evident within representational regimes where the boundaries between one time and another or different spaces were more clear-cut. Manifestations of these tensions abound. This chapter focuses on feminist responses to the intensified, fragmented times of post-Fordist flexible specialization (McDowell 1991; 1997; Massey 1994; Wigfield 2001; Wajcman and Martin 2002). Focusing on just-in-time labour, the chapter challenges the fixed, unitary, relational subject of feminist critique. The theoretical premise of this challenge assumes that there is no essential self, which exists outside of culture and language. The experience of women in the transient time/spaces of post-Fordism's fragmented reality cannot be taken as an unproblematic starting point for feminist theory, because that experience has no overriding, permanent meaning. Chapter 5 introduced deconstruction as a strategy, which subverts the classical oppositions of the metaphysics of presence and in so doing, unsettles the phallocentric binary that it creates. This chapter deconstructs the temporal logic of post-Fordist flexible accumulation. The central aim of this exercise is to reveal an unsettling reconfiguration of gender and narrativity at work, in post-Fordist accumulation, and to examine its consequences.

This chapter is structured into two main sections. The first part theoretically engages with key feminist discourses, which have sought to provide accounts of gender inequality in post-Fordist labour processes. The second draws upon the seminal work of Richard Sennett (1998), to suggest that just-in-time labour is precipitative of systemic disruptions in narrative constructions of social time. The chapter provides some empirical support for Sennett's conclusion. More specifically, the chapter includes an analysis of classified advertisements for marketing vacancies. The empirical data drives from a quota sample of advertisements from the Times Digital Archive 1785–1985. The findings of my document analysis support Sennett's assertions regarding contemporary work and the corrosive effects of the marketing of the self.

Several other writers have also drawn attention to the corrosive effects of just-in-time labour. Adam (1995) describes the flexibilization of working times as having a decontextualizing impact on people's lives. As she puts it, 'The decoupling of work time from the time of the organisation and from the collective rhythms of public and familial activities erodes communal activities in both the public and the private realm' (1995: 103). Castells describes how the 'dissolution of shared identities' has become tantamount to a modern era in which subjects are 'unable to adapt to networking of firms and individualization of work' (2002: 354). He identifies salient feminist challenges to the disembodied spatial flows and timeless times of intensified flexible labour. Castells variously describes how 'feminist sexual identity movements affirm the control of their most immediate spaces, their bodies, over their disembodiment in the space of flows' (2002: 358).

But mainstream feminist analysis has tended to theorize just-in-time labour through the production of dualistic constructions of gender differentiation. Gender, time and post-Fordist labour processes are analysed through fundamental antinomies between male and female experiences. Conversely, deconstruction reveals both feminine and masculine identities to be problematized by the fragmented temporalities of just-in-time labour. Empirical evidence of this complexity is evident in work-preference surveys which variously reveal that 'the long hours culture is criticised by women and men alike for interfering with home life' (EOC 2001: 4). This chapter draws attention to the crucial role played by narrative in the construction and interpretation of gender identity. A focus on narrative reflexivity suggests a way beyond the antinomies of male versus female experiences of post-Fordist labour processes. Conceptualizing the narrative dimensions of gender identity expresses the sedimentation of time in discursive practices and the intersections of different forms of time in the constitution of gendered subjectivity. It is clear that self-identity, in the modern era, presumes a unique form of narrativity. Time is axiomatic to the narrative of self, whereby self-realization involves 'holding a dialogue with time' (Giddens 1991: 77). Our lives are always a process of linking the past with the future by giving a sense of continuity to an ever changing narrative of self. As Heidegger (2006: 456) states, 'temporality is constitutive for Dasein's Being ... as a state-of-Being which belongs to existence, [Dasein] is "at bottom" temporality'. Heidegger makes it clear that not only history but natural processes too are determined 'by time' (2006: 456). It is therefore imperative on us to recognize 'the time "in which" entities are encountered' (2006: 456). This is also to recognize that 'Dasein as temporality temporalizes a kind of behaviour which relates itself to time be taking it into its reckoning' (2006: 457). To this extent, subjective interpretations of time coexist with rationalized systems of time reckoning. Thus, our apprehension of time is interpreted through the process of Being. The plurivocality of Being in Time resolves the potential antinomies between 'sameness' and 'selfhood' (Ricoeur 1990). Narrative mediations weave self-identities in the context of time, but they do so in the context of discursive struggles to define modern selfhood. Indeed, while 'imaginative variations' (Ricoeur 1990) in narrative mediations render the self open to reconfiguration, the historical durability of discourse affects the creative nature of intersubjective meaning (McNay 1999: 325). One can anticipate the argument in terms of gendered subjectivity.

The interpollations of gendered self-consciousness require interpretation and it is in the act of elucidation that narrative acquires its centrality. Discursive identities are interpretative in nature. Meaning is not inherent to the discursive constructs of gendered identity, but is the product of interpretative strategies that agents employ to link action with narrational meaning. This chapter draws attention to disruptions in the narrative time of modern work. It argues that these disruptions have displaced linear time's centrality to the productive economy. The instantaneous times of post-Fordist labour processes invoke a systemic perturbation in the chronological ordering of time, which significantly unsettles both masculine and feminine narrative identities.

Reflections on the implications of post-Fordism for gender relations at work

> Linear, irreversible, measurable, predictable time is being shattered in the network society, in a movement of extraordinary historical significance. But we are not just witnessing a relativisation of time ... The transformation is more profound; it is the mixing of tenses to create a forever universe, not self-expanding but self-maintaining, not cyclical but random, not recursive but inclusive; timeless time, using technology to escape the context of its existence, and to appropriate selectively any value each context could offer to the ever-present.
> (Castells 2000: 433)

Unparalleled advances in information technology have maximized 'knowledge-based productivity' making possible the globalization of the economy. Axiomatic to the revolution of informationalism is the fragmentation of power which 'is no longer concentrated in institutions (the state), organizations (capitalist firms), or symbolic controllers' (Castells 2002: 359). Rather, power is diffused into global networks of capital, information, real and virtual images 'which circulate and transmute in a system of variable geometry and dematerialized geography (2002: 359). Liberated from the linear rationalist boundaries of 'organized capitalism', flows of capital, information, images and symbols dissolve linear time by disturbing the chronological sequence of events. As networks progressively constitute the new social morphology of our societies, distances between networks contract, enabling light-speed operations. 'Space of flows' induce 'systemic perturbation in the sequential order of phenomena', which may assume the form of instantaneity or else 'random discontinuity in the sequence' (Castells 2000: 464).

Industrialization brought linear synchronicity to the assembly lines of Fordist factories. It heralded clock time as the central organizing principle of modernist production. But this linear, predictable time is being radically challenged in post-Fordist production. The linear chronological time of mass production has been displaced by a contextual relativity 'to the temporality of other firms, networks, processes or products' (Castells 2000: 439). And in the 'network society' capital operates globally as a unit 'in real time' (2000: 470), as its subjects and objects circulate at rates of light-speed velocity. Lash and Urry (1994: 2–3) identify the accelerated circulation of objects 'as the stuff of consumer capitalism', whereby a depletion of meaning precipitated by rapid turnover rates ensues a 'homogenization, abstraction, anomie and the destruction of the subject' (1994: 3). Thus the transformed productive economy has specific consequences for work, identity and the labour process.

Just-in-time labour

> Discontinuous reinvention of institutions. Business manuals and magazines today tend to portray flexible behaviour as requiring the desire for change; but in fact it is change of a particular sort, with particular consequences for our sense of time.
> (Sennett 1998: 47)

Harvey (1990) defines post-Fordism as involving a transition from Fordism to 'flexible accumulation', which accelerated the rise of flexible labour markets and flexible geographies of production. Piore and Sabel (1984) identify a demassification of consumer markets as having precipitated a breakdown of Fordist production. Rapidly fragmenting consumer markets are further coupled with advances in flexible technologies (e.g., Computer Aided Manufacturing) enabling low cost, semicustomized commodities. Piore and Sabel identify these transformations in production as evidence of a new post-Fordist technological paradigm defined as 'flexible specialization'. Flexible technologies and economies of scale, enable firms to 'respond to the growth of flexible markets' (1995b: 15). Organizational flexibility is axiomatic to the new technological paradigm and is manifest in the prevalence of 'decentralised management' techniques (Amin 1995b: 2).

It is evident that the application of flexibility to the organization of work translates into two significant forms of operation: functional flexibility and numerical flexibility. Functional flexibility relates to the use of 'labour across functional boundaries' (Reilly 2001: 28). Numerical flexibility refers to the variety of ways 'organisations vary the numerical input to their work to meet the changing demand for labour' (2001: 30). The concept of just-in-time labour relates specifically to numerical flexibility, and describes the use of fixed term contracts, casual seasonal labour, agency labour, freelancers and outsourcing to respond to fluctuating demands for goods and services. Certainly its distinguishing features are not new; flexibility, flexitime and flexible hours have extended historical trajectories. But what is new is the reapplication of flexibility to redefine the worker. Numerical flexibility suggests a form of time/space compression which no longer seeks profitability through 'extracting more time from labor or more labor from time under the clock imperative' (Castells 2000: 437). This indicates quite disturbing transformations in the organization of the labour process. Although a class-based analysis of these trends is a worthy topic, in this chapter it is a stimulant for examining feminist responses to gender differentials in the organization of just-in-time labour.

Just-in-time labour and feminist critique

Wigfield (2001) details the prevalence of women in employment sectors and occupations, characterized by numerical flexibility.[1] She explains these employment patterns in terms of broader inequalities in the domestic division of labour, and their manifestation into gender segregation in post-Fordist work. Women's dual participation in paid employment and unpaid domestic work, means that women often struggle to work full-time and opt for part-time, temporary jobs or home working to accommodate the ascribed domestic constraints on their time. Elsewhere, feminists have described tensions between the ascribed domestic responsibilities of women and the demands of numerical and functional flexibility. Franks (1999) describes how just-in-time labour involves the reconstitution of self to that of a 'freelancer', whose movement between short-term contracts is engineered by a markedly adaptable array of portfolio skills. Similarly Castells describes how the inventory of management procedures for lean production is increasingly dependent on skilled labour 'freed' to make decisions in 'real time' (2000: 437). Moreover, skilled labour is increasingly 'required to manage its own time in a flexible manner, sometimes adding more work time, at other times adjusting to flexible schedules, in some instances reducing working hours and thus pay' (2000: 437). Similarly, Sennett (1998: 48) draws our attention to how short-term flexible change seeks to decisively and irrevocably reinvent institutions so that immediate futures detach the present from the past. Feminist writers describe this decoupling of immediate futures from the collective rhythms of organizational time (public and familial activities), as fundamentally in conflict with the domestic and economic constraints which shape female patterns of employment (McDowell 1991; Coates 1997; Walby 1997; Franks 1999; Wigfield 2001). While sympathetic to these feminist discourses, closer analyses reveals their various contributions to be united by a systemic male versus female dualistic opposition. For example, the dual systems framework adopted by Wigfield (2001) describes how patriarchy in conjunction with capitalism, constrains women's experiences of post-Fordist labour processes.

Elsewhere, Castells quotes Irigaray ([1984] 1993) to illustrate how feminists have sought to gain control of 'their most immediate spaces, their bodies, over the disembodiment in the space of flows' (Castells 2002: 358). He describes how, motivated by patriarchalism, the space of flows facilitates a disembodiment of the female form through 'reconstructed images of the woman, and fetishes of sexuality', which 'dissolve their humanity and deny their identity'. Irigaray ([1984] 1993: 7) promotes 'a change in our perceptions and conceptions of space/time' as we enter the new age. She advances an entreaty for 'the inhabiting of places, and of containers, or envelopes of identity' to subvert women's place in man's history. Franks also vehemently challenges an acceleration towards labour conditions in which time is increasingly sacrificed for money and longer hours at work are equated with personal status. In these situations, 'men have tended to be more inclined to sacrifice time for additional money ... women have been more inclined to seek a trade-off to give them more time' for family responsibilities (Franks 1999: 68). Franks further describes the difficulties encountered by women as they attempt to reconcile the highly variant working patterns and hours of flexible work with the 'relational' temporal rhythms of childcare. She states: 'It is self-evident that if small children are involved, there is a requirement for stability and regular routines, yet the freelance life means there can be periods of intense work and then no work' (1999: 90). Franks identifies the intensity of 'just-in-time' work schedules as particularly problematic for the freelance female employee, who having joined 'to the male working culture, are obliged to rank money before time'. Wajcman and Martin (2002) draw attention to the negation of gender difference in the 'reflexive modernisation' thesis (Giddens 1991; Beck 1992) and Sennett's 'corrosion of character' thesis. Criticism is levied at the centrality ascribed to personal goals in the reflexive shaping of family and career aspirations. Giddens's 'project of self' is described as negating the gendered constraints 'of identities with a strong "traditional" moral content' (Wajcman and Martin 2002: 999). Narrative analysis of 136 managers revealed that while male and female managers converge in the use of 'market' metaphors to construct a coherent narrative of self, a 'deep sense of conflict' distinguished female experiences of juggling familial responsibilities (2002: 994). One gains here a sense of the significance of gendered relations to the temporal logic of numerical flexibility. An equally thought-provoking account of gender, numerical flexibility and identity is provided in recent feminist discussions of the post-Fordist career construct.

Hopfl and Atkinson (2000: 140) provide a brief, but insightful reflection with regards to the gendered impact of numerical flexibility on the career construct. When referring to organizational relations in modernist time(s), they describe a 'period in which women sought to define themselves as quasi-men' (2000: 140). An episteme, which they predict 'is coming to an end [as] the desire for phallic-power (Kristeva 1980) is being seen for what it is and the costs found to be too great' (Hopfl and Atkinson 2000: 140). The erosion of the narrative career is heralded, by Hopfl and Atkinson, as presenting revolutionary possibilities for women. For, 'these changes expose some of the ambivalences which women have experienced in their careers through the duality of commitment to home and work' (2000: 140). These ambivalences relate to incongruences between the ascribed domestic responsibilities of women and the prerequisite of full-time career development. In the writings of Hopfl and Atkinson, female experiences of these incongruences provide a constant threat to the necessary fictions, which sustain the modernist career construct. The logic of rational evaluation, so central to the career construct, is identified as concealing the inherent 'untidiness' of life plans as 'decisions do not always conform to a rational pattern'. Female experiences threaten to expose the irresolvable antinomies of rational action by thrusting into the organizational arena the 'conflicts of authority which confront women who work' (2000: 139). As women articulate the incompatibility of a work time which delineates public from private 'issues of choice, personal responsibilities and personal meaning are thrown into focus'.

The increasing pervasiveness of numerical flexibility and just-in-time labour is argued, by Hopfl and Atkinson, to represent a radical disjuncture from the rationalist logic of the modernist organizational career. The fragmented times of just-in-time labour draw 'more on notions of ambivalence and discontinuity than on clear and sequential series of career advances' (2000: 141). And in so doing this represents a powerful alternative discursive regime, 'one that poses a threat to the notion of a unitary trajectory of career development' and reveals the paradoxes at the root of this masculine orthodoxy. For instance, the forms of contractual agreements associated with the enforcement of numerical flexibility are described, by Hopfl and Atkinson, as producing dramatic disruptions in the reciprocal relations between employer and employee. Consequently employees are beginning to re-evaluate the rationalist career structure and the forms of organizational commitment, which it presupposes. Curiously, Hopfl and Atkinson (2000: 140) describe how, while these changes herald a crisis in masculinity, women are less threatened by the ambivalences and insecurities precipitated by the organizational restructuring required to implement numerical flexibility. Indeed, women have historically struggled to sustain organizational commitment and, thus employment insecurity 'has been a familiar context of women's working experience for a long time' (2000: 140). What is significant here is the inference that numerical flexibility has precipitated a disruption in gendered relations to linear rationalist work models. And more specifically, that the ambivalences and insecurities, which threaten to implode the construct of the modernist career, are apparently less threatening to women. For this 'male'/'female' opposition (or even 'feminine'/'masculine' dualisms which assume each element to have a concrete existence in the world) partake of a tradition which constitutes the feminine as 'Other' to the masculine order (Hekman 1990; Game 1991). In this sense, feminist discourses, which valorize essentialist distinctions, as mediating gendered relations to post-Fordist labour processes, unintentionally reproduce these gendered inequalities (e.g., Hopfl and Atkinson 2000). An alternative perspective involves deconstructing the times/spaces of post-Fordist just-in-time labour. The following section introduces a theoretical account of gender and time, which suggests that gendered relations to post-Fordist numerical flexibility are uniquely linked to systemic disruptions in the prevalence of modernist narrative time(s) at work.

Systemic disruptions in narrative time/space

In *Being and Time* Heidegger's account of *Dasein* informs our comprehension of human identity as stretched across time (Thomas 1996: 51). *Being* is dispersed through the chronicles of time. The existential time of *Dasein* possesses an intense immediacy, uniquely relevant to the person. And yet *Dasein*, as a concept, also draws attention to the way subjectivity is always lived in embodied form (Thomas 1996). Subjects live time/space events as well as being constituted by them. Time is, therefore, inextricably bound up with places, spaces and the body. For people 'do not so much think real time but actually live it sensuously, qualitatively' (Urry 1995: 6). The identity, which emerges in the process of the self, stretches across time as 'the person one is now has a historical connection with the person whom one was yesterday' (Thomas 1996: 45). By reflecting upon previous experience, present contingencies and future desires, the self is consistently bringing itself into existence (1996: 52). Narrativity is thus axiomatic to modern self-identity. Indeed, Giddens (1991: 76) describes how the production of an interpretative self-history is central to self-identity in modern social life. The 'reflexive monitoring' of self 'forms a trajectory of development from the past to the anticipated future' (1991: 75). Giddens describes the future as resonant with possibilities, 'yet not left open to the full play of contingency'. Foucault (1979a), in particular, demonstrates the profound historicity of modern subjectivity. Society and culture provide specific 'technologies of the self' through which identities are constituted. The self is a developing site of cultural inscription (Thomas 1996: 47). Our existential experiences of time are reinscriptive of society's social rhythms rather than mere representations. The modern self as a narrative text is always lived in an embodied form so that 'subjects are dialogical, bringing specific personas, discourses and voices to contexts of negotiation, and domination' (Thrift 1991: 461, quoted in Thomas 1996: 47). But what becomes of narrative time when, as is currently evident, epistemic struggles transform cultural texts into polysemic spaces 'where the paths of several possible meanings intersect'? (Barthes 1987: 37). More specifically, how is narrative time reconfigured amid the just-in-time discontinuities of post-Fordist production?

Concepts such as 'instantaneous time', 'timeless time' and the 'space of flows' alert us to tempo-spatial disruptions, incoherencies and inconsistencies involved in post-Fordism's break with narrative time/space. Lash and Urry (1987: 299) describe how in disorganized capitalism the narrative propensity of time is 'less rational and has come to resemble a succession of disconnected events'. Consequently in post-organized capitalism, 'our temporality is in part then a "calculating hedonism" in which these "mini-rationalities" are packed into a larger and overarching irrationality' (1987: 299). The theme of dislocated 'presentism' is evidenced in Jameson's (1984) discourse. Postmodernity, as the cultural logic of late capitalism, displaces biographical narratives with disembodied spectacles, flattening the unconscious into a pervasively schizophrenic reality (Lash and Urry 1987: 298). Jameson's despair resides with the interminable consequences of instantaneous time. For, the demise of narrativity results in the suppression of history, resulting in 'our identities and especially political and collective identities [being] rendered incoherent' (Lash and Urry 1987: 298). The loss of narrative realism and the self as a coherently reflexive project embedded in time/space events resonates through Castell's (1997) *Network Society*. Castells (1997: 355) describes the 'networkers' (as opposed to the networked), as individualized subjects governed by patterns of 'rational expectations', self-centred strategic calculations and driven by an insatiable Dionysian nomadic existence. The following section attempts to draw attention to the gendered impact of the erosion of narrative realism in post-Fordist time(s). Deconstruction is applied here to reveal how post-Fordist production unsettles key narratives of modernist work and the gendered relations, which are their condition and outcome.

Engendering the demise of the narrative career and work ethic

> The potential loss of a long-term future threatens career, hitherto invested with a future orientation, with an identity crisis, and this in turn will restrict individuals' construction of their future. Thus the future of career will both contribute to and result from the revolutions taking place in the construction and experience of time and space.
>
> (Collin 2000: 93)

Goffman (1959: 123) defines the 'career' as allowing 'one to move back and forth between the self and its significant society'. Elsewhere Heidegger has drawn our attention to the movement of self-stretching across time as axiomatic to the construction of self-identity. Clear affinities exist here between Goffman's account of the career and *being* across time. An indication of this is provided by Collin (2000: 91) whereby the career establishes 'a time-line and a trajectory, around which personal narratives, with their past, present and future could be woven'. In this sense, the self is a story constituted through sets of events in the present, linked with memories of the past and motivated by future anticipation. To the extent that the Western construct of the career is pervasively oriented to the future 'individuals have been able to construct their future, and project their sense of self around the future positions and roles ... from various domains and especially those from the work organization' (2000: 91). However, the centrality of a delineable future time to the modernist construction of the career invokes significant gendered differences.

Examine the following extract derived from an advertisement for a marketing manager published in *The Times* in March 1962:

UNIQUE OPPORTUNITY

Young Marketing Manager wanted to pioneer a new and ambitious project from scratch. It will include mail order of unique 'Do-It-Yourself' products and the opening of new types of retail stores. We are a well-established organisation and have chosen the project because of its immense scope.

This is an unusual career opportunity for somebody who can really think, work, plan, enthuse and get results. Marketing, merchandising, direct mail, mail order, retail organisation, selling and managerial talent are needed for the position.

Starting salary: £1,800 to £2,200. Generous yearly salary reviews based on results achieved. Head office near Kingston Surrey.

Ambitious and conscientious men aged 30 to 42 are invited to send full details of their background and achievements to the Managing Director, Box J.1232, The Times, EC4

> (*The Times*, Tuesday, 13 March 1962, p. 2; Issue 55338; col A.
> University of London Research Library Services.
> The Times Digital Archive 1785–1985)

The advertisement is clearly directed at a masculine subject and this is reinforced by the direct appeal to 'Ambitious and conscientious men'. It is my contention that the advertisement also promotes a gendered representation of the modern career. The reference to an 'unusual career opportunity' and enterprising creativity are resonant with the future-oriented instrumentality presupposed of masculine identity. In Chapter 4, it was argued that modernist masculine identities are discursively aligned up with purposive-rational instrumentality and that this conception of self manifests in the desire to control both self and Other. In this sense masculinity is transient, having to be forever renewed by an infinitesimal range of new conquests and the, often unpredictable, approval of others (Kerfoot and Knights 1996.). Significantly, Bauman (2001) identifies the protestant work ethic as driven by compulsive individualism. He states:

> The instrumental rationality favoured and privileged by the pilgrim's life prompts the search for such means as may perform the uncanny feat of keeping the end of the efforts forever in sight while never reaching proximity, of bringing the end ever closer while preventing the distance from being brought to zero. The pilgrim's life is a travel-towards-fulfilment, but 'fulfilment' in that life is tantamount to the loss of meaning.
>
> (Bauman 2001: 157)

One gains here an image of a ceaseless desire for control. But also an inane futility, as Seidler (1989: 192) expresses it, masculine preoccupations with control translate as a 'desperate striving without ever really experiencing the joy of fulfilment'. Similarly Bauman (2001: 157) goes on to describe how 'travelling towards the fulfilment gives the pilgrim's life its meaning, but the meaning it gives is blighted with a suicidal impulse; that meaning cannot survive the completion of its destiny'. Parallels between the Protestant work ethic and instrumental rationality are no coincidence as both have historical trajectories in rational linear time (Adam 1995). Linear time by definition involves a kind of transcendence that trivializes the specificity of the finite moment. It requires a kind of estrangement from the present that entails dematerialization, abstraction and disembodiment (Ermarth 1992). Every present in linear time is in this way also the future. As Ermarth (1992: 31) states:

> The rationalization of consciousness that supports the continuity of past and future, cause and project necessarily supports kinds of thinking that seek to transcend the present, concrete, arbitrarily and absolutely limited moment.

Linear time's continual transcendence from the present resonates with masculinity's compulsive hyperactivity. As with masculinity, the discursive constructs of linear time's future orientation, encourage ceaseless instrumental planning and compulsive 'possessive individualism' (Macpherson 1962). Masculinity's goal-oriented instrumental planning, encourages the pursuit of abstract instrumental objectives that both reflect and reinforce a disembodied and estranged relationship to the world. This involves acting in such a way as to maximize one's returns with a view to the future. But the future always becomes the present at its point of realization. Consequently, masculinity strives to maximize its returns indefinitely; that is to say into a future that will never be realized. Masculinity's propensity for instrumental rational behaviour, thus, involves means–ends forms of behaviour where the end is always a means towards a future end of exactly the same kind. How brittle and tenuous this narrative reveals itself to be as it contends with the decentring timeless time of just-in-time labour.

Bauman (2001: 135) describes how, with the advent of 'liquid modernity', the modern romance with progress loses its allure as it becomes 'individualized ... deregulated and privatized'. It is now, Bauman argues, 'individual men and women on their own who are expected to use, individually, their own wits, resources and industry to lift themselves to a more satisfactory condition' (2001: 135). While the Protestant work ethic was not renowned for its collectivist endeavour, the 'future present' of just-in-time labour radically disrupts the narrative linearity of the modernist work ethic. Examine the following advertisement for a marketing manager published in the Times Online in 2007:

MARKET DEVELOPMENT MANAGER

Our client is a multi-billion dollar company with almost 100 years of experience in the design and manufacture of fasteners & components and equipment & consumable systems as well as a variety of speciality products for customers all over the world. Their proven strategies of increasing market penetration with product innovations, extending current products to new industries and acquiring businesses that improve customer offerings, provide the foundation for the organization's continued growth. Within this role you will develop and implement long-term strategies for their products by understanding the dynamics and potential opportunities of trade sectors using trade focus and the 5 P's process. You will propose and manage a programme of trade focus studies followed by the collation and review of the data, and provide decisions based on factual information gained from these studies. Identifying and developing relationships with contractors along with possible OEM opportunities within the trade sector and developing new or existing distribution channels is key within this role. You must understand the link between contractor and specialised (sub) contractor and how this affects the buying process through the channel. You will provide continuous intelligence on product performance; competitor activities and general market trends and establish links with relevant and key trade associations. Candidates must be strong communicators, as you will be expected to successfully liaise with managers across the UK. You must have an understanding of the market with the ability to dissect and evaluate opportunities to aid you make strong decisions. You must hold demonstrable experience in marketing/market analysis and ideally hold a degree or equivalent in a relevant subject. A self-starter with good presentation skills, you must be prepared to act independently as you will need to spend time on site and will need to successfully interact with marketing and other key departments.

(The Times Online, Posted: 23 March 2007, http://jobs.timesonline.co.uk)

This advertisement provides an interesting illustration of the form of subjectivity axiomatic with marketing management in post-Fordist times. Of particular significance is the presumption of a self that is stretched across time/space and receptive to a multitude of communication structures. Sennett (1998) describes how modern forms of teamwork are in many ways diametrically opposed to the Protestant work ethic and the development of a coherent narrative of self. He states:

> An ethic of the group as opposed to the individual, teamwork emphasizes mutual responsiveness rather than personal validation. The time of teams is flexible and orientated to specific short-term tasks, rather than the reckoning of decades marked by withholding and

waiting. Teamwork, though, takes us into that domain of demeaning superficiality, which besets the modern workplace. Indeed, teamwork exits in the realm of tragedy to enact human relations as a farce.

(Sennett 1998: 106)

Sennett proceeds to provide a fascinating and highly engaging account of contemporary teamwork and the unparalleled challenges it presents to the linear work ethic of modern times. Central to this challenge is a seemingly irascible 'presentism', which steadily erodes narrative meaning and value. Sennett with his trademark autobiographical, nostalgic style convincingly describes how 'presentism' undermines foundational fictions associated with the Protestant work ethic. Some illustration of the necessary fictions of modern work is provided in the following advertisement for a marketing management position published in *The Times*, in August 1954:

MARKETING MANAGER wanted by S. Simpson Ltd., makers of the world-famous DAKS clothes. Must have knowledge of selling, advertising, presentation, and promotion, with ability to organize and inspire sales force at home and overseas. Knowledge of clothing trade desirable but not essential. The position is important, permanent and progressive. Applications in writing, give full details of experience, age, position held, will be regarded as confidential and should be made to H. Balcon. Deputy Managing Director. S. Simpson Ltd., 92–100. Stoke Newington Road, London N.16.

(*The Times*, Monday, 30 August 1954, p. 2; Issue 53023; col A. University of London Research Library Services. The Times Digital Archive 1785–1985)

The advertisement's reference to the position as 'important, permanent and progressive' can be linked with other narratives of modern work, such as 'effectivity as achieved through accumulated experiences', 'work identity as constructed through embodied organisational relations' and 'commitment to organisational cultural as a road to fulfilment'. These and other narratives struggle to gain credence in a just-in-time context. But what is significant here is how the turnstile dynamics of just-in-time production reconfigures narrative time as it becomes 'sliced into episodes dealt with one at a time' (Bauman 2001: 137).

The long-term horizons of the work ethic are giving way to the immediate rewards of episodic work as 'each episode must be revealed and consumed in full before it is finished and a next episode starts' (Bauman 2001: 137). Although this challenge to the Protestant work ethic is no real tragedy, it leaves a trail of decentred deconstruction in its wake. Masculinity's control ethic struggles to achieve definition in the absence of instrumentally reasoned long-term projects. In such activities instrumentally masculine ways of being gain privilege through displays of stoic resolution, deferred gratification, durability and accumulative rewards. In just-in-time labour processes, the Protestant work ethic is under attack as it becomes increasingly uncertain 'whether the labour and effort invested today will count as assets as long as it takes to reach reward' (Bauman 2001: 162). But the emphasis, thus far, on masculinity should not be interpreted as inferring that masculinity is particularly decentred by the irascible 'presentism' of numerical flexibility.

For many women and some men the culmination of the feminine discursive ideal finds expression in the subordination of self to the 'needs', demands and desires of significant others, be they family members, friends, superordinates, etc. (Davies 1990, 1994). Femininity, then, is an ideal that in emphasizing acquiescence leaves little space for an active and autonomous subject who can place equal demands upon those whose labour and identity are serviced by contemporary heterosexual arrangements. Lorraine states:

> [T]o connectedness, to the fusion experienced by fitting so closely to the desire of an other that she feels that other's desire as her own, thus desiring what the other desires ... She cares very little about the pattern of social positions laid out by the Symbolic ... She cares very little about the 'rational' code for translating and transposing a particular self-identity through the position of the Symbolic. She attends instead to the concrete specificity of the particular individuals in front of her taking whatever shape they give her. It is fine with her if this is within the socially acceptable parameters of the Symbolic. If not, she is perfectly content to subvert those parameters.
> (Lorraine 1990: 185)

In this sense, the feminine ideal is expressive of a 'relational' mode of engaging with the world (Davies 1990, 1994). It is for this reason that the phrase 'no time to call our own' has an immediate resonance for many women. For unlike the projects prevalent within masculine discursive configurations that have finite time scales in which measures of achievement can be imposed, 'feminine' work is unending and almost infinite in its ceaseless circularity. Those whose identities are discursively constituted as feminine invariably derive meaning, purpose and direction from their embeddedness in embodied social relations (see Chapter 4). But while the masculine self's compulsive hyperactivity is motivated by the desire to control self and 'other', the feminine self's actions are motivated by a desire for emotional validation. However, the discursive constructs of feminine identity, as with masculine ways of being, are variously constituted through narrative configurations of social time(s). The inherent narrativity of feminine identities is evident when we reflect on the discourses of self-sacrifice and sensual embodiment, which serve to constitute ideal femininity (Rich 1977). Discourses of ideal femininity suggest meaning, purpose and direction to be obtainable through sensitivity to the situationally contingent needs and desires of significant others. Embodied social relations of this genre are predicated on continuous selfless engagement. But this form of embodied social existence struggles to be realized in the turnstile dynamic of just-in-time labour. Sennett's (1998) seminal work provides a means to illustrate these incongruences between feminine relational time and the fragmented times of post-Fordist numerical flexibility.

Sennett describes contemporary organizational culture as dominated by the imperative of risks. But the contemporary culture of risk is peculiar 'in that failure to move is taken as a sign of failure, stability seemingly almost a living death. Destination therefore matters less than the act of departure' (1998: 87). But the aftermath of continuous risk-taking is a feeling of anomie, of 'meaningless success or the impossibility of reward for effort' (1998: 91). A condition in which 'the person in these toils becomes prisoner of the present, fixated on its dilemmas' (1998: 91). The emphasis here on discontinuity unsettles the narrative self of feminine identity. Those whose identities are discursively constituted as feminine invariably derive meaningful existence, purpose and direction in terms of an embeddness in embodied social relations developed in and through time. While positioned in relation to power and space, feminine identities emerge from a self-interpretation constituted through embodied social relations. The feminine self is a developing site of sensual engagement and embodiment. Conversely, the self of post-Fordist numerical flexibility is 'a pliant self, a collage of fragments unceasing in its becoming, ever open to new experience' (1998: 133). The erosion of organizational narratives precipitates the corrosion of narrative identity as 'there can be ... no coherent life narrative, no clarifying moment of change illuminating the whole' (1998: 133). The notion of the self as 'a collage of fragments', clearly challenges the modernist discursive constructs of feminine identities. But this disjuncture is also of relevance to masculine narrative time(s). This is because the masculine desire for identity, through mastery, is premised on an incessant desire to control the future. The rationalization of the career into a teleological linear project is seductive in its promise of control. But, as past experiences increasingly provide little guide to the present, the 'Casino' (Bauman 2001) culture of contemporary organizations suggest a crisis for both feminine and masculine narrative identities.

Timely reflections

Sociologists have long since recognized the centrality of time to the labour process, identity and subjectivity at work. Indeed, axiomatic to Max Weber's Protestant work ethic is a 'worldly asceticism' which rejects immediate reward and imbues the subject with a relentless ethical and individual responsibility for ensuring their long-term security (Sennett 1998: 105). E. Thompson (1967) argues that the rise of industrial capitalism witnessed a transformation in the dominant 'task-oriented' temporal consciousness, towards a greater synchronization of labour and more exact time routines. These changes entailed the imposition (e.g., through official timepieces) and eventual internalization of a specific 'time orientation' to labour and life. Thompson is of course referring here to the self-imposed rationalization of work time into homogenous blocks of linear time (Adam 1995). Theoretical challenges to the hegemony of linear time, have been vociferous in their desire to reveal linear time as inextricably bound up with relations of power (Thrift 1981, 1988; Hassard 1989; Nowotny 1992; Adam 1994). Feminist challenges to linear time's centrality to the productive economy have been no less dynamic in their critique (Davies 1990, 1994; Hakim 1991; Leccardi 1996; Fagan 2001). Significant distinctions exist with regards to the foci of these feminist critiques. Within the area of 'work time preferences', feminists have sought to highlight and address gender differentiation in employment scheduling (Hakim 1996; Rubery *et al*. 1998; Boulin and Hoffman 1999; Fagan 2001). Here it is generally argued that 'the deregulated nature of the labour market combined with the "breadwinner" ideology embedded in welfare state policies, channel women with children into part-time work and men into very long full-time hours' (Fagan 2001: 241). A similar although significantly distinct assertion is made by those feminists who focus on the production of gendered time and subjectivity at work. These writers variously identify the incompatibility of 'women's time' with a linear perspective, which separates work from leisure, the public from the private, and task from clock-based orientations to time (Forman 1989; O'Brien 1989; Davies 1990, 1994; Leccardi 1996). Elsewhere I have argued that many of these feminist challenges are epistemologically grounded in the very same representational tradition, which has secured the hegemony of linear time (see Chapter 5). For these feminist discourses tend towards either a strategy of reversing the phallocentricity of linear time and/or synthesizing the binary elements of their discourse (i.e., its male/female opposition) into mutually inclusive dualistic pairs. The problem that unites these respective strategies is that they fail to replace the dualistic epistemology that is at the heart of Enlightenment thought.

The emergence of post-Fordist just-in-time labour in the current era compounds the epistemological complexities of gendered time. For, the current 'flexible regime' begets 'a character structure constantly "in recovery"' (Sennett 1998: 135). Conversely, feminine and masculine identities indicate the existence of a conscious subject living in time and capable of uniting the literal with the virtual or linking one temporal order (the present) with others (the past and future). This chapter has been concerned to draw attention to the complexities of narrative time as both medium and context for the production of gender identity in the time/space economy of just-in-time labour. Instrumental rationality, as a discursive construct of masculine identity, and managerialist organizational discourses are radically challenged by the fragmented times of just-in-time labour. As Bauman (2001: 128) states: 'rational choice in the era of instantaneity means to pursue gratification while avoiding the consequences and particularly the responsibilities which such consequences imply'. Embodied social relations are no less suited to the extended present of just-in-time production. Evidence of these complexities is provided in recent surveys which suggest that both males and females would prefer more 'work/life balance' (DTI 2003). Similarly, Fagan's (2001: 260) study of work time preferences has identified similarities between the sexes, stating that 'for both men and women the most popular labour market developments would be more flexible hours, followed by earlier starts and finishes, while night work is definitely unpopular'. One might suggest that, given the findings of these respective studies, a concept of gendered time is simply no longer relevant to the current era. But this would once again involve oversimplifying a complex phenomenon. For example, Fagan (2001: 260) further identifies how 'the reasons why schedules were inconvenient did, however, vary strongly with gender', whereby 'women, particularly part-timers, frequently mentioned childcare problems and the need to fit household chores into their day'. The tensions and contradictions emerging here reinforce the necessity of conceptualizing temporality in terms of multiplicity. In the writings of Henri Bergson, time is defined as a 'multiplicité indistincte ou qualitative'. Roughly translated, our experience of time involve a multiplicity of interpenetration 'and organisation of elements, each one of which represents the whole, and cannot be distinguished or isolated from it except by abstract thought' (Bergson 1950, quoted in Breeur 2001: 181). Our experiences of time are therefore not delineated into linear narrative versus post-Fordist fragmentation, but rather 'simultaneity' and 'juxtaposition' (Bergson 1950). The concept of multiplicity is further substantiated by the suggestion that:

> we do not live, after all once in a pre-modern, once in a modern, once in a postmodern world. All three 'worlds' are but abstract idealizations of mutually incoherent aspects of the single life-process which we try our best to make as coherent as we can manage.
> (Bauman 1992: 11)

One might conclude from Bauman's proposition, a coexistence of narrative and post-Fordist times, simultaneously permeating everyday consciousness. In other words, a kind of synthesis and negotiation of temporalities experienced through continuity and yet inextricably tied to the particularity of context. This provides a means of theorizing gendered relations to just-in-time labour beyond the epistemological problematics of duality and alienation.

Note

1 According to the ECO (2003: 1): 'Only 9 per cent of male employees work part-time, compared with 43 per cent of female employees.' Moreover, women constitute around 69 per cent of administrative, personnel services and customer service occupations while men constitute around 69 per cent of managers, officials and skilled trade persons.

PART IV

Global Times

Twining (Her)Stories in Global Futures.
Reproduced by Permission of Getty Images,

8

Women, work and inequality in the global assembly-line

Capitalist accumulation in the global economy

In recent decades there have been unprecedented transformations in the rhythms of capital circulation. 'For the first time in history, the capitalist mode of production shapes social relationships over the entire planet' (Castells 2000: 471). Marx and Engels (1985: 37) had long since anticipated that 'the need of a constantly expanding market' would chase 'the bourgeoisie over the whole surface of the globe'. Since the 1970s, flexibility has developed as an efficacious adumbrate of capital accumulation. Flexible accumulation has broken down the vertically integrated rigidities of Fordist production. And this has been an integral condition for the transition to a more technologically dynamic circulation of capital. In as much as capitalist accumulation depends on the production of surplus value, the circuits which capital travels 'appear as the time of devaluation' (Marx 1973: 538). This is because the speed of circulation directly determines 'the speed with which the production process is repeated' (1973: 538). Since this is the case, the fundamental operation of the capitalist economy is to multiply 'how often capital can be realized in a given period of time' (1973: 538). Indeed, businesses which fail to accelerate turnover time risk surrendering their profits to competitors. Consequently capital must, on the one hand, strive to eradicate spatial barriers to exchange and, on the other, strive to 'annihilate this space with time, i.e., to reduce to a minimum the time spent in motion from one place to another' (1973: 593). The more advanced the capital, the more predicated it is upon the continuous expansion of market relations and the more it strives for 'greater annihilation of space by time' (1973: 539). To this extent capitalist accumulation 'cannot exist without constantly revolutionizing the instruments of production' (Marx and Engels 1985: 37). This translates into continuous transformations in the modes of production as all fixed relations are swept away and 'all newly-formed ones become antiquated before they can ossify' (1985: 37).

Considered remuneratively, the laws of motion of capitalist development dictate a continuous revolution in circulation time. If one imagines the ideal rate of capital circulation, the 'velocity of circulation' would be absolute, 'i.e., no interruption in production resulting from circulation' (Marx 1973: 544). This would mean that circulation generated no delay, and capital was able to immediately begin the repetition of the production process. But this could only be enabled by 'an increase in the forces of production' (1973: 545). Such economies of time are closely linked to the acceleration and abbreviation of time in the 24-hour global economy. Capitalist accumulation is increasingly built on a 24-hour economy of just-in-time deliveries, compressed down time, round-the-clock retailing, real time customer-facing and instant communications. Neoclassical economic traditions regularly promote the benefits of unfettered flows of goods and resources across national boundaries. With the expansion of flexible accumulation, national economies have become integrated into a world economy, driven by global streams of commerce and financial capital. Alongside these global transformations, in the organization of capital, is occurring a disaggregation of labour.

It is clearly evident that in the 24-hour global economy decentralized production intensifies the systematic use of subcontracting as a mechanism for 'deskilling, wage depression and labour intensification' (Taplin 1996: 192). This is because subcontracting establishes patterns of decentralized production, in which firms can 'export labor-intensive and low value-added tasks' to other firms integrated in a global hierarchical network (1996: 192). Trends in the flexibilization of global production initially mapped onto the 'sequential transformation of goods-in-production from low value-added activities to high value-added activities' (Hoogvelt 2001: 137). The concept of value-added refers to 'the market value of a firm's output minus the market value of the inputs it purchases from other firms' (2001: 137). The notion of the value-added chain describes the transformations involved in the processing of raw material into a retailed finished object. In economic terms the commodity-object becomes increasingly more expensive as it proceeds through each stage of production. Each stage in the value chain also represents a point of intervention in which capitalist entrepreneurs can intervene and maximize the profitability of their service. Consequently it has been recognized that 'the concept of a value-added chain expresses a sequential progression from lower value-added to higher value-added activities' (2001: 137). In the history of capitalist development, low value-added activities have been located in unskilled labour markets (within the Third World). Conversely, high value-added activities have been undertaken in labour markets closer to the final destination consumer markets (the First World). Such patterns fitted with capitalism's need to construct sustainable consumer markets, capable of affording high-value products and thus staving off its tendency towards intermittent crises in accumulation.

Advances in technology are radically disrupting traditional value chains. It is now possible to divide up the value chain in new ways and 'locate the labour-intensive slices in the production of those goods traditionally viewed as skill-, capital- or technology-intensive, in low-wage locations' (2001: 138). In such circumstances flexibility means the speedy delivery of goods in working conditions in which skill development is seen as a costly and time-consuming luxury. Consequently:

> The global division of labour is rendering a core–periphery relationship that cuts across national and geographic boundaries, bringing on board, within the core, segments of the Third World and relegating segments and groups in both the traditional core of the system and in the Third World to peripheral status. Core–periphery is becoming a social relationship, no longer just a geographical one.
> (Hoogvelt 2001: 138)

To this extent, globalization has been described as a new international division of labour (Frobel *et al.* 1980). In academic circles it is defined by its distinction from a previous international division of labour, associated with the colonial period through to the late 1960s. It had been in the interest of metropolitan colonial powers to establish and maintain an international division of labour, which relied on colonies to produce raw materials for factories located in Europe. This required a social revolution in forms of indigenous domestic production, particularly in agriculture. Colonial settlers were largely responsible for the displacement of subsistence and semi-commercial farming by the large-scale cultivation of commercial crops. The invasion of capitalism into subsistence farming rapidly modernized agricultural production but this was at the expense of increased social differentiation and proletarianization. The subsistence farming systems that the colonizers encountered were inhabited according to a distinct sexual division of labour. Studies of women and economic development in pre-colonial societies, identify the widespread existence of farming systems populated entirely by women. European settlers showed little regard for the female farming systems they encountered in their newly acquired colonies. Such disinclination was often brutal and destructive. Boserup observes how in 'parts of Africa, where female farming predominated, women were eliminated by European-styled land reforms, and the land was given to their husbands' (1989: 60). European colonial administrators clearly believed that 'male farming ought to be promoted to replace female farming' (1989: 54). Consequently, the existing female agricultural labour force was purposely neglected when colonial settlers introduced modern technology and cash crops into agricultural production. Such developments exacerbated income differentials between the sexes. Cash crop production attracted financial investment, while women were relegated to subsistence farming and 'continued with traditional low-productivity methods' (1989: 56). The forfeiture of women's right to land was clearly an effect of the old international division of labour. Unfortunately, it is evident that women have fared little better in the new international division of labour. In this system, technological advances enable transnational corporations to disaggregate the value chain and export labour-intensive processes to the developing world for production, and the final results are then exported to the industrial heartland.

Offshore production has been linked to the accelerated growth of many Third World economies but it has also created serious social dilemmas. Biotechnology has empowered multinational agro-businesses 'to package, extend and redirect the ... quality and content of the product' (Arce and Marsden 1993: 294). Indeed, the interconnections between global distribution channels and advanced biotechnology enable the production and reproduction of freshness and naturalness over expansive distances of time and space. Such developments have enhanced the control of multinationals over indigenous farmers and precipitated the 'proletarianization of indigenous and rural peoples who mainly relied on subsistence agriculture' (Munoz 2004: 22). Alongside these changes has been an explosion of female workers within the new international division of labour. This is particularly apparent within the Export Processing Zones (EPZs), which appeared as a consequence of the global spread of neoclassical liberalist economic policies. EPZs are an aggregate of free trade zone and industrial park, established to advance export-oriented industries. They are an integral feature of global manufacturing, most especially because they provide businesses with an abundance of low cost labourers. Businesses also enjoy limited duties on both the importing of raw materials and exporting of finished goods. These tax incentives are coupled with generous government subsidies on factory residence and unobstructed access to state-owned transportations systems. Consequently the free trade industrial estates of EPZs are hugely attractive ventures for multinationals. But the huge profit savings EPZs offer are achieved at a cost. It has been observed that the majority of the employees in EPZs are female. This is partly because women are the primary recruitment target for third party subcontractors. In these circumstances, factory owners are all too keen to play on fallacious ideologies which define unskilled, standardized activities as a natural extension of the roles women adopt in the domestic division of labour (Mies 1996; Wichterich 2002). Indeed, a succession of highly reputable studies have identified that 'women endure super-exploitation in factories that do not abide by the most minimum standards of worker protection' (Munoz 2004: 21). Consequently women find themselves ghettoized in the most poorly paid, routinized enclaves of the new international division of labour. Of particular concern is the experience of women in the global textile industry.

This chapter argues that globalization precipitates the 'spatial degradation' of the production process. It is a disconcerting fact of contemporary textile manufacturing that accelerated turnover gains have become increasingly dependent on the exploitation of a spatially disaggregated, feminized global assembly-line. This chapter is divided into three main sections. The first section described globalization as an accentuation of the time/space compression directly associated with flexible accumulation. The second section theoretically examines gender and inequality in the 24-hour global economy. The final section provides a case study of the international clothing company Burberry and its closure of the Treorchy textile factory in South Wales. In March 2007, this plant was closed and production was relocated to Asia. It is reported that over 309 (mainly female) workers were made redundant. The closure of the Treorchy plant generated a spectacular global campaign and was the focal feature of the Welsh Affairs Committee's enquiry into 'Globalization and Its Impact on Wales'. The case study contains a detailed document analysis of parliamentary papers and witness evidence presented by Burberry to the Welsh Affairs Committee in February 2007. The case study argues that the closure of the Treorchy plant and the global disaggregation of production are directly linked to the feminization of labour in the new international division of labour.

The 24-hour global economy

Globalization refers to the intensification of worldwide processes integrating national economies through increasingly unfettered flows of commerce, and financial capital across national boundaries. The tendency for capitalist processes to converge in the production of a global market place has been well observed. An international division of labour and international market exchange accompanied the rise of industrial capitalism in the eighteenth century. International trade accelerated the maturation of capitalism in the early twentieth century. And even capitalism's historic post-1945 rapid decolonization forced newly independent nations into a global economic order in which they were expected to adopt export-led trade as a primary vehicle of fiscal development. Thus capitalism has a legacy of global divisions of labour. Nevertheless, the deepening international connections of contemporary global processes suggest that we are entering a new economic order driven by the powerful forces of financial liberation, and the rapid diffusion of information technologies.

The 1970s marked the meteoric ascendancy of neo-liberalism and the reduction of trade barriers separating industrial economies. In the United Kingdom and the United States the economic nationalist agenda of the post-war era gave way to the neo-liberalist ideals of the General Agreement on Tariffs and Trade (GATT). In the 1980s, further measures were introduced geared towards curtailing tariffs and other barriers to the free flow of trade between member nations. Neo-liberalism's blueprint soon extended into the fiscal policies of developing nations, most especially because the G7 ascribed the World Bank and International Monetary Fund

(IMF) a more prominent role in global development policy. Since the mid-1970s, the IMF has been providing developing countries with financial assistance on concessional terms. These agreements initially took the form of Trust Funds. Commencing in March 1986, concessional financial assistance was enabled through the Structural Adjustment Facility, SAF (IMF 2004). The concessional terms of SAF were geared to the implementation of supply-side fiscal polices which many low income member countries adopted as part of the rubric of Structural Adjustment Policies (SAPs). For these nations SAPs provided a mechanism to rescue them from a crippling debt repayment crisis. In 1987, the apparent successes of SAPs led to the emergence of the Enhanced Structural Adjustment Facility (ESAF). In due course ESAF evolved into a primary driving force of globalization. This is because ESAF's concessional terms emphasize the overwhelming need for Third World nations to replace state-led import-substitution with market-led export-substitution. ESAF also provided the IMF with immense control over low income member countries and this was a source of significant contention. In 1999, ESAF was replaced by the Poverty Reduction and Growth Facility (PRGF). The IMF describes this as a 'low interest lending facility for low income countries' (IMF 2006). PRGF is supported by the necessity for low income member states to submit a Poverty Reduction Strategy Paper (PRSP) as part of the IMF's concessional terms of finance assistance. It is intended that PRSPs will produce a 'country-led mechanism to more sharply focus countries' poverty reduction efforts' (2006). And this will be achieved by the adoption of policies more closely focused on achieving 'a full integration between the poverty reduction and macroeconomic elements of the program, and greater degrees of participation by civil society and national ownership, which in turn would lead to more consistent policy implements' (IMF 2004). But the PRGF continues to extol the imperative for developing nations to accept the liberalization of trade and capital flows, as a condition of economic advancement. As the IMF states:

> The Poverty Reduction and Growth Facility (PRGF) remains the IMF's main facility for assisting low-income countries ... The Fund recently completed its review of the design of PRGF-supported programs among the more economically stable low-income members ... The recent review confirmed the importance of macroeconomic stability and openness for sustained growth. It highlighted the central roles of private investment and exports, and also focused attention on the importance of sound institutions.
>
> (IMF 2005)

To this extent, free trade promises to stimulate economic development and this is supposedly accentuated when market-led export-substitution drives economic growth. This is because production and trade, predicated on market-based exchange, are expected to generate larger economies of scale. Likewise deregulated trade barriers advance 'internal and external competition', as the unimpeded free mobility of goods stimulates technological development and labour market participation (Peterson and Lewis 1999: 404). Conversely, critics of Third World market liberalization accuse Western nations of hypocrisy. Western nations entice developing economies to open their markets, while instituting restrictions on their own barriers, thus, 'preventing developing countries from exporting their agricultural products and so depriving them of desperately needed export income' (Stiglitz 2002: 6). Consequently, free-trade policies are seen as duplicitous in their principles of 'comparative advantage' when the primary beneficiaries of export-led industrialization have been Transnational Corporations (TNCs).

Alongside liberalization and the growth of global corporations has been an unprecedented advance in the application of information technologies. Revolutionary advances in IT have dramatically effaced the formidable time and space barriers, which separated national markets. According to Castells, a defining feature of global capitalism is that 'agents in this economy' are fundamentally dependent 'upon their capacity to generate, process and apply efficiently knowledge-based information' (Castells 2000: 66). It is self-evident that information and knowledge have always been axiomatic to capitalist economies. But it is also evident that we are witnessing the evolution of an advanced technological paradigm configured around new formidable information technologies. The information-driven environment of global capitalism 'makes it possible for information itself to become the product of the production process' (2000: 67). To this extent capital has achieved an unprecedented mobility. Unlike 'organized capitalism' with its synchronous flows of capital and labour circulating on a national scale, global capitalism is 'disorganized' (Lash and Urry 1994). Fragmented, flexible production, indomitable networks of financial flows now circulate on an international scale. In global capitalism, accumulation proceeds and profit are generated 'increasingly in the global financial markets enacted by information networks in the timeless space of financial flows' (Castells 2000: 472). A revolution in information technology and a dramatic restructuring of world capitalism have brought into being 'a new social structure, the network society; a new economy, the informational global economy' (2000: 472). Flows of commercial trade and financial capital circulate globally irrespective of national boundaries. The velocity of circulation now assumes unprecedented speed. Indeed, the application of information technologies has dramatically reduced the cost of production internationally, thus linking ever-expanding markets into global transnational networks. These innovations have tremendously advanced the mobility of capital and shifted the impulse of business from the pursuit of economies of scale, to an emphasis on economies of time.

The globalized woman

New technologies enable TNCs to set up decentralized production networks, by outsourcing to different parts of the globe. Outsourcing is a generic term that refers to contracting out a precise function to another business organization that specializes in that function. Such flexibilization enables manufactures to minimize costs either by relocating standardized labour-intensive portions of manufacturing processes to cheaper labour markets or by 'creating global electronic outworking in services that were previously non-tradable' (Peterson and Lewis 1999: 403). By decentralizing production networks globally, manufacturers externalize a vast proportion of the costs linked with the labour process.

Evidence also suggests that the global economy enables firms to achieve production efficiencies, by subcontracting specialized functions to smaller firms which 'results in labour market segmentation between rather than within firms' (Taplin 1996: 192). This is because the post-Fordist pattern of vertically integrated firms is being superseded by an organized pattern of subcontracting to smaller firms 'who remain dependent upon them in a hierarchically structured network' (1996: 192). The resulting interlocking mesh of contracts and subcontracts creates a paradox in which flexible accumulation is achieved alongside Fordist labour processes. Traditionally decentralization was the preserve of deskilled tasks in inflexible industrial plants. In the current era, technological advances make it feasible to standardize complex operations 'that previously were subject to the friction of space and therefore regarded as non-tradable' (Hoogvelt 2001: 135). New technologies enable the transformation of complex immobile tasks into portable, 'real time' activities. Firms can now relocate a, seemingly unlimited, range of complex operations where cost-effective labour markets can guarantee profitability.

It is clear that women are the primary workers in the global economy's 'vertically disintegrated' (Sayer 1989) methods of production. Women constitute the majority of part-time and impermanent workers in developing countries (Chen et al. 2005: 9). TNCs actively encourage the recruitment of young females in export-processing enclaves (Sklair 2002). Plus, females achieve a lower rate of pay than their male counterparts. Such observations concur with the feminization of poverty thesis. The focus here is on the formal spaces of globalization and the exclusion of economic and cultural spheres, associated with domestic labour, from the analysis of the new international division of labour.

Feminist theorists have responded to gender exclusion by beginning from 'the informal spheres marginalised under global capitalism' and using this as 'a strategic way to reveal how informal economies of production and caring subsidize and constitute global capitalism through cheapening production in sweatshops and homework' (2002: 261). In this body of work, globalization is axiomatic to a new era of crises in capital accumulation. In order to offset a crisis in accumulation, capital has engineered a global restructuring of the labour process and encouraged a series of spatial displacements (from factory production to sweatshops and, more controversially, home working). Alongside these spatial displacements, global capital has attempted to tether the tide of declining profitability through ideological shifts, which have involved a transition 'from family-wage work to poorly paid feminized work' (2002: 261). To this extent, feminists have sought to highlight the significant role that cultural ideologies of domestic labour, gender identity and sexuality play in defining the composition of the new international labour market. Maria Mies (1996: 358) argues that the restructuring of the global economy, towards the direction of export-led industrialization, has 'created an enormous expansion of what has been called the "informal sector" in rural and urban areas'. She argues that 'the exploitation and over-exploitation of women's labour in this informal sector, enable people in rich countries to buy inexpensive garments, handicrafts and year-round flowers, fruit and vegetables from Asia, Africa and Latin America' (1996: 358). Similar observations are evident in Barrientos et al. (2004). A vast proportion of the employment in global production is informal, non-contracted flexible work. During the Fordist era, it was possible to clearly separate the labour market into distinct formal and informal segments. Deregulated global production has blurred this boundary and it is increasingly evident that there are 'increasing numbers of both men and women now employed in "informal" types of employment as the share of secure permanent, full-time jobs declines throughout the world' (2004: 1). The impact of gender and informal labour is further evident when one considers global value chains. At the high-value ends of global value chains, formal employment is a prominent feature. But this is less evident as the supply end becomes more proliferated. At this lower end of the continuum contract labour and home workers pervade labour markets.

Women have a higher propensity than men to be concentrated in the informal enclaves of global value chains. This is because the technology used in decentralized production depends on the existence of labour market differentiation among the skilled and unskilled (Balakrishnan 2002). Firms downsizing and subcontracting to smaller operators create 'labour market segmentation between firms in networks' (Taplin 1996: 192). The extent to which this segmentation translates into gender segregation depends on the distribution of skills between the sexes and the resilience of prevailing labour law. Given that the compulsive logic of 'vertical disintegration' is towards the automation of high skilled, high paid jobs, the emerging labour process tends towards a blend of work intensification and low skilled batch production. Consequently, work in these markets 'is inevitably seen as part of secondary labour markets, with low pay, few benefits, and little job security' (1996: 197). Women are particularly over-represented in these labour markets. This is because skill distribution is often differentiated by sex. On a global scale, most subcontracted, labour intensive work is carried out by women, who have historically been marginalized from skill development and training. It is important, therefore, to recognize that the continuous-flow infrastructure of the 24-hour global economy is driven by a reservoir of female labour power. The complexity of this gender dynamic is particularly intriguing when we consider the global economies of time and space in contemporary clothing production.

Women and the global assembly-line

Throughout the 1950s and 1960s, the clothing industry continued to be predominated by female employees. It also continued to be characterized by labour-intensive activities and low wages. This squeeze on salaries enables companies to be profitable despite only investing a small capital outlay. Pay conditions were further exacerbated by the method of piece-work payment, and the application of scientific management in the form of time and motion studies. Since the 1970s the most pervasive system of payment, in the industry, has been 'payment by results', which establishes a bench-mark 'for each operation known in the trade as "the standard performance" for each operation' (Coyle 1984:8). This is operationalized as the rate of output that a qualified worker would achieve, in the absence of excessive exertion, over an average of the working period. Time and motion studies aim to devise expedient procedures by which a garment can be assembled. In accordance with Fordist operations, this involves breaking down complex procedures and recreating them in a sequence of simple operations 'with a specific method established for each operation' (1984: 9). From this schema evolved the system of progressive bundling, which has since pervaded the textile industry's basic operational technology.

Progressive bundle systems involve the gradual sequential assemblage of garments as they are transferred through a succession of subassembly and main assembly operations. Such processes have the advantage of being stable systems with regards to the regularity of output. Nevertheless, progressive bundle systems are extremely cumbersome in operation and require vast quantities of work in progress. Increased levels of reliability are achieved in straight-line or 'synchro' systems (Cooklin 2000). As indicated by its name, this operating system is based on the synchronized flow of work through each phase of the garment's manufacture. Time and motion studies are an essential component of this system because the synchro system is inhibited if there are significant variations in the standard times allowed for the entirety of operations performed in the assembly-line. This system of work study provides management with detailed information regarding the standard performance of employees. Management can access performance rates over a working day or even over the duration of less than an hour. It is invariably female workers who are subject to these acute economies of time and motion. This is because enduring parallels exist between the organization of the textile process in the nineteenth century and its organization in Fordist and neo-Fordist production. But important distinctions also need to be recognized. The twentieth century witnessed the rise of fashion as signifying practice and the growth of the fashion industry. By the 1970s, textile manufacture had to contend with accelerated cycles of fashion. It has been observed that seasonal fashion changes meant 'that long production runs [were] difficult to achieve and often undesirable' (Coyle 1984: 11). In response, manufacturers emphasized a distinct form of flexibility. In contrast with the technical investments in flexible accumulation, which has come to define globalization, textile manufacturers achieved flexibility 'though the flexibility of labour' (1984: 11). In this era, low capital investment in machinery limited the flexibility of production systems and their ability to be responsive to rapid market changes. Consequently manufacturers placed emphasis on work intensification and the 'flexibility of human labour' (1984: 10). It was this form of numerical flexibility which attracted a generation of female workers into the textile industry. Throughout the twentieth century, female employees provided the industry with 'an irresistible combination of flexibility and skill and cheapness' (1984: 11).

In more recent times the textile industry has become increasingly automated, particularly in Third World countries. Its primary activities continue to consist of spinning, weaving and finishing, but these three functions are frequently undertaken in integrated plants (Kyvik Nordas 2004). Technology is also functioning to enhance the integration of textile and clothing. Both industries are inevitably closely related. Nevertheless, technological developments have advanced this integration through developments in vertical supply chains, and also in instituting progressive distribution and sales activities. Examples of these developments include the establishment of retail corporations, such as the US company, Wal-Mart in the 1970s. Wal-Mart demanded that suppliers instrumented information technologies to enable the exchange of sales data and insisted that they adopted quality controls for labelling and handling material (Kyvik Nordas 2004: 1). Such practices have spread throughout the textile industry and have shifted the competitive advantage of suppliers from production costs to 'a question of costs in combination with lead time and flexibility'. Indeed, it has been argued that 'the textile and clothing sectors can be seen as a supply chain consisting of a number of discrete [interrelated] activities' (2004: 3). This is because the supply chain is transforming into an 'integrated production network' in which the production process is 'sliced into specialised activities and each activity is located where it can contribute the most to the value of the end product' (2004: 3). The ensuing spatial disaggregation of textile production produces an economically powerful global core, from which manufacturing jobs flow eastwards. Indeed, contemporary textile production involves the creation of Export Processing Zones spread throughout the global periphery, where labour-intensive factories produce clothing for exportation back to the core (Hu-Dehart 2003: 246). In this new global economy, 'finance capital from the global core flows unfettered across international borders, to locate sources of cheap labor where eager local elites in control of pliant states act as "middlemen" to facilitate what is euphemistically termed global economic integration' (2003: 246).

Case study – Burberry's Treorchy Factory, 1988–2007

While writing this chapter, my attention has been drawn to a pertinent illustration of the relationships between multinational textile corporations and spatially disaggregated feminized labour markets. In September 2006, the international clothing company Burberry announced the closure of its factory at Treorchy, in Rhondda, in the heart of South Wales. Just weeks previously Burberry had reported that:

> In the financial year to 31 March 2006, the Group generated total revenue of £743m across its retail, wholesale and licensing channels. For that period, the Group estimates the total retail value of products sold bearing the Burberry brand was in excess of £2.7 billion.
> (Burberryplc.com 2007: 1)

Nevertheless, in March 2007, the plant at Treorchy was closed and 309 (mainly female) workers lost their jobs. The factory had been producing clothing since 1939 and was assimilated into the Burberry emporium in 1988. Established in 1856, Burberry has a compelling reputation for the production of luxury British designer apparel. Burberry markets itself to this effect, its website promotion states that 'The brand has a rich heritage associated with Britain' (Burberryplc.com 2007: 1). Burberry's headquarters are based in London, and this is the central location of its supply chain management activities. Burberry employs approximately 2000 people in the UK, 600 of whom are engaged in the manufacturing of its iconically 'British' polo shirts and trench coat. Treorchy produced 25 per cent of Burberry's polo shirt range with the rest manufactured in Portugal, Turkey and Asia. Here and elsewhere, Burberry epitomizes the growth of a more integrated global textile industry. Ever since the 1990s, Burberry has repositioned its manufacturing strategy in order to develop an international brand. Following the appointment, in 1997, of a new CEO (Rose Marie Bravo) Burberry began reversing its previous strategy of licensing its brand. Up until this time Burberry had licensed its trademark to countries, such as Hong Kong, Singapore and Spain, instead of owning its retail stores and investing in the development of its brand. With the appointment of Rose Marie Bravo, Burberry embarked on the shrewd move of purchasing all its licenses so that the company could retain control over the development of the brand and manufacturing processes. Axiomatic to this strategy was the use of technology to streamline the supply chain and consolidate manufacturing operations.

The intrinsic technology of clothing production has changed little over the past century. Production technology is still widely organized according

Women, work and inequality in the global assembly-line 163

a progressive bundle operating systems. Although advances in the systematizing of operations have reduced the time and motion of each operation, the basic system embodies a work design which employs low skilled workers to perform simplified tasks to produce standardized products. While it is evident that basic technology is consistent with the mechanized systems of Fordism, advances in information technology have improved efficiency at each stage and streamlined the interface between them (Kyvik Nordas 2004). To this extent, firms have been able to escape the rigidities implicit in Fordism and adopt 'flexible production systems that are better suited to fluctuating demand, the need for shortened product development time, and competition based on quality rather than price' (Taplin 1996: 192). These innovations are best suited to the global market place in which 'production runs are short and flexibility means speedy delivery of goods to market' (1996: 193). On 27 February, Burberry's Chief Executive (Angela Ahrendts), its Director of Corporate Affairs (Michael Mahony), Chief Financial Officer (Stacey Cartwright) and its Chairman (John Peace) addressed the Welsh Affairs Committee and its Chairman (Hywel Francis). Burberry was asked to address the Welsh Affairs Committee as part of its 2007 enquiry into *Globalization and its Impact on Wales*. The Committee had started obtaining oral evidence in January 2007 and by February 2007; it had begun examining the impact of globalization on employment in Wales. A principal focus here was the relocation of work and 'the impact of eastern and southern Asia on manufacturing and services industries in Wales' (Welsh Affairs 2007). Consequently the closure of the Treorchy factory coincided with the Welsh Affairs Committee's major enquiries and it stands to reason that senior members of the Burberry Corporation were summoned to address the committee.The issue of global supply chains was raised as part of Burberry's defence testimony. More specifically, it was stated that:

> It is the quality of the manufacturing process as well as the quality of the finished garment, so what we have been able to do is to significantly upgrade the fabric, upgrade the dying and washing facilities to decrease the shrinkage, upgrade the trim, so we are able to give the consumer a much higher quality product ... at a significantly reduced cost. From the supply chain perspective as well, with the suppliers that we are using, they are what we call wholly vertical suppliers: they do 20 different processes, if you will, from sourcing yarns to laser printing et cetera, whereas our facility in Treorchy really just does one or two services. As we continue to grow the business – we are getting quite large – we really need to consolidate with wholly vertical suppliers worldwide.
>
> (Parliamentary Papers 2007: 5)

It is also evident that lean production requires increased capital investment. This imposes financial constraints on manufacturers, which can either be absorbed (thus producing reduced profit margins), passed up the supply chain, displaced by contracting lead times or displaced by relocating manufacturing to lower cost countries. It would appear that Burberry's decision to close the Treorchy factory is a response to price-based competitive pressures and the need to adopt flexible systems to reduce production costs. In advance of its scheduled appearance in front of the Welsh Affairs Committee, Burberry submitted a memorandum. It contained an official statement, which declared that the September 2006 announcement of closure was precipitated by a year-long review of Burberry's supply chain and manufacturing process. Burberry had concluded from the review that:

> Treorchy was not commercially viable and that as a number of other clothing retailers have also found, it is now possible to source certain products of greater quality overseas at a significantly lower cost, from suppliers who will nearly always take on the complete management, purchase, production and distribution requirements.
> (Burberry 2007: 2)

The memorandum further stated that the year-long review had investigated ways in which the complex supply chain could be improved and standardized. However, 'there was found to be no case for re-equipping Treorchy to make different items when capacity exists elsewhere in the UK and Europe' (2007: 2). On this basis Burberry decided to relocate production to 'other existing and more competitive sources of supply in the European Union and Asia' (2007: 2).

But there is considerable contention as to whether Burberry was actually losing money. Representatives of the General Municipal and Boilermakers (GMB) union have since calculated that the Treorchy factory was making Burberry £22m a year. GMB estimates that a polo shirt cost £11 to produce at the Treorchy factory and it was making 600,000 of these a year at an average minimum retail price of £55. According to the GMB this 'equates to about £30 million revenue' (Parliamentary Papers 2007: 33). They further argue that 'If you take the manufacturing costs and the overheads costs, which come to about £7.2 million, that still leaves a hefty profit of somewhere around £22 million to £23 million' (2007: 33). The GMB are adamant that these calculations showed that 'the factory was viable'. However, Burberry presents an alternative calculation, which factors in the cheaper production costs of polo shirts in China, i.e., £4 per unit. When pressed about the overall savings that will be achieved by relocating the Treorchy plant, Burberry's Chief Financial Affairs Officer stated that:

> There was a transfer price that was being paid internally by our merchandising division to acquire the product from Treorchy; that transfer price was not sufficient to cover the extra costs at the location and therefore in local terms we were still generating a manufacturing loss of £1.5 million. By then being able to source the polo shirts at a

Women, work and inequality in the global assembly-line

more affordable rate and add to the quality, there will be somewhere around £3 million worth of benefits on top.

(Parliamentary Papers 2007: 14)

Thus keeping the Treorchy factory open would result in financial losses of £3m a year. This version of financial loss and profit is peculiar to global capitalism's political economies of time and space. I shall substantiate this contention in the following discussion.

Wage negotiations in global times

Global cultural processes are entering our daily lives and presenting formidable pressures for 'individuals and groups and even national governments, to conform to international standards of price and quality' (Hoogvelt 2001: 134). To this extent, global competition introduces into our consciousness a 'shared phenomenal world' (2001: 134). Media coverage, and even our own global interpersonal relationships, make immediate the competitive environment of global capitalism. We internalize these conditions and develop a reluctant appreciation of the trials, and tribulations, of TNCs. Our attention is even more aroused by media coverage of local financial crises precipitated by global market processes. Evidence of this process was particularly apparent in the redundancy negotiations between the GMB and Burberry. The GMB consistently emphasized that the closure of the Treorchy branch would have a devastating impact on the local community. As Mervyn Burnett (Senior Officer with GMB) stated in his witness testimony to the Welsh Affairs Committee:

> *Mrs James*: I would like to turn to the effects of the planned closure of Treorchy. You describe the impact of the closure as 'devastating' for the local community. What is being done to mitigate the effect of this?
>
> *Mr Burnett*: It has been extremely difficult. Burberry has been the largest employer in the Rhondda Valley for many, many years. Even when it was Polikoffs and Burberry took it over in 1987, there were over 309 people employed there. The community relies upon Burberry to provide stabilisation, if you like, within the community. There are families who have worked there, not just the mother and father but sometimes the son or daughter work there as well. People like to work within the community. It cuts down on the commuting and even though many of these people are only on the minimum wage being able to walk to work in the morning makes it more viable for them to stay in the community, work in the community and spend their hard-earned money in the community and the community benefits from that.
>
> (Parliamentary Papers 2007: 34)

The concerns raised by Mervyn Burnett are well judged and appropriately observed. The closure of Burberry's Treorchy factory will have a devastating impact on the local community. It will also irreparably damage the long heritage of textile manufacture in this area. Chapters 1 and 2 examined the establishment of the British textile industry in the nineteenth century. Several of the historical patterns highlighted in these chapters provide a foundation for understanding how it came to be that women constituted a large portion of the Treorchy workforce. Up until the mid-nineteenth century, woollen manufacturing had been one of the most prominent rural industries in Wales (Jenkins 1976). South Wales, in particular, had an abundance of raw wool and clear running water, both providing ideal conditions for the development of a textile industry. Even more relevant were the traditional skills handed down from generation to generation. In pre-industrial times the spinning of woollen yarn was a domestic art practised in most Welsh cottages and farmhouses. Wool manufacture was an essential component of the rural community and it has been observed that there was hardly a parish in Wales that did not have a repertoire of spinners, carders, weaves and fullers (1976: 96). Spinning was also a craft practised, almost entirely, by women and oral histories have reported that 'not a female was to be seen unemployed in knitting' (Davies 1933). Nevertheless, this was a domestic industry and although most working-class women were engaged in spinning wool, little was manufactured for sale except for a few stockings and certainly not enough to clothe a whole county.

In due course the domestic production of wool exceeded the stage of supply for self-sufficient rural communities. And in the eighteenth century, textile production was being transferred from the homestead to the workshops of capitalist clothiers. But for Wales, the technological revolution in textile production appeared much later than it had done in England. This is because woollen manufacturers were delayed in adopting the mechanical inventions which had revolutionized textile production in North-West England. It has been observed that until the latter part of the eighteenth century, carding, spinning and weaving remained within domestic production, but fulling was mechanized and relocated in newly emerging fulling mills. Nevertheless, spinning remained a female responsibility and continued to be practised by women in the homestead. While the possession of a spinning wheel involved low capital investment, ownership of a loom was much more expensive. In prosperous village areas one or two looms would be located in the *ty-gwydd* (loom house) and this marked the beginning of the transition of wool production from the homestead to the factory. In 1770, James Hargreaves had established a patent for his spinning jenny, nevertheless women in Southern Welsh towns were still mainly operating hand spinning wheels. Indeed, for most of the eighteenth century, the only machines employed were hand cards, humble hand spinning wheels and hand looms. With regards to the latter, Welsh weaving traditions mapped onto national customs and favoured male operatives. However, the employment of male weavers was limited by the slow adoption of mechanical inventions. Thus, for example, in 1835 there were only four power looms in the South Wales towns of Montgomeryshire (Cundall and Landman 1925: 96). Conversely, in 1820, mainland England had already exceeded this with a recorded 12,500 power looms (1925: 9). These statistics suggest that the Welsh textile industry experienced a protracted period of domestic production, which had the effect of sustaining traditional patterns of gender segregation in domestic production.

Arkwright's inventions eventually transferred the weaving labour process into textile factories. Arkwright operated his machines by waterpower and this meant that the early textile factories were located, in the hill country, where running water was in abundance. It was only until waterpower was replaced by the steam engine that the wool industry was transferred from the village and small town to the great cities of the nineteenth-century textile revolution. It has been observed that the woollen industry in South Wales continued to flourish until the end of the First World War, and that between 1914 and 1918 the price of wool achieved record levels (Jenkins 1976: 98). But the end of the war brought disaster to wool manufacture and many mills were forced to close down. This first wave of economic decline dramatically impacted on the community. Renovations to dwellings were forestalled, 'buildings decayed and many were completely abandoned' (1976: 105). Weavers were made redundant and employees were forced to migrate to industrial areas in pursuit of work. The following decades witnessed a continued decline 'with the number of mills decreasing from 250 in 1926, to 81 in 1947, and to 24 in 1974' (1976: 106). Nevertheless, the market for Welsh textiles had expanded impressively especially with the invention of double weave ('tapestry') and light tweeds. Indeed, the Welsh textile industry's expertise and extensive heritage appear to have been the initial motivation for Burberry's acquisition of the Treorchy factory in the 1980s. And it was this traditional heritage which also defined the gender division of labour within the Treorchy plant.

The Welsh Clothing and Textile Association (WCTA) was closely involved in the GMB union negotiations with Burberry. Consequently I contacted WCTA to acquire factual data about the Treorchy plant. During a telephone interview with a member of the WCTA, I was informed that women outnumbered men on the shop floor, but at the level of management there was an equal distribution of men and women. I was also informed that machinists, within the Treorchy plant, tended to be female. This pattern of gender and employment was confirmed during an extended telephone interview with the GMB official Mervyn Burnett. According to Mervyn Burnett, females constituted 75 per cent of the Treorchy factory workforce. Approximately 170 of these women worked as sewing machinist (seamstresses). The fact that women outnumbered male employees concurs with employment statistics for this area. By the 1970s manufacturing had significantly declined in Wales, but this still represented the largest category of male employment. Thus in 1971, metal manufacturing and engineering constituted 20.5 per cent of male employment (Williams 1995: 300). Conversely, male employment in textile production witnessed a more accelerated decline. Between 1851 and 1911 the numbers of males employed in the dress sector declined from 5.5 per cent in 1851 to just over 2 per cent in 1911 (1995: 300). Between 1921 and 1971, this decline continued and in absolute figures resulted in a drop 6600 (1995: 300). Conversely, in 1851, the dress sector constituted 21.5 per cent of female employment and in 1911, 15.5 per cent of working women were employed in this sector. The concentration of women in textile manufacturing continued throughout the twentieth century. And according to Mervyn Burnett, in the past and present of Welsh textile production, women have constituted 75–80 per cent of the workforce. Suffice it to say that while the mode of textile production may vary from century to century, the notion persists that women are suited to textile work. Indeed, recent decades have witnessed an intensification of the processes by which feminized labour is created and kept cheap.

It is widely believed that the 1970 Equal Pay Act inadvertently contributed to the gender segregation of women into the low paid, semi-skilled enclaves of the textile industry. This is because the legal requirement for employers to provide equal pay precipitated a division of skilled labour, which disinclined the recruitment of women, into the more skilled and higher paid jobs of cutting textiles and pressing operations. With little professional training, female workers struggled to break through into the higher paid employment structures of the Treorchy factory. Moreover, as Mervyn Burnett describes, 'Cutting room jobs and pressing jobs are manual jobs which didn't involve female dexterity'. Mervyn is astute in his observations. It is evident that capitalist entrepreneurs routinely appropriate family ideologies and biological myths in order to inculcate, and legitimate, insidious disparities in the sexual division of labour. 'Female dexterity' is, all too often, used to justify unskilled, low paid, feminized labour. Women are assumed to be innately endowed with the capabilities required to do dexterous tasks. It has been observed that 'employers find girls quick to achieve proficiency because they are already trained in the art of manual dexterity' (Elson 1983: 6–7). To this extent girlhood is constituted as a time of preparatory labour in which young girls become practised in 'flexing their fingers before they enter the job market' (1983: 6). But 'female dexterity' invariably fails to translate into occupational status and 'women, it's often argued, just do not have that natural affinity with machines that men have. They can operate simple machines – but they can't understand how the machine works' (1983: 7). Such observations concur with the sexual division of labour in the Treorchy factory.

During our extended interview, Mervyn Burnett was keen to highlight the dual responsibilities, which determined the employment patterns of the female sewing machinists. Here, and elsewhere, it seems that employment careers mirrored 'the expectation that women workers will perform both jobs – at work and at home – for the price of one' (Joekes and Baud 1983:

55). Indeed, the persistence of the 'double day' necessitates 'the on-going interaction between two social structures ... the factory and the family' (1983: 55). Such covalence was apparent in the Treorchy factory. According to Mervyn, many of the female sewing machine operatives opted for the family-friendly working hours, made available by their employers and worked a '7:30a.m. to 4:30p.m. shift'. There were also opportunities to work part-time and flexible hours. The provision of flexible working times was obviously particularly attractive for female employees. This is because the pressures of domestic labour time could be accommodated with the necessities of paid work. Given the volatile pace of the fashion industry, it would appear that Burberry required a flexible army of sewing machinists. And this need was covalent with the expectation that women should juggle paid labour time with informal labour time. The provision of flexible working options mapped onto the fashion industry's volatile economies of time, and secured employment for a generation of unskilled female sewing machine operatives.

Mervyn was particularly keen to state that in the aftermath of the factory's closure, many of the female sewing machinists have struggled to find forms of work, which can accommodate their childcare responsibilities. According to Mervyn, although these female workers have been offered retraining, 'a legacy of women and textile history' has been lost. Suffice it to say that the closure of the Treorchy plant devastated a long-established tradition of female employment.

In January 2007, Burberry announced that it would give the Treorchy plant to the South Wales community in which it was located. The GMB criticized this gesture, dismissing it as hollow and avaricious. The GMB's incredulity was no doubt heightened by the fact that the Treorchy plant's closure came at a time when Wales had lost 46,000 jobs in manufacturing in just over a decade (GMB 2006). To this extent the closure of the Treorchy plant is set to advance concerns regarding the economic plight of families and communities in the Rhondda Valley. Burberry later agreed to pay £150,000 a year into a special Trust Fund for the Rhonda Valley. The GMB were also successful in achieving a multimillion pound improvement on Burberry's initial redundancy packaged announced in September 2006. This improvement took the form of a loyalty bonus for Burberry's Treorchy staff. But on 29 January 2007, the GMB reported that it had adamantly rejected a claim made by Burberry (published in the *Daily Telegraph*) that the Save Burberry campaign had been hijacked by militant tendencies. The GMB was particularly incensed by statements from unknown Burberry insiders who allegedly had said, 'The fact is that most of the workforce at the company [Treorchy] are not up in arms about the closure. They are happy with the deal being offered them' (quoted in Telegraphy.co.uk 2007). Such claims appeared to be part of an intriguing counter-offensive, clearly intended at dissuading further increases in the redundancy settlement. On 3 March, BBC news reported that CBI Wales Director, David Rosser, told BBC Radio Wales that international corporations were closely observing the Treorchy union campaign. He further stated that 'Wales as a business location looks a little less friendly, a little less attractive than it used to' (quoted in BBC News 2007). Asked whether the campaign will affect the business community, David Rosser remarked that members had already enquired, 'Are we going to go through that if we end up in Wales?' (2007). Similar reservations were expressed by Burberry's Chairman (John Peace) when he addressed the Welsh Affairs Committee in February 2007:

> *Chairman*: Mr Stephen Crabb wishes to make a brief intervention.
>
> *Mr Crabb*: Were you taken by surprise by the extent of the campaign against the proposed closure of the Treorchy site? Did you anticipate the level of concern expressed?
>
> *Mr Peace*: I was not surprised nor disappointed at a campaign against the closure of the factory.
>
> *Albert Owen*: Embarrassed?
>
> *Mr Peace*: Forgive me, sir. I was bitterly disappointed at the campaign aimed at damaging the Burberry brand, I thought that was most inappropriate. I was not embarrassed. I was very sad about the fact that 300 people were losing their livelihoods. I come from a mining community so I can feel for those people and if I could have found a way of saving those jobs in a sustainable way I would have been much happier than people losing their livelihoods.
>
> (Parliamentary Papers 2007: 27)

Such remarks are obviously geared towards engendering a shared experiential world, in which global flows of capital impact on local consciences in order to subdue resistance to plant closures.

On 24 March 2007, pop stars and celebrities headlined a concert at Ystrad Rhondda Leisure Centre as part of the campaign to save the Treorchy factory. The campaign achieved international coverage and provided Burberry with a worldwide platform to present its case that the Treorchy plant was no longer commercially viable. Burberry's CEO had already been summoned to a Commons Select Committee, to justify the closure of the Treorchy plant. But most savvy marketing managers realize the enormous potential of international coverage. The Burberry brand is over a century old, and its association with the 'chavvy' enclaves of British culture, has hindered the possibilities of developing an international brand. Thus, the Save Burberry campaign provided the company with a unique opportunity to 'inject a bit of scandal and vivacity into the brand' (Cadwalladr 2007: 43). Evidence of Burberry's international counter-publicity campaign at work is apparent when it states that:

> Globalisation has meant that to remain internationally competitive, it is important to operate at the most appropriate and efficient locations.

Our experience of the luxury branded goods sector shows that this calculation is a function of unit cost, skill levels, and brand value. For 'iconic' and high price-point garments such as Burberry trench coats and our other luxury outerwear products it is important to maintain British manufacture. For goods such as polo shirts, unit cost is more important than place of manufacture, which appears to have limited relevance to the consumer given that at present only 25 per cent of our polo shirt output is made in Treorchy, with the rest being made in Portugal, Turkey and Asia.

(Burberry 2007: 2)

Such claims appeal to a global collective conscious and provide for a uniquely imposing rhetorical repertoire. National interests provide a limited challenge when the weight of global market forces is piled on your doorstep. Consequently it is unsurprising that despite the resounding protests of the workforce, on 30 March 2007, Burberry closed its Treorchy branch and transferred production overseas to China.

Feminizing the global assembly-line

It is clear that Burberry is operating in a highly volatile global market in which competitive pressures have intensified the imperative to manufacture highly differentiated product lines, through shorter lead times and substantially reduced production costs. It is also evident that Burberry has responded to these competitive pressures by emphasizing flexibility. A portion of this flexibility has been achieved through the adoption of advanced microprocessing technologies to automate the activities of skilled workers and standardize less technically skilled functional processes. As Burberry states: 'A lack of flexibility in our supply chain would limit our ability to respond efficiently to changing circumstances and fashion trends ... The Project Atlas programme is designed to deliver both business process improvements and the technology to provide better visibility over the supply chain' (Burberryplc.com 2007: 2). Advances in microprocessing technologies enable firms to adopt just-in-time strategies, reduce inventories and accelerate the delivery of goods to market. Such advances enable firms to decentralize the production process. But flexible forms of decentralized production, result in increased labour market segmentation and threaten the security of workers at both the core and periphery. As firms abnegate vast portions of the production system to subcontractors, 'they also utilize new technology to reduce their need for all but a few skilled workers' (Taplin 1996: 196). Thus 'production workers under a flexible "networked" system often have no mobility within a firm because career ladders have been externalized' (1996: 196). Moreover, it has been observed that:

> while work in the subcontractor firm is inevitably seen as part of secondary labour markets, with low pay, few benefits, and little job

security, what we are now witnessing is a downgrading of hitherto primary labour market jobs in core firms.

(Taplin 1996: 197)

It is evident that multinational corporations are using advanced technology to routinze and deskill the activities of workers in core firms, while cultivating an elite 'core' of multiskilled labourers (Barrientos et al. 2004). Some evidence of this relationship between elite core and periphery is demonstrated by Burberry:

> The Treorchy experience is an obvious example where Wales has found it very challenging to compete against some other economies in manufacturing operations. Our own experience demonstrates that whilst globalisation can significantly impact upon lower valued-added production in the UK, it has allowed global companies such as Burberry to grow our business around the world and has resulted in higher-skill, higher value-added jobs in the UK in design and marketing of our higher value garments. Whilst we are a global business with less than 10 per cent of our sales in the UK, our ability to compete successfully globally in our key markets generates value in the UK. Therefore, the answer, recognized by politicians of all parties, is to seek to attract higher value-added operations and employment, whilst also focusing on up-skilling the workforce.
>
> (Burberry 2007: 5)

It has been observed that it is primarily men who are assumed to possess the levels of human capital necessary to manage the advanced technologies, in the elite core of multinational enterprises (Barrientos et al. 2004). Consequently they represent the majority of employees in the elite core. And even where there is some parity in numbers between the sexes, it is evident that organizational cultures reproduce masculine ways of being (Kerfoot and Knights 1996). Conversely, it is evident that, in the global textile industry, the application of new technologies outside of the primary core has dramatically reduced the labour process 'to the status of a mere component, one of many, in the production process' (Mitter and van Luijken 1983: 62). Technological applications have accelerated the fragmentation and deskilling of hitherto primary jobs in textile manufacturing. Processes that once required considerable time for skilled operatives to learn are now downgraded to the automated components of standardized processes. Indeed, automation has meant that few of the traditional textile processes require hand finished expertise. The crafts of designing, weaving, cutting and finishing have been significantly automated and it is mainly the process of sewing the garments, which has endured as a labour-intensive skill. Automation has also enabled the disaggregation and global relocation of these processes. And this has been accompanied by the enforced unemployment of a predominantly female workforce. But just as textile factories, in the industrial heartland, continue to make women redundant in the primary core, women in Third World countries are being rapidly recruited into the clothing industry. Indeed, women in the Third World are overly represented within the labour force of the subcontractors that service the low value-added segments of the supply chain. Over the past two decades this pattern of labour market feminization has been rapidly advanced by the deregulation and liberalization of development polices.

While it is evident that global economic integration has the potential to facilitate global development policies, it also needs to be appreciated that global flows of decentralized production have been accompanied by neo-Fordist flexibility (Taplin 1996). The post-war Fordist assembly-line epitomized capital-intensive, heavy industry. And the Fordist worker was invariably a white Western, unskilled or semiskilled male. This worker expected access to a union, employee protection and a salary that would constitute a 'family wage'. Conversely, technology and liberalized Third World labour markets have 'enabled firms to reorganize jobs and production and externalize many activities that in the past had sustained internal labour markets' (Taplin 1996: 196). The typical worker in the global assembly-line is 'likely to be a young single Asian woman employed in labour-intensive, low value added stages of production, paid wages too low to cover a household's basic costs and enjoying very little social protection' (Barrientos *et al.* 2004: 4). In the 'tiger economies' of South-East Asia, unparalleled rates of economic growth have largely been achieved through the efforts of millions of female workers, employed to accomplish low paid, insecure, labour-intensive work (Wichterich 2002: 2). It has been observed that mainstream global developmental policy is quick to identify women as the victors of world market integration. Indeed, 'export production and liberalized trade ... serve as the engine of female employment' (2002: 2). But it is also evident that 'women have been paid a high price for this in the shape of appalling working conditions, few rights, meagre pay and no social security or sustainable livelihood' (2002: 2).

Part of the problem involves the process of subcontracting to third parties. While the multinational corporation might well be committed to well-regulated, unionized plants, there is little guarantee that third party subcontractors will be bound by such regulations. It has been observed that 'around the world some 27 million workers are in "free trade" or "export processing" zones that are frequently precluded by law from regulating wages, hours and working conditions' (Brown 2002: 13). In February 2007, the GMB made representations to the International Textile, Garment and Leather workers Federation (ITGLWF), requesting an inquiry into the terms of employment and working conditions at the two third party plants where the Burberry merchandise will be produced. According to the GMB, the ITGLWF have elsewhere witnessed the existence of 'textile employees in China working 12 to 14 hours per day, seven days per week, often for less than £1 per day' (GMB 2007: 1). Burberry appears cognizant of these problems, thus in its memoranda presented to the Welsh Affairs Committee it states that:

> Burberry does not own factories in China, Hong Kong or any other Asian countries. Burberry uses third party suppliers which, after implementation of the proposed changes in sourcing, will supply less than 10 per cent of Group production. Burberry will ensure high standards of corporate and social responsibility from these suppliers, with regular expert third party audits to ensure continued compliance. Burberry also collaborates with other international brands to underpin adherence from third party suppliers to its Corporate Social Responsibility compliance standards.
>
> (Burberry 2007: 3)

Although this evocation of corporate social responsibility is convincing, when repeatedly questioned by the Welsh Affairs Committee, Burberry's position appeared less guaranteed. As is evident in the following extract from Burberry's witness testimony:

> *Albert Owen*: ... You say that you had concerns as well about the minimum wage in various countries, and indeed pulled out of production in Bangladesh and the Philippines. What is the minimum wage in, say, Singapore in comparison to Britain and are you sure that your suppliers are adhering to those minimum standards?
>
> *Mr Mahony*: As part of our audit process our auditors are aware of the local regulations in each country to make sure that not only is our own policy complied with but the local legal standards are met as well.
>
> *Albert Owen*: In countries where there is no minimum wage, what would you say to be a decent threshold level, how would you negotiate that with your third parties?
>
> *Mr Mahony*: Most countries in fact do have a minimum wage but the overall standard —
>
> *Albert Owen*: Is that the case, does Singapore have a minimum wage?
>
> *Mr Mahony*: Most of the countries that we operate in do have a minimum wage, but the standard that we operate to is what we call a living wage, which is a combination of meeting essential needs plus some discretionary income.
>
> *Albert Owen*: I am not sure that every country that you operate in does have a statutory minimum wage; what I am saying is do you take that into the equation, is that something that you would look for when you are looking to set up with a third party supplier, that that social responsibility would include paying a decent living wage?

Mr Mahony: Yes, it does. As I say, our overall policy is that there must be a living wage paid, but we look at both our own policy plus local legal requirements and make sure both are met.

Albert Owen: You monitor that on a regular basis?

Mr Mahony: We do, yes.

(Parliamentary Papers 2007: 17–8)

The concept of a 'living wage' is an uncomfortably ambiguous construction. Indeed, our confidence in this principle is further undermined by the following disclaimer, presented on Burberry's website, 'In key emerging markets, particularly China, we are dependent upon third party operators with the associated lack of direct control and transparency' (Burberryplc.com 2007: 3). Given that women are overly represented among the labour force in the emerging 'tiger economies' of South-East Asia, it is conceivable that this global assembly-line will be predominated by low paid female workers. Indeed, the global textile industry is characterized by this tendency. It has been observed that multinationals actively recruit young females and this recruitment drive is supported by a belief in the 'manual dexterity' of this group. Such assumptions were evident in an official Malaysian investment brochure which stated that 'The manual dexterity of the Oriental female is famous the world over. Her hands are small and she works with extreme care. Who therefore, could be better qualified by nature and inheritance to contribute to the efficiency of a production line than the Oriental girl (Elson 1983: 5–6). This disconcerting racial stereotype operates to stigmatize female workers as 'cheap labour'. It even suggests a racialized functional fit between the emerging Asian economy and the supposed 'manual dexterity' of the Oriental female. Nevertheless, and despite their implausibility, such claims are widespread and they act as an effective adumbrate to wage inequalities.

Women are invariably paid less than their male equivalents and this inequality is perpetuated by the endurance of patriarchal ideologies, which profess that men should be paid a 'family wage' and that female workers are only 'supplementary earners' (Wichterich 2002: 2). In fact, the 'family wage' is an illusion. Most dual earning families will appreciate that it is unusual for a man to earn enough to achieve a decent standard of living, for himself and his family. Invariably women have to contribute to the household income. To this extent the 'family wage' appears to be a necessary patriarchal fiction rather than a woman's reality (Elson 1983). Nevertheless, this fable continues to sustain global labour markets and its obvious agenda is that of reinforcing the financial dependence of women on men. Moreover, the perpetuation of these patriarchal ideologies enables itinerant executives to ameliorate their conscience as they shop among global labour markets for low cost, exploitable labour.

Timely reflections

The integration of national economies through global flows of commerce and financial capital has endowed capitalism with heightened dexterity. Capital is increasingly detached from the spatial frictions which separate national markets. New technologies have boosted the speed of capital flows across the globe. And the spread of neoclassical economics, through industrial and Third World economies, has liberalized trade and enabled TNCs to increase revenues by outsourcing routinized manufacturing processes to low cost labour markets in developing countries. The proponents of neoclassical globalization economics celebrate the adoption, by Third World countries, of export-oriented strategies. But the widely extolled high growth rates of the 'tiger economies' in South-East Asia have been achieved by the hard toil of millions of female workers. Multinationals based in the industrialized northern hemisphere initially gravitated to the East as a location for the lucrative outsourcing of labour-intensive segments of manufacturing processes. It has been observed that the 'tiger economies' recorded a sharp rise in exports between 1970–1990 and that during this period 'the percentage of women in the total labour force also shot up to new highs: from 25 to 44 per cent in South-Asia, for example' (Wichterich 2002: 2). The latest phase in the globalization process is driving a growth in the manufacturing industry in Latin America, the Caribbean, and regions of Sub-Saharan Africa (Barrientos et al. 2004: 4). It is estimated that women represent in excess of 'one-third of the manufacturing labour force in developing countries and nearly a half in some Asian countries' (Barrientos et al. 2004: 4).

This chapter's case study aimed to reveal how the globalization of markets has intensified competitive pressures to produce clothing at lower costs, with contracted lead times and increasingly differentiated product lines. It was argued that companies have responded to these pressures through technological innovations and the adoption of flexible employment structures. This has precipitated a new wave of outsourcing, enabled by technological advances, directed towards making the labour process more versatile. Consequently, competition between multinationals operates not simply between North and South but wherever higher profit margins can be achieved by exploiting low wage countries. In conjunction with these processes has been a resurgence in the outsourcing of standardized clothing production to auxiliary workers situated in their homes and sweatshops. It is usual for firms to combine technologically engineered flexibility with versatile forms of employment. The use of temporary, part-time casual employment as a basis for flexibility is not a new thing. We have already mentioned such measures as they predominated in clothing production in the 1960s and 1970s. Nevertheless, in recent times it has become apparent that the textile industry's reservoir of flexible workers is both globally dispersed and located in the informal enclaves of the primary core. Indeed, every time multinationals use third party subcontractors, they affirm the inevitability that informal production subsidizes capital accumulation in the global economy. And in so doing, secure the illicit activities of itinerant manufacturers who are shielded from the regulations of factory legislation, employee protection and union organization. Suffice to say that ancillary working for the clothing industry has become 'a black hole in the industrialised economies, with piece rates equivalent to much less than the legal minimum wage' (Wichterich 2002: 22). These conditions are compounded by the fact that producers are entirely responsive to market demands, and will shorten or lengthen the working day as required. Consequently producers encourage the use of flexible employees, paid on piece rate and to whom they have little responsibility when orders subside.

Women are often encouraged into the industry because it appears to offer a solution to the problems of combining domestic responsibilities with the need to contribute to the household income. But this decision is invariably accompanied by additional hardship. The economic pressures which force women into home working suggest that they are unlikely to have access to ample spaces, which can be designated as workspaces. Consequently home areas become workspaces and *vice versa*. In this situation 'the pressure to work constantly is intense' (Mitter and van Luijken 1983: 65). These complexities are also compounded by the limited recognition ascribed to the labour of home workers, by family members. The illegality of this form of enterprise means that the home worker's 'job may not be seen as proper work' (1983: 65), thus further compounding the tenuous status and vulnerability of the isolated home worker.

Such harsh conditions of work bear little resemblance to the glossy brand image presented by the big clothing manufacturers located further up the supply chain. These multinationals subcontract to smaller companies, which may then use home workers to service the low value-added aspects of the production process. Multinationals then use third party disclaimers to deny accountability for the failure of subcontractors to comply with labour laws. It is without doubt that these workers constitute an easily exploited group, and the vulnerability of this group is compounded by the reasons why they are unable to obtain employment in the formal economy. Consequently women working in the informal sector present particular problems to union organization. Within academic circles the expansion of the informal sector, in the global economy, is categorical evidence that for many women, 'The Third World exists in the First' (Wichterich 2002: 22). Thus flexibility integrates both First World and Third World women into a global assembly-line of feminized production.

Technological advances in the clothing industry have intensified, hitherto patterns of flexible accumulation, and brought into being a new international system of labour characterized by a globally disaggregated predominately female proletariat. In this context formal and informal market sectors exist alongside each other as multinationals become ever more dependent on women as a source of low cost labour. This suggests the importance of highlighting the informal spheres in which women come to be marginalized in global capitalism, and utilizing this strategy as a method of revealing how informal economies of production and domestic labour subsidize and create capitalist accumulation.

Conclusion
Towards a politics of gender, work and time

When Harvest comes, into the Field we go,
And help to reap the Wheat as well as you;
Or else we go the Ears of Corn to glean;
No Labour scorning, be it e'er so mean;
But in the Work we freely bear a Part,
And what we can, perform with all our Heart.
To get a Living we so willing are,
Our tender Babes into the Field we bear,
And wrap them in our Cloaths to keep them warm,
While round about we gather up the Corn;
And often unto them our Course do bend,
To keep them safe, that nothing them offend:
Our Children that are able, bear a Share
In gleaning Corn, such is our frugal Care.
When Night comes on, unto our Homes we go,
Our Corn we carry, and our Infant too;
Weary, alas! But 'tis not worth our while
Once to complain, or rest at ev'ry Stile;
We must make haste, for when we Home are come,
Alas! We find our Work but just begun.
   Mary Collier ([1739] 1985: 9–10)

We began our analysis of gender and work with Mary Collier's poetic epistle *The Woman's Labour*. Her poem vividly describes the social and material ramifications of women's work, and sets this within the historical context of primitive accumulation. Collier depicts a bleak picture of rural labouring women in the eighteenth century. Time and time again she returns to the double burden endured by women as they endlessly toil in the fields and at home. Over two hundred years later feminists continue to publicize the audacious exploitation of women in capitalist economies. Collier's testimony extolled the double dispossession of the labouring woman as her body and labour became the property of a landowner. Capital accumulation requires the appropriation of nature as a source of raw materials and labour power (Luxemburg 1971: 368). But the logic of capitalism inevitably produces contradictions in the form and intensity of nature's appropriation. In primitive societies where 'natural economy' prevails, production responds to internal demand and thus there is no surplus production (1971: 368). Conversely the logic of capitalism seeks to achieve the maximum appropriation of surplus value. Thus, the relationship between nature and capital is never founded on the harmonious exchange of equivalents. Indeed, it has been argued that the process of commodifying nature is enforced by structural 'violence' (Mies 1996: 355). This tenacity was theoretically examined in Part I of this book. With the rise of industrial capitalism, time was translated into economic terms, it became a medium in which labour could be intensified to previously unimagined rates of growth (Nowotny 1976). Marx identified the commodification of time as a guiding principle of capitalism. Surplus value can be accrued through extracting more time from a labourer than is required to produce goods to the value of his/her wages (Marx 2003). 'In the crucial equation linking acceleration and accumulation, a human value could be placed upon time' (Hassard 2001: 133). Time became a major symbol for the production of economic wealth. When time was deemed as an economic object, a symbol of production, it, like the individual, 'became a commodity of the production process' (Hassard 2001: 133). In Marx's analysis, the expropriation of labour time is accomplished by the immanent laws of capitalist production itself. Labour time is an integral feature of capitalist accumulation as it alone produces surplus value. Nevertheless, in Marxist theory, men and women have been positioned differently with respect to the meaning of productive labour. Orthodox Marxists reinforce this partitioning with the claim that domestic labour's 'relation with capital is not direct (i.e., it is not a wage labour) and second, it does not create more value than it itself possesses' (Seccombe 1974: 11).

Conversely, Part I described the patriarchal structure of domestic textile production as evidence of the centrality of gender to industrial capitalism's political economy of time. In this era, the woman assumed responsibility for her family's well-being and her time was divided between domestic labour and paid work in accordance with the family's economic requirements (Alexander 1989: 40). Home was very much a workplace for women and their input to the family economy was considerable. Nevertheless, the woman's domestic labour took precedence over her work in social production and in a patriarchal culture this was assumed 'to follow naturally from her role in biological reproduction' (1989: 40). But the transfer of production to the market place irreparably disrupted this equilibrium. Capitalism brought about transformations in the cultivation system as well as private forms of land ownership and the introduction of modern textile technologies. Such developments precipitated a shift in the logic of production away from the 'production of use' towards the 'production for exchange' (1989: 40). This is because the invasion into domestic textile economies, by capitalism, placed an emphasis on cash crops to the neglect of subsistence production. In due course primitive accumulation consumed these domestic economies. And this formed the setting for 'the struggle of capital against natural economy' (Luxemburg 1971: 368). The ever-growing capacity of capital production necessitated 'a non-capitalist social strata as a market for its surplus value' (1971: 368). For these purposes capitalism either annihilated, or ceased possession of, pre-capitalist economies and introduced into these areas a commodity economy, which separated the means of production from labour power. The resulting decline of domestic textile production as a fundamental source of capital, coupled with its substitution by industrial capital, undermined the socioeconomic position of women and guaranteed their exploitation under capitalism.

This gendered experience of primitive accumulation was further confounded by the refusal of capital to be 'ever content with the means of production which it can acquire by way of commodity exchange' (Luxemburg 1971: 370). In conjunction with the profits accrued through the expropriation of land and other natural resources, labour required in capitalist production was sourced from among the local dispossessed. Having dismantled women's primary role in subsistence production, capital remained fully determined to move women into subordinate and auxiliary positions in the textile industry. And the time-disciplined exploitation of these labouring women was a clear extension of 'the struggle of capital against natural economy' (Luxemburg 1971: 369).

Because housework is not based on commodity production, and since it is located outside the market place, it is excluded from Marx's economic categories of labour. Consequently, orthodox Marxists fail to recognize the centrality of gender to capitalism's political economy of time. In the 1960s and 1970s, left-wing feminists became increasingly vocal about the gender myopia of orthodox Marxist theory. Part II of this book, empirically examined gender and subjectivity within the context of the norms and behaviours associated with capitalist production. To the extent that domestic labour is unpaid, it is, with difficulty, reconciled with the competitive pressure of the salaried labour market. Feminist writers have variously defined domestic labour as motivated by 'nurturing, love and altruism' (Beneria 2003). The routinized circularity and repetitiveness of domestic labour encapsulated by the phrase 'a woman's work is never done' exemplify the incompatibility of women's work with linear conceptions of time (Davies 1990; Le Feuvre 1994).

Working women are usually disadvantaged in the career stakes because of their engagement in a multiplicity of simultaneous 'need'-centred responsibilities and, therefore, cannot always show the same amount of commitment to paid employment as their male counterparts. Labour market statistics support this, with 42 per cent of women employees in part-time employment compared with 9 per cent of male employees (EOC 2006: 11). Further evidence of the ways in which women attempt to negotiate the clock time of work with domestic labour, is evident in the higher proportion of women opting for flexible working arrangements. According to the EOC, 57 per cent of women employees, compared with only 23 per cent of male employees, use one or a combination of the following arrangements: part-time, flexitime, annualized hours, term-time working, job share and home working (2006: 11). It is quite often the case for males that they manage excessive time demands at work as a result of this labour being serviced domestically by a woman (i.e., partner, wife, maid or mother). Increasing rates of formal employment by women have meant that they are faced with the task of managing the most demanding temporal constraints of economic labour during precisely the same periods of their life cycle when domestic pressure is at its greatest (Le Feuvre 1994; Deem 1996). For many women, the accumulative temporal constraints of paid and domestic work negatively impact on their promotion opportunities and frequently result in broken or part-time employment.

Part III examined whether women's relation to the productive economy was changing as they enter the labour market in post-Fordist times. Chapters 6 and 7 identified post-Fordism with an insidious new form of time-disciplined labour process. In post-Fordist organizations, our subjective experiences of time have become integral to capitalist accumulation. Productivity in just-in-time systems entails an acute time/space compression geared at producing more in less time. And the *sine qua non* of just-in-time systems is the transformation of organizational cultures into team-based 'learning cultures', in which workers are self-disciplined into achieving the optimum standardized task performance (Jenkins 1994: 24). Indeed, the classical Fordist model of management, which sought to separate cognition from physical labour, is abandoned in the lean management processes of post-Fordist production (Rifkin 1996: 97). In contrast to classical Fordism, post-Fordism's implementation of co-operative managerial approaches (e.g., production teams) is designed to harness the mental capabilities and communicative skills of everyone involved in the labour process. This is because language has gained a key role in every facet of the production process (Gorz 1999: 41). Under the broad rubric of re-engineering, corporations are transformed from pyramidal uncommunicative structures into horizontal networks transferring flows of activity. And new information technologies, coupled with digitization, increase the emphasis placed on abstract cognition in production. This denotes a specific instance in the subjectivization of labour to capital. For language is put to work in the time-compressed culture of post-Fordist production and the workers' communicational capacities have become valuable resources for capitalist production (Gorz 1999: 41). Indeed, the deliberate engagement with the worker's personality, as it becomes woven into the 'learning culture', triumphs in linking the social background of labourers with the behavioural codes of corporate capitalism. It is within this context that the qualitative times of social reproduction have been integrated into capital's expropriation of surplus labour time. The organizational ethnography in Chapter 6 identified time-disciplined reflexivity as axiomatic to capital accumulation in post-Fordist production. The flexibly organized space of post-Fordist interfirm networks invokes changes in self and subjectivity. While vertically integrated geographical dispersed production operates according to objective linear time, capital accumulation is increasingly reliant on the qualitative times of embodied social relations as a source of exploitation. This places gender at the heart of post-Fordism's political economy of time.

Part IV examined unprecedented transformations in the pace and scope of capitalism. Of particular significance has been the accelerated pace of textile production. Since the 1950s, a series of technological and legal changes have transformed retail clothing supply. In the immediate post-war era, Fordism pioneered the diffusion of new technologies, together with the monopolistic regulation of clothing manufacture by the capitalist state. The resulting regime of 'intensive accumulation' (Jessop 1991) relied upon the intensification of clothing production and the Taylorization of the labour process. In cotton- and wool-producing districts, Fordism promoted the use of chemical fertilizers and synthetic pesticides designed to maximize the utility value of land-based production. This 'mode of development' (Lipietz 1988) was sustained by state investment, uniform production methods, converging product lines and 'standardized global markets' (Arce and Marsden 1993: 293). These regularities set in motion synchronicities across the whole economy. Patterns of industrial production echoed the knowledge base of trading firms, enabling the propitious regulation of consumer demand. And centralized government agencies secured capitalist accumulation by the commercial management of clothing manufacture networks. To this extent clothing manufacturing's synchronous circuits of productive capital extended across the scope of entire national economies. Indeed, it is evident that these synchronous flows of capital provided the infrastructure for the emergence of an international system of clothing production. Nevertheless, the greatest challenges to Fordist clothing manufacture were presented by the increasing capacity of commercial networks to exceed synchronous circuits of capital organized on a local and global scale. Oligopolistic markets strained in the context of maturing information technologies. And pioneering advances in clothing technology set in motion a precipitous plunge in the economic power of national companies.

The application of information technologies has significantly reduced the cost of communication internationally and substantially effaced the time and space distances, which separated national markets (Peterson and Lewis 1999: 403). These innovations have significantly advanced the mobility of capital. New technologies enable TNCs to set up decentralized production networks, by outsourcing to different parts of the globe. Such flexibilization enables manufacturers to minimize costs, either by relocating standardized labour-intensive portions of manufacturing processes to cheaper labour markets or by 'creating global electronic outworking in services that were previously non-tradable' (1999: 403). By decentralizing production networks globally, manufacturers externalize a vast proportion of the costs tethered to the labour process (Balakrishnan 2002). Proponents of globalization highlight the labour market 'benefits' associated with decentralization. The increasingly unfettered flow of goods and resources across national boundaries is described, in neoclassical economic traditions, as promoting a 'greater growth and a rise in standards of living everywhere through a better division of labour, bigger economies of scale, the flow of investment toward activities with the highest returns, and lower prices' (Peterson and Lewis 1999: 404).

Such enthusiasm is largely impervious to the gender, race and class inequities which are quite evidently consequences of globalization. Chapter 8 critically examined the emergence of a new international division of labour that concentrates women, in low paid employment enclaves. The adoption, by Third World countries, of concessional funding through the Poverty Reduction and Growth Facility (PRGF) is a major driving force in the liberalization of trade barriers and the global extension of the new international division of labour. Third World countries initially entered into these agreements by their adoption of Structural Adjustment Policies (SAPs), which were economic policies designed to enable qualification for debt relief loans, distributed by the World Bank and the International Monetary Fund. In 1999, the IMF replaced its Enhanced Structural Adjustment Facility (ESAF) with the Poverty Reduction and Growth Facility (PRGF). For many Third World countries the adoption of PRGF's concessional terms has provided an expedient means of addressing the stifling fiscal burdens precipitated by heavy international debt. But PRGF continues to be driven by an economic agenda keen to inculcate a common guiding principle which promotes 'export-led growth; privatisation and liberalisation and the efficiency of the market' (Whirled Bank Group 2003). It has been observed that the PRGF's concessional terms invariably result in countries having to devalue their currencies against the dollar, 'lift import and export restrictions; balance their budgets and not overspend; and remove price controls and state subsidies'. With few exceptions, these trade agreements have increased the participation of women in the industrial labour force and across employment sectors. This trend has led observers to note a direct link between the expansions of export orientation in Third World economies and the feminization of employment. There is growing consensus that the comparative advantages gained by Third World countries, from the decentralization of production in the First World, has been to the disadvantage of women. The impact of TNCs entering Third World economies and capitalizing on cheaper labour markets is compounded by the rigidity of traditional domestic divisions of labour. In most Third World countries the responsibility for domestic labour is ascribed to the female members of the household. TNCs quite clearly trade upon the substitution of low paid women workers for men workers as part of the deskilling and feminization of the labour process (Peterson and Lewis 1999: 407). And the exploitation of women by TNCs in the 24-hour global economy, clearly results in the intensification of women's unpaid labour time. But addressing these problems is not quite as clear. This is mainly because a vast proportion of macroeconomic analysis, of capitalist economies, assumes domestic labour time to be a 'non-produced input to economic growth' (1999: 407). The central objective of this book has been to challenge this assumption. For this book argues that the expropriation of the formal and informal labour time of women is integral to capitalist accumulation.

References

Adam, B. (1993) Within and beyond the time economy of employment relations; conceptual issues pertinent to research on time and work, *Social Science Information*, 32: 163–84.
Adam, B. (1994) Running out of time: environmental crisis and the need for active engagement, in T. Benton and M. Redclift (eds) *Social Theory and the Environment*. London: Routledge.
Adam, B. (1995) *Timewatch: The Social Analysis of Time*. Cambridge: Polity Press.
Addy, J. (1976) *The Textile Revolution*. Kent: Longman Group Ltd.
Alexander, S. (1989) Women's work in nineteenth-century London: a study of the years 1820–50, in E. Whitelegg, M. Arnot, V. Beechy, L. Birke, S. Himmelweit, D. Leonard, S. Ruehl and M. Speakman (eds) *The Changing Experience of Women*. Oxford: Blackwell.
Amin, A. (1995a) Post-Fordism: models, fantasies and phantoms of transition, in A. Amin (ed.) *Post-Fordism: A Reader*. Oxford: Blackwell.
Amin, A. (1995b) *Post-Fordism: A Reader*. Oxford: Blackwell.
Apostol, S. (1996) Are call centres the sweatshops of the 20th-century? *Call Centre Focus*, 2(5).
Arce, A. and Marsden, T. (1993) The social construction of international food: a new research agenda, *Economic Geography*, 69(3): 291–311.
Arkin, A. (1997) Hold the production line, *People Management*, 6 February.
Balakrishnan, R. (2002) *Gender Dynamics of Subcontracted Work in a Global Economy*. Connecticut CT: Kumarian Press.
Baldry, C. (1998) Space, the final frontier, paper presented at 16th Annual International Labour Process Conference, School of Management, University of Manchester Institute of Science and Technology, April.
Baldry, C., Bain, P. and Taylor, P. (1998) 'Bright satanic offices': intensification, control and team Taylorism, in P. Thompson and C. Warhurst (eds) *Workplaces of the Future*. London: Macmillan Business, 163–83.
Barratt, M. and McIntosh, M. (1989) The family way, in E. Whitelegg, M. Arnot, V. Beechy, L. Birke, S. Himmelweit, D. Leonard, S. Ruehl and M. Speakman (eds) *The Changing Experience of Women*. Oxford: Blackwell.
Barrientos, S., Kabeer, N. and Hossain, N. (2004) The gender dimensions of the globalization of production. Working Paper 17. Geneva: Policy Integration Department

World Commission on the Social Dimension of Globalization International Labour Office. Available at: www.ilo.org/publns
Barthes, R. (1987) Theory of the text, in R. Young (ed.) *Untying the Text*. London: Routledge and Kegan Paul, 31–47.
Bate, S.P. (1997) Whatever happened to organizational ethnography, *Human Relations*, 50(9): 1147–75.
Bauman, Z. (1992) *Mortality, Immortality and Other Life Strategies*. Cambridge: Polity Press.
Bauman, Z. (1997) *Postmodernity and its Discontents*. Cambridge: Polity Press.
Bauman, Z. (2001) *Liquid Modernity*. Cambridge: Polity Press.
BBC News (2003) Working mums 'harm child's progress'.
BBC News (2007) Burberry's fight 'puts off' firms. Available at: http://news.bbc.co.uk
Beck, U. (1992) *Risk Society*. London: Sage.
Becker, G. (1971) *The Economics of Discrimination*. London: Chicago Press.
Becker, G. (1981) *A Treatise on the Family*. Cambridge, MA: Harvard University Press.
Bee, A. (2000) Globalization, grapes and gender: women's work in traditional and agro-export production in Northern Chile. *The Geographical Journal*, 166(3): 255–65.
Beechey, V. (1977) Some notes on female wage labour in capitalist production, *Capital and Class*, 3: 45–66.
Beechey, V. (1979) On patriarchy, *Feminist Review*, 3: 72–6.
Bell, D. (1976) *The Cultural Contradictions of Capitalism*. London: Heinemann.
Belt, V. (1999) Are call centres the new sweatshops? The Thursday Review, *The Independent*, 14 January, 4.
Belt, V. and Richardson, R. (1999) Work opportunities for women in the information society. Call Centre Teleworking Interim Report. London: Centre for Urban and Regional Development.
Beneria, L. (2003) *Gender, Development and Globalization*. London: Routledge.
Beneria, L. and Bisnath, S. (2001) Gender and poverty: an analysis for action, in F.R. Lechner and J. Boli (eds) *The Globalization Reader*. Oxford: Blackwell.
Benston, M. (1989) The political economy of women's liberation, *Monthly Review*, 41(7): 31–43.
Berg, M. (1993) What difference did women's work make to the Industrial Revolution? *History Workshop*, 35: 22–44.
Bergson, H. (1950); *Matter and Memory*, trans. N.M. Paul and W. Scott Palmer, London:George Allen & Unwin.
Blake, W. ([1804] 1991) *Jerusalem*. London: Morton D. Paley.
Boserup, E. (1989) *Woman's Role in Economic Development*. London: Earthscan Publications.
Boulin, J-.Y. and Hoffman, R. (eds) (1999) *New Paths in Working Time Policy*. Brussels: European Trade Union Institute.
Boulton, M. (1983) *On Being a Mother*. London: Tavistock Publications.
Bowlby, J. (1950) *Childcare and the Growth of Love*. London: Penguin.
Bradley, H, (1998) *Gender and Power in the Workplace; Analysing the Impact of Economic Change*. Basingstoke: Macmillan.
Brannen, J. and Moss, P. (1991) *Managing Mothers: Dual Earners Households After Maternity*. London: Unwin Hyman.
Braverman, H. (1974) *Labour and Monopoly Capital: The Degradation of Work in the Twentieth Century*. London and New York: Monthly Review Press.
Breeur, R. (2001) Bergson's and Sartre's account of the self in relation to the transcendental ego, *International Journal of Philosophical Studies*, 9(2): 177–98.
Brinkley, I. (2000) *The Future of Work: Looking Ahead to the Next Ten Years*. Trade Union Congress Published Report. London: Congress House.
British Telecom Global Networked IT Services (2006) Global locations. Available at: http://www.btglobalservices.com

References

Brittan, A. (1989) *Masculinity and Power*. Oxford: Blackwell.
Brown, G. (2002) The global threats to workers' health and safety on the job, *Social Justice*, 29(3): 12–25.
Brown, G., Andrews, B., Harris, T., Alder, Z. and Bridge, L. (1986) Social support, self-esteem and depression, *Psychological Medicine*, 16: 813–31.
Bruegel, I. (1986) The reserve army of labour 1974–1979, in *Feminist Review (ed.) Waged Work: A Reader*. London: Virago.
Brunskell, H. (1999) Feminist methodology, in C. Seale (ed.) *Researching Culture and Society*. London: Sage.
Bryant, A. (1971) *English Saga 1840–1940*. London: Collins.
Burberry (2007) *Memorandum Submitted by Burberry (Glob 19)*. Welsh Affairs Committee. Available at: http://www.publications.parliament.uk/pa/cm200607/cmselect/cmwelaf/ucglobal/m9.htm
Burberryplc.com (2007) Company overview and strategy. Available at: www.burberryplc.com
Burchell, G. (1990) *The Organisation of pleasure*, unpublished working paper, University of Warwick.
Burnette, J. (1997) An investigation of the female-male wage gap during the Industrial Revolution in Britain, *Economic History Review*, 2: 257–81.
Busfield, D. (1988) Skill and the sexual division of labour in the West Riding textile industry 1850–1914, in J. Jowitt and A. McIvor (eds) *Employers and Labour in the English Textile Industries 1850–1939*. London: Routledge.
Butler, J. (1990) *Gender Trouble: Feminism and the Subversion of Identity*. London: Routledge.
Butler, J. (1992) Contingent foundations: feminism and the question of 'postmodernism', in J. Butler and J. Scott (eds) *Feminist Theorize the Political*. London: Routledge.
Butler, O. (1987) *Dawn: Xenogenesis*. New York, NY: Warner Books.
Cadwalladr, C. (2007) Squaring up to Burberry. *The Observer Magazine*, 25 March.
Caffentzis, G. (1995) *The Fundamental Implications of the Debt Crisis for Social Reproduction in Africa*. London: Zed Books.
Casey, C. (1995) *Work, Self and Society: After Industrialism*. London: Routledge.
Castells, M. (1998) *The Information Age: Economy, Society and Culture. Vol. II. End of Millennium*. Malden, MA: Blackwell.
Castells, M. (2000) *The Rise of the Network Society*. Oxford: Blackwell.
Castells, M. (2002) *The Power of Identity*. Oxford: Blackwell.
Chambers, D. (1986) The constraints of work and domestic schedules on women's leisure, *Leisure Studies*, 5(3): 309–25.
Chandra, R. (1992) *Industrialization and Development in the Third World*. London: Routledge.
Chang, G. (2000) *Disposable Domestics: Immigrant Women Workers in the Global Economy*. Boston, MA: South End Press.
Chapkis, W. and Enloe, C. (1983) *Of Common Cloth: Women in the Global Textile Industry*. Amsterdam: Transnational Institute.
Chapman, S. (1987) *The Cotton Industry in the Industrial Revolution*. Basingstoke: Macmillan.
Chen, M., Vanek, J., Lund, F., Heintz, J., Jhabuala, R. and Bonna, C. (2005) *Progress of the World's Women 2005: Women, Work, Poverty*. New York, NY. United Nations Development Fund for Women.
Clark, P. (1985) A review of the theories of time and structure for organisation sociology, in S. Bachrach and S. Mitchell (eds) *Research in the Sociology of Organisations*. Greenwich, CT: JAI Press. 35–79.
Clarke, J. and Critcher, C. (1990) *The Devil Makes Work: Leisure in Capitalist Britain*. Basingstoke: Macmillan.
Clough, P. (1994) *Feminist Thought: Desire, Power and Academic Discourse*. Oxford: Blackwell.
Coates, G. (1997) Organisation Man – Women and Organisational Culture *Sociological*

Research Online, 2(3). Available at: http://www.socresonline.org.uk/socresonline/2/3/7.html
Collier, M. ([1739] 1985) *The Woman's Labour*. The Augustan Reprint Society. Publication Number 30. Los Angeles, CA: William Andrews Clark Memorial Library.
Collin, A. (2000) Dancing to the music of time, in A. Collin and R. Young (eds) *The Future of Career*. Cambridge: Cambridge University Press.
Collins, P. (1991) *Black Feminist Thought*. London: Routledge.
Collinson, D. and Collinson, M. (1989) Sexuality in the workplace: the domination of men's sexuality, in J. Hearn, D.L. Sheppard, P. Tancred-Sheriff and G. Burrell (eds) *The Sexuality of Organisations*. London: Sage, 91–109.
Collinson, D. and Collinson, M. (1997) Delayering managers: time/space surveillance and its gendered effects. *Organisation*, 4(3): 375–407.
Cooklin, G. (2000) *Introduction to Clothing Manufacture*. Oxford: Blackwell Science.
Cooper, R. and Law, J. (1995) Organisation: distal and proximal views, in S. Bocharach, P. Gaghardi and B. Mundell (eds) *Research in the Sociology of Organisations*. Greenwich, CT: JAI Press.
Costa, M. and Dalla Costa, G. (1995) *Paying the Price: Women and the Politics of International Economic Strategy*. London: Zed Books.
Cousins, M. and Hussain, A. (1984). *Michel Foucault*. London: Macmillan.
Coyle, A. (1984) *Redundant women*. London: The Women's Press.
Cundall, L. and Landman, T. (1925). *Wales: An Economic Geography*. London: Routledge.
Dalla Costa, M. and James, S. (1975) *The Power of Women and the Subversion of the Community*. Bristol: Falling Wall Press.
Davidoff, L. (1976) The rationalization of housework, in D. Barker and S. Allen (eds) *Dependence and Exploitation in Work and Marriage*. London: Longman.
Davies, D. (1933) *The Economic History of South Wales Prior to 1800*. Cardiff: University of Wales Press Board.
Davies, K. (1990) *Women and Time: Weaving the Strands of Everyday Life*. Aldershot: Avebury.
Davies, K. (1994) The tension between process time and clock time in carework: the example of day nurseries, *Time and Society*, 3(3): 259–77.
Davies, K. (2001) Responsibility and daily life: reflections over time/space in J. May and N. Thrift (eds) *Timespace Geographies of Temporality*. London: Routledge.
Davies, R. (1975) *Women and Work*. London: Hutchinson & Co.
Deem, R. (1996) No time for a Rest? An exploration of women's work: engendered leisure and holidays, *Time and Society*, 5(1): 5–25.
Derrida, J. (1979) *Spurs/Eperons*. Chicago, IL: University of Chicago Press.
Derrida, J. (1984) *Margins of Philosophy*, trans. A. Bass. Chicago, IL: The University of Chicago Press.
Derrida, J. (1997) *Of Grammatology*, trans. G. Spivak. London: The Johns Hopkins University Press.
Dex, S. (1984) *The Sexual Division of Work*. Brighton: Wheatsheaf.
Dex, S. and Joshi, H. (1999) Careers and motherhood: policies for compatibility. *Cambridge Journal of Economics*, 23: 641–59.
DTI (2003) More people want flexible hours than cash, company car or gym. London: DTI.
Du Bois, B. (1983) Passionate scholarship: notes on values, knowing and method in feminist science, in G. Bowles and R. Dueilli Klein (eds) *Theories of Women's Studies*. London: Routledge and Kegan Paul.
Duck, S. ([1736] 1985) *The Thresher's Labour*. The Augustan Reprint Society. Publication Number 30. Los Angeles, CA: William Andrews Clark Memorial Library.
Edwards, M. and Lloyd-Jones, R. (1973) N.J. Smelser and the cotton factory family: a

reassessment, in N.B. Harte and K.C. Ponting (eds) *Textile History and Economic History*. Manchester: Manchester University Press.

Ehrenreich, B. and Hochschild, A.R. (2002) *Global Woman: Nannies, Maids and Sex Workers in the New Economy*. NewYork, NY: Metropolitan Books.

Elchardus, M. (1991) Flexible men and women: the changing temporal organization of work and culture: an empirical analysis, *Social Science Information*, 30: 701–26.

Elson, D. (1983) Nimble fingers and other fables, in W. Chapkis and C. Enloe (eds) *Of Common Cloth: Women in the Global Textile Industry*. Amsterdam: Transnational Institute.

Engels, F. ([1845] 1971) *The Condition of the Working Class in England*, trans. W.O. Henderson and W.H. Chaloner. Oxford: Basil Blackwell.

Engels, F. ([1884] 1985) *The Origin of the Family, Private Property and the State*. Harmondsworth: Penguin.

Engels, F. (1968) The origin of the family, private property and the state, in *Marx and Engels, Selected Works*. London: Lawrence and Wishart.

Equal Opportunities Commission (2001) *The Work-Life Balance: Women and Men in Britain*. Manchester: Equal Opportunities Commission.

Equal Opportunities Commission (2003) *Facts About Women and Men in Great Britain*. Manchester: Equal Opportunities Commission.

Equal Opportunities Commission (2006) *Facts About Women and Men in Great Britain*. Manchester: Equal Opportunities Commission.

Ermarth, E. (1989) The solitude of women and social time, in F. Forman and C. Sowton (ed) *Taking our Time: Feminist Perspectives on Temporality*. Oxford: Pergamon Press, 37–46.

Ermarth, E. (1992) *Sequel to History: Postmodernism and the Crisis of Representational Time*. Princeton, NJ: Princeton University Press.

Ernest, M. (1967) *La formation de la penseé économique de Karl Marx, de 1843 jusqu' à la rédaction du "Capital" : étude génétique*, Paris : Maspero

Ezzy, D. (1997) Subjectivity and the labour process: conceptualising 'good work', *Sociology*, 31(3): 427–44.

Fagan, C. (2001) Time, money and the gender order: work orientations and working/time preferences, *Gender, Work and Organisation*, 8(3): 239–67.

Ferguson, M. (1995) *Eighteenth-Century Women Poets: Nation, Class and Gender*. Albany NY: State University of New York Press.

Fernie, S. and Metcalfe, D. (1997) *(Not hanging on the telephone): payment systems in the new sweatshops*. London: Centre for Economic Performance, LSE.

Firat, F. (1994) Gender and consumption: transcending the feminine? in J.A. Costa, (ed.) *Gender Issues and Consumer Behaviour*. London: Sage.

Foreman, A. (1978) *Femininity as Alienation: Women and the Family in Marxism and Psychoanalysis*. London: Pluto.

Forman, F. (1989) Feminizing time: an introduction, in F. Forman and C. Sowton (eds) *Taking Our Time: Feminist Perspectives on Temporality*. Oxford: Pergamon Press.

Forman, F. and Sowton, C. (1989) *Taking Our Time: Feminist Perspectives on Temporality*. Oxford: Pergamon Press.

Forman, M. (1994) 'Movin' closer to an independent funk': black feminist theory, standpoint and women in rap, *Women's Studies*, 23: 35–55.

Foucault, M. (1979a) *Discipline and Punish: The Birth of the Prison*, trans. A. Sheridan. New York, NY: Vintage/Random House.

Foucault, M. (1979b) *The History of Sexuality*: Volume 1: An Introduction, trans. Lane, A., London: Penguin.

Foucault, M. (1980) *Power/Knowledge: Selected Interviews and Other Writings 1972–1977*. Colin Gordon (ed.). Harvester: Hemel Hempstead.

Foucault, M. (1982) The subject and power, in H.L. Dreyfus and R. Rabinow (eds) *Michel Foucault: Beyond Structuralism and Hermeneutics*. Chicago, IL: University of Chicago Press.

Foucault, M. (1984) *The History of Sexuality, Vol. 3. The Care of the Self*, trans. Robert Hurley. New York, NY: Pantheon.

Franks, S. (1999) *Having None of It: Women, Men and the Future of Work*. London: Granta Books.

Frenkel, S., Tam, M., Korczynski, M. and Shire, K. (1998) Beyond bureaucracy? Work organization in call centres, *The International Journal of Human Resource Management*, 9(6): 957–79.

Frobel, F., Kreye, F. and Heinrichs, O. (1980) *The New International Division of Labour*. Cambridge: Cambridge University Press.

Game, A. (1991) *Undoing the Social: Towards a Deconstructive Sociology*. Buckingham: Open University Press.

Gane, N. (2001) Zygmunt Bauman: liquid modernity and beyond, *Acta Sociologica*, 44(3): 267–75.

Gardiner, J. (1971) The economic roots of women's liberation, paper presented at International Socialism Conference on Women, June.

Gardiner, J. (1976) The political economy of domestic labour in capitalist society, in D. Barker and S. Allen (eds) *Dependence and Exploitation in Work and Marriage*. Harlow: Longman.

Garrod, E. (1996) Call centre sweatshops? *Call Centre Focus*, 3(3).

Gaskell, P. (1836) *Artisans and Machinery: The Moral and Physical Condition of the Manufacturing Population Considered with Reference to Mechanical Substitutes for Human Labour*. London: John W. Parker.

General Municipal Boilerworkers Union (2006) GMB in talks with Burberry management regarding proposed 300 job losses at Treorchy. 6 September. Available at: http://www.gmb.org.uk

General Municipal Boilerworkers Union (2007) GMB calls on international textile trade union federation to help to discover pay and conditions at two textile factories in Guangdong, China that will supply Burberry. 13 February. Available at: http://www.gmb.org.uk

Giddens, A. (1991) *Modernity and Self-Identity*. Cambridge: Polity Press.

Gittins, D. (1994) *The Family in Question: Changing Households and Familiar Ideologies*. Basingstoke: Macmillan.

Goffman, E. (1959) The moral career of the mental patient, *Psychiatry*, 22(2): 123–42.

Goldman, R. (1995) *Reading Ads Socially*. London: Routledge.

Gorz, A. (1999) *Reclaiming Work: Beyond the Wage-Based Society*. Cambridge: Polity Press.

Hakim, C. (1991) Grateful slaves and self-made women: fact and fantasy in women's work orientation, *European Sociological Review*, 12(3) 227–50.

Hakim, C. (1996) *Key Issues in Women's Work: Female Heterogeneity and the Polarisation of Women's Employment*. Atlantic Highlands, NJ: Athlone Press.

Hall, S. (1988) 'Brave New World', *Marxism Today*, October: 24–9.

Harris, C.C. (1983) *The Family and Industrial Society*. London: George Allen & Unwin.

Harte, N.B. and Ponting, K.C. (1973) *Textile History and Economic History*. Manchester: Manchester University Press.

Hartmann, H. (1981) The unhappy marriage of Marxism and feminism: towards a more progressive union, in H. Hartmann, and L. Sargent (eds) *Women and Revolution: The Unhappy Marriage of Marxism and Feminism: A Debate on Class and Patriarchy*. London: Pluto Press.

Harvey, D. (1990) *The Condition of Postmodernity: An Inquiry into the Origins of Cultural Change*. Oxford: Basil Blackwell.

Hassard, J. (1989) Time and industrial society, in P. Blyton, J. Hassard, S. Hill and K. Starkey (eds) *Time, Work and Organization*. London: Routledge.

Hassard, J. (1990) *The Sociology of Time*. Basingstoke: Macmillan.

Hassard, J. (2001) Commodification, construction and compression: a review of time metaphors in organizational analysis, *International Journal of Management Reviews*, 3(2): 131–40.

Heidegger, M. (1997) *Plato's Sophist*, trans. R. Rojcewicz and A. Schuwer. Bloomington, IN: Indiana University Press.

Heidegger, M. (2006) *Being and Time*, trans. J. Macquarrie and E. Robinson. Oxford: Blackwell.

Hekman, S. (1990) *Gender and Knowledge: Elements of a Postmodern Feminism*. Cambridge: Polity Press.

Henley Centre (1996) *Teleculture Futures*. Study commissioned by BT.

Hewitt, P. (1993) *About Time: The Revolution in Work and Family Life*. London: Rivers Oram Press.

Hill, S. (1991) Why quality circles failed but total quality management might succeed, *British Journal of Industrial Relations*, 29: 541–68.

Hochschild, R. (1983) *The Managed Heart*. Berkeley, CA: University of California Press.

Hollis, P. (1979) *Women in Public: The Women's Movement 1850–1900*. London: George Allen & Unwin.

Holloway, G. (2005) *Women and Work in Britain Since 1840*. Abingdon: Routledge.

Honeyman, K. (2000) *Women, Gender and Industrialisation in England, 1700–1870*. Basingstoke: Macmillan.

Hoogvelt, A. (2001). *Globalization and the Postcolonial World*. London: The Johns Hopkins University Press.

Hopfl, H. and Atkinson, P. (2000) The future of women's career, in A. Collin and R. Young (eds) *The Future of Career*. Cambridge: Cambridge University Press, 130–44.

Hu-Dehart, E. (2003) Globalization and its discontents, *Frontiers*, 24(2/3): 244–60.

Humphries, J. (1991) Lurking in the wings . . .: women in the histography of the industrial revolution, *Business & Economics*, 20: 32–44.

IBG (1984) *Explorations in Feminism: Geography and Gender: An Introduction to Feminist Geography*. Women and Geography Study Group of the IBG. London: Hutchinson.

IMF (2004) *IMF Concessional Financing Through the ESAF*. A fact sheet. International Monetary Fund, April. Available at: http://www.imf.org

IMF (2005) *Strengthening the IMF's Support for Low-Income Countries*. International Monetary Fund. Available at: http://www.imf

IMF (2006) *The Poverty Reduction and Growth Facility*. A fact sheet. International Monetary Fund, August. Available at: http://www.imf.org

Irigaray, L. (1980) When our lips speak together, *Signs*, 6(1): 69–79.

Irigaray, L. ([1984] 1993) *An Ethics of Sexual Difference*. trans. C. Burke and C. Gillian. London: Athlone Press.

Jameson, F. (1984) *Postmodernism or the Cultural Logic of Late Capitalism*. London: Verso.

Jenkins, A. (1994) Just-in-time 'regimes' and reductionism, *Sociology*, 28(1): 21–30.

Jenkins, G. (1976) *Life and Tradition in Rural Wales*. London: J.M. Dent and Sons.

Jessop, B. (1991) *Fordism and Post-Fordism: A Critical Reformulation*. Lancaster: Lancaster Regionalism Group.

Joekes, S. and Baud, I. (1983) The double day, in W. Chapkis and C. Enloe (eds) *Of Common Cloth: Women in the Global Textile Industry*. Amsterdam: Transnational Institute.

Jordan, E. (1989) The exclusion of women from industry in nineteenth-century Britain, *Comparative Studies in Society and History* 31: 273–96.

References

Kates, S. and Shaw-Garlock, G. (1999) The ever entangling web: a study of ideologies and discourses in advertising to women, *Journal of Advertising*, XXVIII (2): 33–49.

Kaye, K. (1977) Towards the origin of dialogue, in H. Rudolph Schaffer (ed.) *Studies in Mother-Infant Interaction*. London: Academic Press, 89–117.

Kerfoot, D. and Knights, D. (1993) Management, masculinity and manipulation from paternalism to corporate strategy in financial services in Britain, *Journal of Management Studies*, 30(4): 659–77.

Kerfoot, D. and Knights, D. (1994) Into the realm of the fearful: power, identity and the gender problematic, in L. Radtke and H.J. Stam (eds) *Power/Gender Social Relations in Theory and Practice*. London: Sage.

Kerfoot, D. and Knights, D. (1995): *The Organisation of Social Division, Constructing Identities in Managerial Work*, paper delivered at the 12th European Group on Organisation Studies (EGOS) Colloquium, Istanbul, Turkey, 6–8 July.

Kerfoot, D. and Knights, D. (1998) Managing masculinity in contemporary organizational life: A 'managerial project' *Organisation,* 5(1): 7–26.

Kerfoot, D. and Knights, D. (1996) The best is yet to come: searching for embodiment in managerial work, in D. Collinson and J. Hearn (eds) *Masculinity and Management*. London: Sage.

Knights, D. (1995) Hanging out the dirty washing: labour process theory in the age of deconstruction, paper delivered at the 13th Annual International Labour Process Conference, 5–7 April.

Knights, D. and McCabe, D. (1998a) 'Ain't misbehavin?': opportunities for resistance within bureaucratic and quality management innovations, *Sociology* 34(3): 421–37.

Knights, D. and McCabe, D. (1998b) 'Another one bites the dust': engender'ing the problems of masculinity in the management of innovation, *Zeitschrift für Personalforschung*, 12(2): 187–209.

Knights, D. and McCabe, D. (2001) 'A different world': shifting masculinities in the transition to call centres, *Organization*, 8(4): 619–46.

Knights, D. and Odih, P. (1995) It's about time!: the significance of gendered time for financial service consumption, *Time and Society*, 4(2): 205–33.

Knights, D. and Odih, P. (1995) *Demographic Profiles of the Consumer Market up to and Beyond the Year 2000*. London: Financial Services Forum.

Knights, D. and Odih, P. (1997) 'From here to eternity': a masculine project theorizing time, space and risk within the classical, modern and postmodern epistemological regimes, in H. Rasmussen (ed.) *Proceedings of the AOS, Accounting Time and Space Conference*. Copenhagen. 4–6 September.

Knights, D. and Odih, P. (2002) 'Big Brother is watching you!': call centre surveillance and the time disciplined subject, in G. Crow and S. Heath (eds) *Social Conceptions of Time: Structure and Process in Work and Everyday Life*. London: Palgrave Macmillan, 144–59.

Knights, D., Calvey, D. and Odih, P. (1998) Report Stages 1–5 unpublished reports. University of Keele.

Knights, D., Calvey, D. and Odih, P. (1999) Social managerialism and the time disciplined subject: quality–quantity conflicts in a call centre, paper presented at 17th Annual International Labour Process Conference, School of Management, Royal Holloway, University of London, 29–31 March 1999.

Kreitzman, L. (2004) *The 24 Hour Society*. Cheltenham: Edward Elgar.

Kristeva, J. (1980) *Powers of Horror*, trans. L. Roudiez. New York, NY: Columbia University Press.

Kyvik Nordas, H. (2004) *The Global Textile and Clothing Industry Post the Agreement on Textile and Clothing*. WTO Publications. Available at: www.wto.org

Landry, D. (1990) *The Muses of Resistance: Laboring-Class Women's Poetry in Britain, 1739–1796*. Cambridge: Cambridge University Press.

Lash, S. and Urry, J. (1987) *The End of Organized Capitalism*. Cambridge: Polity Press.
Lash, S. and Urry, J. (1994) *Economies of Signs and Space*. London: Sage.
Leach, J. (1844) *Stubborn Facts from the Factories by a Manchester Operative*, published and dedicated to the working classes by William Rashleigh, M.P. London: John Ollivier 11–5.
Leccardi, C. (1996) Rethinking social time, feminist perspectives, *Time and Society*, 5(2): 169–86.
Leccardi, C. and Rampazi, M. (1993) Past and future in young women's experience of time, *Time and Society*, 2(3): 353–81.
Le Feuvre, N. (1994) Leisure, work and gender: a sociological study of women's time in France, *Time and Society*, 2(3): 151–79.
Lee, M. (1993) *Consumer Culture Reborn: The Cultural Politics of Consumption*. London: Routledge.
Lemert, C. (1994) Poststructuralism and sociology, in S. Seidman (ed.) *The Postmodern Turn: New Perspectives on Social Theory*. Cambridge: Cambridge University Press.
Linstead, S. (1999) Deconstruction in the study of organisations, in J. Hassard and M. Parker (eds) *Postmodernism and Organisations*. London: Sage.
Lipietz, A. (1988) Gouverner l'économie, face aux défis internationaux : du développementisme nationaliste à la crise nationale. Paris : Centre d'études prospectives d'économie mathématique appliquées a' la planification.
Lloyd, G. (1984) *The Man of Reason 'Male' and 'Female' in Western Philosophy*. London: Methuen.
Lorraine, T. (1990) *Gender Identity and the Production of Meaning*. Oxford: Westview.
Luxemburg, R. (1971) *The Accumulation of Capital*. London: Routledge and Kegan Paul.
Macpherson, C.B. (1962) *The Political Theory of Possessive Individualism*. Oxford: Clarendon Press.
Marx, K. ([1887] 2003) *Capital, Volume I; A Critical Analysis of Capitalist Production*, Frederick Engels (ed.); trans. from the third German edn by Samuel Moore and Edward Aveling London: Lawrence and Wishart.
Marx, K. (1967) *Essential Writings of Karl Marx* ed. D. Caute. London: Panther.
Marx, K. (1973) *Grundrisse: Introduction to the Culture of the Critique of Political Economy*. London: Penguin.
Marx, K. (1978) *Capital: A Critique of Political Economy*, vol. 2, trans. D. Fernbach. Harmondsworth: Penguin.
Marx, K. (1981) *Capital: A Critique of Political Economy*, vol. 3, trans. D. Fernbach. Harmondsworth: Penguin.
Marx, K. and Engels, F. (1985) *The Communist Manifesto*. London: Penguin.
Massey, D. (1994) *Space, Place and Gender*. Cambridge: Polity Press.
McDowell, L. (1991) Life without father and Ford: the new gender order of post-Fordism, *Transactions, Institute of British Geographers*, 16: 400–19.
McDowell, L. (1997) *Capital, Culture, Gender at Work in the City*. Oxford: Blackwell.
McNay, L. (1999) Gender and narrative identity, *Journal of Political Ideologies*, 4(3): 315–36.
Meek, R. (1979) *Studies in the Labour Theory of Value*. London: Lawrence and Wishart.
Mies, M. (1983) Towards a methodology for feminist research, in G. Bowles and R. Dueilli Klien (eds) *Theories of Women's Studies*. London: Routledge.
Mies, M. (1996) Women and work in a sustainable society, *Ecumenical Review*, 48: 354–68.
Mitchell, J. (1974) *Psychoanalysis and Feminism*. London: Allen Lane.
Mitter, S. (1986) *Common Fate, Common Bond: Women in the Global Economy*. London: Pluto Press.
Mitter, S. and van Luijken, A. (1983) A woman's home is her factory, in W. Chapkis and C. Enloe (eds) *Of Common Cloth: Women in the Global Textile Industry*. Amsterdam: Transnational Institute.

References

Morgall, J. (1986) New office technology, in M. Snell and M. McIntosh (eds) *Waged Work: A Reader*. London: Virago.

Morgan, P. (1997) *Who Needs Parents? The Effects of Childcare and Early Education on Childhood Development*. London: IEA Health and Welfare Unit.

Morris, L. (1990) *The Working of the Household*. Cambridge: Polity Press.

Mouffe, C. (1992) Feminism and radical politics, in J. Butler and J. Scott (eds) *Feminists Theorise the Political*. New York, NY: Routledge, 369–85.

Mumford, L. (1934) *Technics and Civilisation*. New York, NY: Harcourt, Brace and World.

Mumford, L. (1955) The monastery and the clock, in *The Human Prospect*. Boston, MA: Beacon Press.

Munoz, C. (2004) Mobile capital, immobile labour: inequality and opportunity in the tortilla industry. *Social Justice*, 31(3): 21–39.

Munro, R. (1998) Identity, culture and organisation, course outline, Department of Management, Keele University.

Nagar, R., Lawson, V., McDowell, L. and Hanson, S. (2002) Locating globalization: feminist (re)readings of the subjects and spaces of globalization, *Economic Geography*, 78: 257–84.

News.bbc.co (2007) Rock acts play for Burberry staff. Available at: http://news.bbc.co.uk

Nicholson, P. (1993) Motherhood and women's lives, in D. Richardson and V. Robinson (eds) *Introducing Women's Studies*. Basingstoke: Macmillan.

Nowotny, H. (1976) Time structuring and time measurement: on the interrelation between time keepers and social times, in J.T. Fraser and N. Lawrence (eds) *The Study of Time 2*. New York, NY: Springer Verlag.

Nowotny, H. (1992) Time and social theory: towards a social theory of time, *Time and Society*, 1:421–54.

Oakley, A. (1981) *Subject Women*. Oxford: Martin Robertson.

O'Brien, M. (1989) 'Periods', in F. Forman and C. Sowton (eds) *Taking Our Time: Feminist Perspectives on Temporality*. Oxford: Pergamon Press, 11–20.

O'Brien, S. (1991) Structural adjustment and structural transformation in Sub-Saharan Africa, in C. Gladwin (ed.) *Structural Adjustment and African Women Farmers*. Gainesville, FL: University of Florida Press.

Odih, P. (1998) *Gendered time and financial services consumption*, PhD thesis, University of Manchester Institute of Science and Technology.

Odih, P. (1999a) Gendered time in the age of deconstruction, *Time and Society*, 8(1): 9–38.

Odih, P. (1999b) The women's market: marketing fact or apparition? *Consumption, Markets and Culture*, 3(2): 165–93.

Odih, P. (2003) 'Gender, Work and Organisation in the Time/Space Economy of Just-in-Time Labour'. *Time and Society* 12: 293–314.

Odih, P. and Knights, D. (2002) 'Now's the time!' Consumption and time (space) disruptions in postmodern virtual worlds, in B. Adam and R.Whipp (eds) *Time and Management*. Oxford: Oxford University Press.

Odih, P. (2007) *Advertising in Modern and Postmodern Times*. London: Sage.

Omvedt, G. (1997) Rural women and the family in an era of liberalization: India in comparative Asian perspective, *Bulletin of Concerned Asian Scholars*, 29(4): 33–44.

ONS (2007a) Employee jobs by industry and sex, June 1998–June 2002. Short-term turnover and employment survey. Office of National Statistics. Available at: http://www.statistics.gov.uk

ONS (2007b) Annual population survey employment levels by occupation and gender Wales. Available at: http://www.statswales.wales.gov.uk/

Pahl, J. (1989) *Money and Marriage*. London: Macmillan.

Palmer, M. and Neaverson, P. (1994) *Industry in the Landscape, 1700–1900*. London: Routledge.

References

Parliamentary Papers (1816) Select Committee on State of Children Employed in Manufactories of United Kingdom: *Minutes of Evidence* Chair/author: Peel, Robert, Sir. Session: 1816 Paper Series: House of Commons Papers; Reports of Committees, Paper Number, (397), Volume/Page, III.235.

Parliamentary Papers (1833) Royal Com. On Employment of Children in Factories. *First Report, Minutes of Evidence*, App; Reports of District Coms. Chair/Author. Tooke, Thomas. Session: 1833, Paper Series: House of Commons Papers; Reports of Commissioners Paper Number: (450), Volume/Page: XX.1 CH.

Parliamentary Papers (1835) Select Committee on Petitions of Hand-Loom Weavers Report, *Minutes of Evidence*, Chair/author:Maxwell, John. Session: 1835 Paper Series: House of Commons Papers; Reports of Committees Paper Number: (341), Volume/Page: XIII.1 CH Microfiche Number: 38.100–3.

Parliamentary Papers (1840) Royal Com. on Hand-Loom Weavers. *Report by Mr. Hickson on Condition of Hand-Loom Weavers.* Chair/author: Hickson, W.E. Session: 1840 Paper Series: House of Commons Papers; Reports of Commissioners Paper Number: (639) Volume/Page: XXIV.639 CH Microfiche Number: 43.183–4.

Parliamentary Papers (1892); Royal Com. on Labour. Digest of Evidence (Group C) Volume I. Textile Chair/author:cavendish, Spencer Compton, 8th D. Devonshire Session:1892 Paper Series: command papers; reports of commissioners Paper Number: [C.6708-III] Volume/Page: XXXIV.209 CH Microfiche Number: 98.255–256

Parliamentary Papers (1898) Report by Miss Collet on Changes in Employment of Women and Girls in Industrial Centres. *Part I. Flax and Jute*, Session: 1898 Paper Series: Command Papers; Accounts and Papers. Paper Number[C.8794]. Volume/Page: LXXXVIII.305 CH Microfiche Number: 104.734–735.

Parliamentary Papers (2007) Globalization and its impact on Wales: minutes of evidence taken before Welsh Affairs Committee. uncorrected transcript of oral evidence to be published as HC 281–iv. Tuesday 27 February. Available at: http://www.publications.parliament.uk

Peterson, J. and Lewis, M. (1999b) *The Elgar Companion to Feminist Economics*. Cheltenham: Edward Elgar.

Pettinger, L., Parry, J., Taylor, R. and Glucksmann, M. (2005) *The New Sociology of Work*. Oxford: Blackwell.

Pietrykowski, B. (1995) Fordism at Ford: spatial decentralization and labour segmentation at the Ford Motor Company, 1920–1950, *Economic Geography*, 71: 383–401.

Pike, E. (1966) *Human Documents of the Industrial Revolution in Britain*. London: George Allen & Unwin.

Pinchbeck, I. (1969) *Women Workers in the Industrial Revolution, 1750–1850*. London: Cass.

Piore, M. and Sabel, C. (1984) *The Second Industrial Divide: Possibilities for Prosperity*. New York, NY: Basic Books.

Plumb, J. (1968) *England in the Eighteenth Century (1714–1815)*. Harmondsworth: Penguin.

Postan, M. (1939) Revisions in Economic History: The Fifteenth Century, *The Economic History Review*, 9(2): 160–7.

Punday, D. (2000) Derrida in the world: space and post-deconstructive textual analysis, *Postmodern Culture*, 11(1): September.

Quennell, M. and Quennell, C. (1933) *A History of Everyday Things in England 1733–1851*. London: Batsford.

Rauber, P. (1997) To every fruit there is a season, *Sierra*, January/February, 20–1.

Ravenhill, J. (2005) *Global Political Economy*. Oxford: Oxford University Press.

Reilly, P. (2001) *Flexibility at Work: Balancing the Interests of Employer and Employee*. Aldershot: Gower.

Ribbens, J. and Edwards, R. (2000) *Feminist Dilemmas in Qualitative Research: Public Knowledge and Private Lives*. London: Sage.

References

Rich, A. (1977) *Of Woman Born: Motherhood as Experience and Institution*. London: Virago.
Richardson, D. (1993) *Women, Motherhood and Child Rearing*. London: Macmillan.
Ricoeur, P. (1990) *Time and Narrative*. Chicago, IL: The University of Chicago Press.
Rifkin, J. (1996) *The End of Work: The Decline of the Global Labour Force and the Dawn of the Post-Market Era*. New York, NY: Tarcher Putman.
Rose, M. (1996) *The Lancashire Cotton Industry: A History Since 1700*. Lancashire: Lancashire County Books.
Rose, N. (1999) *Power of Freedom: Reframing*. Cambridge: Cambridge University Press.
Rowbotham, J. (1973) *Woman's Consciousness, Man's World*. Harmondsworth: Pelican Books.
Rubery, J. (1994) *Employers, Strategy and the Labour Market*. Oxford: Oxford University Press.
Rubery, J., Smith, M. and Fagan, C. (1998) Gender, societal effects and working time regimes, *Feminist Economics*, 4(1): 71–101
Sayer, D. (1989) *Readings from Karl Marx*. London: Routledge.
Schutz, A. (1967) *Collected Papers: The Problem of Social Reality*. The Hague: Martinus Nijhoff.
Scott, A. (1988) Flexible production systems and regional development, *International Review of Urban and Regional Research*, 12(2): 171–85.
Seccombe, W. (1974) The housewife and her labour under capitalism, *New Left Review* 83, January February, 3–24. Available at: http://www.newleftreview.net/IssueI82.asp?Article=01
Seidler, V. (1989) *Rediscovering Masculinity: Reason, Language and Sexuality*. London: Routledge.
Sennett, R. (1998) *The Corrosion of Character: The Personal Consequences of Work in the New Capitalism*. New York, NY: W.W. Norton & Company.
Sewell, G. and Wilkinson, B. (1992) Someone to watch over me: surveillance, discipline and the just-in-time labour process, *Sociology*, 26(2): 271–91.
Shutz, A. (1972) *Phenomenology of the Social World*. London: Heinemann Educational Books.
Sklair, L. (2002) *Globalization, Capitalism and Its Alternatives*. Oxford: Oxford University Press.
Smelser, N. (1959) *Social Change in the Industrial Revolution: An Application of Theory to the Lancashire Cotton Industry 1770–1840*. London: Kegan Paul.
Smith, A. (1937) *The Wealth of Nations*. New York, NY: Modern Library.
Stanley, L. and Wise, S. (1983); *Breaking Out: Feminist Consciousness and Feminist Research*. London: Routledge and Kegan Paul.
Stanworth, C. (2000) Women and work in the Information Age, *Gender, Work and Organisation*, 7(1): 20–33.
Stiglitz, J. (2002) *Globalization and its Discontents*. London: Penguin.
Stoppard, M. (1984) *The Baby Care Book*. London: Dorling Kindersley.
Strauss, A. and Corbin, J. (1990) *Basics of Qualitative Research: Grounded Theory Procedures and Techniques*. London: Sage.
Streeten, P. (1971) Book Review: 'Industry and Trade in Some Developing Countries: A Comparative Study', *The Economic Journal*, 81 (321): 144–8.
Taplin, I. (1996) Rethinking flexibility: the case of the apparel industry, *Review of Social Economy*, LIV (2): 191–220.
Taylor, P. and Bain, P. (1998) 'An assembly line in the head': the call centre labour process paper delivered at the 16th Annual International Labour process Conference, 30 March–1 April, UMIST, Manchester.
Telegraph.co.uk (2007) Fashionistas versus sandalistas as the battle to check Burberry goes global. *Sunday Telegraph*, 27 January. Available at: *http://www.telegraph.co.uk/news*

Thomas, C. (2005) Globalization and development in the South, in J. Ravenhill (ed.) *Global Political Economy*. Oxford: Oxford University Press.
Thomas, J. (1996) *Time, Culture and Identity: An Interpretive Archaeology*. London: Routledge.
Thompson, E. (1967) Time, work-discipline and industrial capitalism, *Past and Present*, 38 (December): 56–97.
Thomson, D. (1971) *England in the Nineteenth Century*. Harmondsworth: Penguin.
Thrift, N. (1981) Owners' time and own time: the making of a capitalist time consciousness, 1300–1800, in A.R. Pred (ed.) *Space and Time in Geography*. Liun: Gleerup, 56–84.
Thrift, N. (1988) Vico voco: ringing the changes in historical geography of time consciousness, in M. Young and T. Schuller (eds) *The Rhythms of Society*. London Routledge and Kegan Paul, 53–94.
Thrift, N. (1991) For a new geography 2, *Progress in Human Geography*, 15: 456–65.
Toffler, A. (1981) *The Third Wave*. London: Pan Books.
Tong, R. (1992) *Rosemarie: Feminist Thought: A Comprehensive. Study*. London: Routledge.
Trevelyan, G. (1973) *English Social History: A Survey of Six Centuries: Chaucer to Queen Victoria*. London: Book Club Associates.
Turner, C. (1992) *Living by the Pen: Women Writers in the Eighteenth Century*. London: Routledge.
Urry, J. (1981): *The Anatomy of Capitalist Societies: The Economy, Civil Society and the State*. London: Macmillan.
Urry, J. (1995) *Consuming Places*. London: Routledge.
Valenze, D. (1995) *The First Industrial Woman*. Oxford: Oxford University Press.
Van Dijk, J. (1999) The one-dimensional network society of Manuel Castells, *New Media and Society*, 1(1): 127–38.
Wadsworth, A.P. and Mann, J. (1931) *The Cotton Trade and Industrial Lancashire 1600–1780*. Manchester: Manchester University Press.
Wainwright, D. (1997). Can sociological research be qualitative, critical and valid? *The Qualitative Report*, Vol. 3, No. 2. Online. http://www.nova.edu/ssss/QR/QR3-2/wain.html
Wajcman, J. and Martin, B. (2002) Narratives of identity in modern management: the corrosion of gender difference? *Sociology*, 36(4): 985–1002.
Walby, S. (1990) *Theorizing Patriarchy*. Oxford: Basil Blackwell.
Walby, S. (1997) *Gender Transformations*. London: Routledge.
Walby, S. (2007) *Gender (In)equality and the Future of Work*. Manchester: Equal Opportunities Commission.
Wearing, B. (1984) *The Ideology of Motherhood*. London: Allen and Unwin.
Weedon, C. (1987) *Feminist Practice and Poststructuralist Theory*. Oxford: Blackwell.
Welsh Affairs Committee (2007) Welsh Affairs Committe Inquiry Page: Globalisation and its impact on Wales http://www.parliament.uk/parliamentary-committees/welsh_affairs_committee
Westwood, S. (1984); *All day, every day : factory and family in the making of women's lives*, London : Pluto Press
Whipp, R. (1994): A Time to be Concerned: A Positional Paper on Time and Management, *Time and Society*, 3: 99–116
Whirled Bank Group (2003) Structural Adjustment Program. Available at: http://www.whirledbank.org/development/sap.html
Wichterich, C. (2002) *The Globalized Woman*. London: Zed Books.
Wigfield, A. (2001) *Post-Fordism, Gender and Work*. Burlington, VA: Ashgate.
Williams, C.C. (1988) *Examining the Nature of Domestic Labour*. Hampshire: Gower.
Williams, J. (1995) *Was Wales Industrialised?* Cardiff: Gomer Press.

Index

24-hour global economy 155–9

'abstract' labour, Marx, Karl 9–11
accumulation
    see also capitalist accumulation
    capital accumulation 75–7
    by dispossession 27–30
    gender 16
    in non-economic times 75–7
    primitive 16, 27–41
Admin. Officer, domestic division of labour 95–6
advertisements, marketing management jobs 141–4
attrition, call centre 124–5, 128
automation, clothing industry 161

barriers, trade 155–6, 157
    Bauman, Z. 141, 142, 148
    brand reputation, call centre 116–17
    Burberry Treorchy factory
    case study 162–75
    commercial viability 162–4
    corporate social responsibility 173–5
    globalization 155, 162–75
    timely reflections 175–7
    wages negotiations 164–71
    WCTA 167
Burchell, G. 86
Burnette, Joyce 53–7

call centre
    analytic themes 118–19
    attrition 124–5, 128
    brand reputation 116–17
    customer advisers 122–3, 124–5
    emotional labour 119–22
    empathy 119–20, 126–7
    ethnography 118–22
    gender identities 120–1
    gendered time 129
    masculinities 121
    performance monitoring 123–4, 128
    post-Fordist production 115–30
    process orientation 118–19
    process tensions 122–4
    process time 119–22
    quality assurance 124–5
    resistances 124–5
    senior advisers 124–5
    task orientation 122–4
    team manager 127
    technological determinism 115–17
    temporal clashes 124–5
    time discipline at work 117
    time-disciplined 115–30
    trainer 119–20, 123
    training 118–20, 124
capital accumulation, in non-economic times 75–7
capital development, Marx, Karl 70–2

Index

capital/nature relationships 179
capitalist accumulation 1–24
  gender 1–24
  global economy 151–5
  Industrial Revolution 6–7
  subcontracting 152
  theorizing 6–7, 11–14
  value-added chain 152
  velocity of circulation 152
case study, Burberry Treorchy factory 162–75
Castells, M. 134
clothing industry
  see also textile...
  automation 161
  Burberry Treorchy factory 155, 162–75
  EPZs 161
  flexibility 161
  global economy 160–4
  progressive bundle systems 160
  Wal-Mart 161
  women 160–4
Collier, Mary 1–6, 179–80
Collin, A. 140
commercial viability, Burberry Treorchy factory 162–4
conditions, working 50–2
core-periphery relationships, global division of labour 153
corporate social responsibility
  Burberry Treorchy factory 173–5
  global economy 173–5
  subcontracting 173–5
Crompton mule 44–5
customer advisers, call centre 122–3, 124–5

Dalla Costa, M. 69–70, 75–6
Davies, K.
  emotional labour 120
  linear time 92–3
dental nurse, linear time 90
Derrida, J. 109, 110
development assistance, global economy 155–6
discrimination, gender 57–61
dispossession
  accumulation by 27–30
  integral nature 28–9

textile innovation 34–41
division of labour
  domestic 93–6
  EPZs 154
  farming 153–4
  global 153
  international 154
  motherhood 93–6
DLPLS see Domestic Labour as Productive Labour School
domestic division of labour 93–6
Domestic Labour as Productive Labour School (DLPLS) 67–8
domestic labour time 179–80
  family 65–75
  housework 72–5
  Marx, Karl 66
  as productive labour time 67–9
  surplus value 69–72
dual temporal burden
  employment patterns 102–5
  motherhood 102–5
Duck, Stephen 2–3, 5

economic categories, Marx, Karl 63–5
emotional labour, call centre 119–22
empathy, call centre 119–20, 126–7
employment patterns
  dual temporal burden 102–5
  motherhood 98–107
  reserve army of labour 99–100
  voluntary worker 101–2
  women 98–107
enclosure, textile production 30–4
Engels, F. 27–8
  domestic labour time 65–6
EPZs see Export Processing Zones
Ermarth, E. 142
ethnography, call centre 118–22
exploitation
  global economy 159
  women 159
Export Processing Zones (EPZs)
  clothing industry 161
  division of labour 154

factory production
  family factories 38–41
  gendered time 47
  space economies 46–7

textile innovation 38–41
time economies 46–7
family factories, textile innovation 38–41
farming, division of labour 153–4
female rationality, timely reflections 109–10
femininity 146–7
    linear time 88–96
feminist critique, just-in-time labour 136–9
feminist perspectives 17
    see also gender; motherhood; women
    global times 23–4
    modern times 19–20
feminizing, global assembly line 171–5
flexibility at work, post-Fordism 20–2
flexibility, clothing industry 161
flexibilization, TNCs 157–8
flexible accumulation 135
flexible work
    gender identities 131–48
    post-Fordism 131–48
    timely reflections 146–8
Fordist production, modern times 18–19
Foucault, M. 82, 84, 126

Gaskell, P. 27, 43–4, 52, 55–6
gender
    see also feminist perspectives; women
    accumulation 16
    capitalist accumulation 1–24
    discrimination 57–61
    feminist perspectives 17
    industrial capitalism 63–77
    inequalities 57–61
    male displacement 44–5
    political economy of time 1–24
    primitive accumulation 16
    textile industry 42–62
    theorizing 11–14
    time economies 63–77
    time work discipline 50–7
gender differences
    timely reflections 107–11
    valuing work 101–2
    wages 15–16, 53–7, 102
gender identities 81–97
    call centre 120–1

flexible work 131–48
    just-in-time production 131–4
    power 83–5
    restructuring 131–48
    subjectivity 83–5
gender relations
    see also relational time
    post-Fordism 134–9
gendered time
    call centre 129
    factory production 47
    power/knowledge 105–7
    relational time 105–7
    resistance 105–7
global assembly line
    feminizing 171–5
    women 160–1
global capitalism, global economy 157
global division of labour 153
global economy
    24–hour 155–9
    capitalist accumulation 151–5
    clothing industry 160–4
    corporate social responsibility 173–4
    development assistance 155–6
    exploitation 159
    global capitalism 157
    globalized woman 157–9
    hypocrisy, Western 157
    IMF 155–6, 183
    off-shore production 154
    outsourcing 157–9, 183
    PRGF 156, 183
    TNCs 157–9, 184
    trade barriers hypocrisy, Western 157
    trade barriers reduction 155–6
    vertically disintegrated production 158
global times 23–4, 149–77
    wages negotiations 164–71
globalization 183–4
    Burberry Treorchy factory 155, 162–75
    Wales 155
globalized woman, global economy 157–9

Hoogvelt, A. 153
housework 72–5, 180

see also domestic labour time
Humphries, J. 55
hypocrisy, Western, global economy 157

identity, gender see gender identities
IMF see International Monetary Fund
industrial capitalism
　gender 63–77
　time economies 63–77
Industrial Revolution 14–17
　capitalist accumulation 6–7
　political economy of time 6–7
　technological advances 14–15
Information Development Officer, motherhood 93–4
information technologies, impact 183–4
innovation, textile see textile innovation
international division of labour 154
International Monetary Fund (IMF), global economy 155–6, 183

James, S. 69–70, 75–6
jenny factories, textile innovation 37–8
just-in-time labour 147–8
　corrosive effects 132–3
　feminist critique 136–9
　numerical flexibility 135–6
　post-Fordism 22, 135–9
just-in-time production 148
　gender identities 131–4

Kerfoot, D. 76–7, 82, 86–7, 120
Knights, D. 76–7, 82, 86–7, 120

labour market statistics 181
labour theory of value 7–8
　Marx, Karl 7–11
labour time 179
　buying/selling productive 8–11
　domestic labour time 65–75
　productive labour time 8–11
Leach, James 51
lecturer, motherhood 103
librarian, domestic division of labour 96
linear time 126
　femininity 88–96

masculinities 87–8, 142
phallocentricity 147
liquid modernity 142

machine-minding 50
male displacement 44–5
Mann, J. 37–8
marketing management jobs, advertisements 141–4
Marx, Karl 7–14
　capital development 70–2
　domestic labour time 66
　economic categories 63–5
　labour theory of value 7–11
　productive labour time 8–11
　surplus value 12–14, 63–4
masculinities 85–8, 147
　call centre 121
　linear time 87–8, 142
mechanization 50
modern times 18–20
　feminist perspectives 19–20
　Fordist production 18–19
　Taylorism 18
　timely reflections 96–7
modern work, timely reflections 107–11
motherhood
　domestic division of labour 93–6
　dual temporal burden 102–5
　employment patterns 98–107
　lecturer 103
Mouffe, C. 84–5

narrative career, demise 140–6
narrative time/space, systemic disruptions 139–46
nature/capital relationships 179
negotiations, wages 164–71
numerical flexibility, just-in-time labour 135–6

off-shore production, global economy 154
outsourcing
　global economy 157–9, 183
　TNCs 157–9

patriarchy, private to public 57–61
pay see wages

Index

performance monitoring, call centre 123–4, 128
phallocentricity, linear time 147
physiotherapist 81
political economy of time 1–24
　gender 1–24
　Industrial Revolution 6–7
　theorizing 6–7, 11–14
　time as currency 2–6
post-Fordism 20–2
　flexibility at work 20–2
　flexible work 131–48
　gender relations 134–9
　just-in-time labour 22, 135–9
　temporal issues 134–5
　time-disciplined call centre 115–30
Postan, M. 31
Poverty Reduction and Growth Facility (PRGF), global economy 156, 183
power
　gender identities 83–5
　subjectivity 83–5
power/knowledge
　gendered time 105–7
　relational time 105–7
　resistance 105–7
power sources, textile production 48–50
PRGF see Poverty Reduction and Growth Facility
primary school teacher, linear time 90–1
primitive accumulation 27–41
　gender 16
process orientation, call centre 118–19
process tensions, call centre 122–4
process time, call centre 119–22
production for exchange 29–30
productive labour time
　buying/selling 8–11
　domestic labour time as 67–9
　Marx, Karl 8–11
progressive bundle systems, clothing industry 160
public patriarchy 57–61

quality assurance, call centre 124–5

receptionist, temporal disempowerment 104–5

relational time
　see also gender relations
　gendered time 105–7
　power/knowledge 105–7
　resistance 105–7
relationships
　core-periphery 153
　nature/capital 179
reserve army of labour, employment patterns 99–100
resistance
　gendered time 105–7
　power/knowledge 105–7
　relational time 105–7
resistances, call centre 124–5
responsibility, corporate social see corporate social responsibility

Seccombe, W. 72–4
senior advisers, call centre 124–5
Sennett, Richard 132–3, 135, 143–4, 146
Smelser, N. 34–6, 40
social responsibility, corporate see corporate social responsibility
social time 126
space economies, factory production 46–7
spinning jenny
　adoption 44
　jenny factories 37–8
statistics, labour market 181
steam-powered textile production 49–50
subcontracting
　capitalist accumulation 152
　corporate social responsibility 173–5
subjectivity
　gender identities 83–5
　power 83–5
surplus value
　domestic labour time 69–72
　Marx, Karl 12–14, 63–4
systemic disruptions, narrative time/space 139–46

task orientation, call centre 122–4
Taylorism, modern times 18
team manager, call centre 127
technological advances, Industrial Revolution 14–15

Index

technological determinism, call centre 115–17
temporal clashes, call centre 124–5
temporal disempowerment
  dual temporal burden 102–5
  receptionist 104–5
  voluntary worker 106
temporal issues, post-Fordism 134–5
textile industry
  see also clothing industry
  gender 42–62
  nineteenth century 42–62
  rise of 42–62
textile innovation
  dispossession 34–41
  family factories 38–41
  jenny factories 37–8
  time-disciplined production 38–41
textile production
  see also clothing industry
  domestic 32–4
  enclosure 30–4
  power sources 48–50
  steam-powered 49–50
  weaving time 48–50
  women 32–4
textile revolution
  time 42–50
  work-discipline 42–50
Thompson, E.P. 39
time as currency 2–6
time discipline at work, call centre 117
time-disciplined call centre, post-Fordist production 115–30
time-disciplined production, textile innovation 38–41
time economies 16–17
  factory production 46–7
  gender 63–77
  industrial capitalism 63–77
time, linear
  femininity 88–96
  masculinities 87–8, 142
time, weaving
  textile revolution 42–50
  work-discipline 42–50
time work discipline, gender 50–7
timely reflections
  Burberry Treorchy factory 175–7
  female rationality 109–10

flexible work 146–8
gender differences 107–11
modern times 96–7
modern work 107–11
TNCs *see* transnational corporations
trade barriers
  hypocrisy, Western 157
  reduction, global economy 155–6
trade unions *see* unions
trainer, call centre 119–20, 123
training, call centre 118–20, 124
transnational corporations (TNCs)
  global economy 157–9, 184
  globalized woman 157–9
  outsourcing 157–9
Trevelyan, G. 30

unions 57–61
'useful' labour, Marx, Karl 9–11

value
  labour theory of value 7–11
  surplus value 12–14, 63–4, 69–72
value-added chain, capitalist accumulation 152
valuing work, gender differences 101–2
velocity of circulation, capitalist accumulation 152
vertically disintegrated production, global economy 158
voluntary organization manager, linear time 89
voluntary worker
  employment patterns 101–2
  temporal disempowerment 106

Wadsworth, A.P. 37–8
wages
  gender differences 15–16, 53–7, 102
  negotiations, Burberry Treorchy factory 164–71
  negotiations, global times 164–71
Wal-Mart, clothing industry 161
Wales
  Burberry Treorchy factory 155, 162–75
  globalization 155
  WCTA 167
WCTA *see* Welsh Clothing and Textile Association

weaving machine 25
weaving time
   textile production 48–50
   textile revolution 42–50
   work-discipline 42–50
Welsh Clothing and Textile Association (WCTA), Burberry Treorchy factory 167
women
   see also feminist perspectives; gender; motherhood
   clothing industry 160–4
   employment patterns 98–107
   exclusion 57–61
   exploitation 159
   global assembly line 160–1
   globalized woman 157–9
   textile production 32–4
work-discipline
   textile revolution 42–50
   time 42–50
work ethic, demise 140–6
work/life balance 148
working conditions 50–2